MONROE COLLEGE LIBRARY

3 7340 01070168 5

Breakthrough IT
Change
Management
How to Get Enduring Change Results

WITHDRAWN from
Monroe College Library

MONROE COLLEGE LIBRARY
2468 JEROME AVE

Breakthrough IT Change Management

How to Get Enduring Change Results

Bennet P. Lientz

John E. Anderson Graduate School of Management
University of California, Los Angeles (UCLA)

Kathryn P. Rea

The Consulting Edge, Inc.
Beverly Hills, California

ELSEVIER
BUTTERWORTH
HEINEMANN

AMSTERDAM • BOSTON • HEIDELBERG • LONDON • NEW YORK • OXFORD
PARIS • SAN DIEGO • SAN FRANCISCO • SINGAPORE • SYDNEY • TOKYO

HD
58.8
.L527
2004

Elsevier Butterworth–Heinemann
200 Wheeler Road, Burlington, MA 01803, USA
Linacre House, Jordan Hill, Oxford OX2 8DP, UK

Copyright © 2004, Bennet P. Lientz and Kathryn P. Rea

All rights reserved.

No part of this publication may be reproduced, stored in a retrieval
system, or transmitted in any form or by any means, electronic,
mechanical, photocopying, recording, or otherwise, without the prior
written permission of the publisher.

Permissions may be sought directly from Elsevier's Science &
Technology Rights Department in Oxford, UK: phone: (+44) 1865
843830, fax: (+44) 1865 853333, e-mail:
permissions@elsevier.co.uk. You may also complete your request
on-line via the Elsevier Science homepage
(http://elsevier.com), by selecting "Customer Support" and then
"Obtaining Permissions."

∞ Recognizing the importance of preserving what has been written, Elsevier prints
its books on acid-free paper whenever possible.

Library of Congress Cataloging-in-Publication Data

British Library Cataloguing-in-Publication Data
A catalogue record for this book is available from the British Library.

ISBN: 0-7506-7686-8

For information on all Butterworth–Heinemann publications
visit our website at www.bh.com

03 04 05 06 07 08 09 10 9 8 7 6 5 4 3 2 1

Printed in the United States of America

Contents

Part I
Select Your Change Management Strategy and Approach

Chapter 1
Introduction

Chapter 2
Dynamics of Change and Work

Chapter 3
Politics and the Resistance to Change

Chapter 4
Develop Your Change Goals and Strategy

Chapter 5
Prepare Your Change Management Framework

Part II
Get Ready for Change

Chapter 6
Determine Activities for Change

Chapter 7
Collect Information on Today's Work

Chapter 8
Define Your Long-Term Solution and Quick Hits

Chapter 9
Develop Your Change Implementation Strategy

Chapter 10
Plan Ahead for Change

Part III
Implement Change

Chapter 11
Get Quick Hit Results

Chapter 12
Carry Out Major Change

Chapter 14
Prevent Deterioration and Expand the Change Effort

Part IV
Address Specific Situations and Issues

Chapter 15
Implement New Technology and Systems

Chapter 16
Achieve Success in E-Business

Chapter 17
Common Issues in Change Management

Preface

COMMENTS ABOUT CHANGE

What do the following things have in common?

- Industrial engineering
- Implementing a new IT system
- New government program
- Reengineering
- Six Sigma
- Inventions

Note the wide range of the items listed. All of these and many others have the goal of change and improvement in common. Human beings have been concerned about change since the written word. Some societies were afraid of change while others have embraced it. The above methods were created to address change.

With all of the books written on change and work performed, you would think that there should be a high success rate. Yet, that is not the case. Look at the above list and you will find that half or more of these things either fail to be implemented or fail to deliver the change. Moreover, in many cases where there is change, the change is not persistent. Instead, the work or the process falls back to what was previously there. It is no wonder that there is a great deal of management frustration in getting and keeping changes in place.

There have been many books written about change and change management. A number of these have some good ideas. However, most suffer from the following shortcomings.

- *There is an overdependence on jargon.* This makes use of such methods problematic. There are already enough problems with change implementation and sustenance without having to deal with a new vocabulary.

- *The methods are too complex to fit in in many organizations.* What is needed is a common sense approach that is flexible and adaptive.
- *There is a restriction to getting the change in—rather than keeping it in.* Yet, the key is implementing lasting change.
- *There is too much emphasis on a top-down, management-driven approach.* Management at the top comes and goes. Yet, the people doing the work where the change was focused remain.
- *There is little or no recognition of deterioration after change has occurred.* Yet, as employees come and go and as the business changes and adapts, change in the work continues.

We can also learn from some old adages.

- *You cannot teach an old dog new tricks.* This is a reference to resistance to change.
- *You can lead a horse to water, but you cannot make him drink it.* This refers to management telling employees that they must change and then thinking that change will follow—often doesn't happen.
- *The more things change, the more they stay the same.* This is an interesting statement. When you implement change, many detailed steps and activities remain the same.

CHANGE MANAGEMENT SUCCESS DEFINED

Before even starting to read this book, we need to have a commonly understood definition of success for change management. The typical measure of success in most books is that change has been successfully defined and implemented.

Experience over many change efforts shows that these objectives are insufficient. If these are all that you achieve, it is highly probable that the work will either partially or totally revert back to its previous state. Our goals for you are more ambitious and include:

- Gain support for change from employees and managers.
- Implement change along measurements for the work so that the results of the change are clearly determined.
- Implement a new culture of collaboration where employees share more information and work more in teams.
- Raise the level of awareness of the process and work so that there is less of a tendency for reversion.
- Implement an ongoing measurement process for the work to detect any problems.

You can see the difference in scope between the two approaches. Here you want to instill a culture that will sustain the change without massive management intervention. People are self-motivated to keep the changes in place and to even look for improvements.

AN EFFECTIVE CHANGE MANAGEMENT APPROACH

The above discussion provides a lead-in to our approach. Our fundamental theme is that positive change can improve people's lives at work and at home. This is a simple statement, but is one that helps you through problems and issues. There is also the enjoyment of seeing people define the details of change, gain self-confidence, and see positive results. That is why we have been so interested and involved in change over many projects and years. A basic lesson learned here is that change management can be fun and a real source of satisfaction. You really feel good when change has been carried out successfully and is working.

This approach has been used successfully in over 70 organizations in over 20 countries in a variety of organizations and country cultures and languages. We have employed the term "Breakthrough" in the title for good reason. When compared with existing methods, there are major differences including these critical success factors:

- *Participation and collaboration.* Change must be supported from the bottom and middle as well as from the top. People at all levels have to believe that they and their organization will benefit from change.
- *Recognition of the need for change.* This is a key to getting people turned on to change.
- *Implementation of change in stages.* Rather than a "big bang" approach, change is accomplished in discrete phases so that at each phase people see the benefits and gain confidence to move to the next phase.
- *Ongoing team and teamwork.* Not only must you have teams for implementing change, but you need them for ongoing support as well.
- *Measurement of the work.* In order to determine the situation before change, during, and after change, you must implement measurements. You also need this to detect deterioration and reversion.
- *Change is political.* To treat change management as technical or strictly business ignores the political resistance and other factors involved.
- *Common sense and jargon free.* The methods can be and have been employed without massive training or consultants doing it for you.
- *Sensitivity to the culture of the country and organization.* You cannot impose some canned method on an organization and expect it to work. Effective methods have to be sensitive to the culture of the organization and country.
- *Focus on implementation and sustaining change.* Most of the book deals with implementing change and keeping the changes in effect to prevent reversion.

- *Use of systems and technology in a planned and organized manner.* There are two chapters dealing with the interrelationship between systems and technology on the one hand, and change management on the other.

AUDIENCE OF THE BOOK

Managers and employees who are involved in projects and work to implement improvements and change are one major audience. Consultants and advisors are a second group that will find this book useful. Another group consists of individuals who are considering carrying out change and have not done so, but are seeking guidelines for successfully implementing change. The book contents have been used in courses and seminars in change management, reengineering, and process improvement. The materials have also been employed in courses dealing with systems implementation and design as well as E-Business implementation.

ORGANIZATION OF THE BOOK

The book is organized into four parts. In the first part you will develop your change management strategy by considering alternative approaches, the political and cultural factors in your organization, and your goals with respect to change. Part II deals with getting ready for change. Here you will identify how the work will be performed after the change as well as Quick Hits to get you from where you are now to the future changed environment. You will develop an implementation strategy for change as well as an implementation plan. The implementation strategy is very important since it provides a roadmap to everyone as to where changes are leading and how the multiple changes interact and combine. Continuing with implementation, Part III deals with getting the change established and keeping it going.

Throughout the book you will find numerous examples. These cross a number of industries and government agencies. Part IV deals with applying the materials to several commonly encountered situations: systems and technology implementation and E-Business. This part also contains a chapter in addressing commonly encountered problems in change management.

WHAT YOU WILL GET OUT OF THE BOOK

Most of the chapters are organized in a parallel structure that includes an introduction, method, approach, lessons learned, issues, what to do next (how to use the materials in the chapter), and summary. Our goal is to include many lessons learned from over 40 years of implementing change. In addition, we will be giving examples of failures.

Putting this all together, you will receive specific lessons learned, guidelines, and directions and suggestions for dealing with issues and problems such as resistance to do the following:

- Determine what activities should be changed.
- Get employees and managers on your side to support change.
- Overcome resistance to change.
- Define your change management goals.
- Develop your change management strategy.
- Identify your long-term work and processes.
- Organize teams and create a collaborative, sharing atmosphere that supports change.
- Create Quick Hits that support the long-term work and processes.
- Determine your change implementation strategy.
- Build your change implementation plan.
- Implement change and Quick Hits.
- Measure the results and work.
- Keep the momentum of change alive.
- Prevent the work from reverting or falling back to what it was.

There are several example firms used. There are over 200 specific guidelines. In addition, we have provided many checklists, score cards, and other aids to help you use the material right away.

Here are some of the questions that will be addressed in this book.

- How do you deal with high management expectations for change results?
- What steps should you take to establish support for change among lower level employees?
- How should you handle long-term department employees whose power is derived from the current, long standing work and rules?
- How do you cope with management wanting change, but not willing to provide support?
- What do you do if a key management sponsor leaves?
- What approach do you take if major IT and infrastructure changes are needed to generate business change?
- How do you address the many exceptions, workarounds, and "shadow systems" that exist in departments alongside normal work?
- How do you manage implementing change across multiple locations, cultures, and countries?
- What if you have to make changes that affect customers or suppliers?
- How do you sustain people's interest in change?
- How do you prevent reversion and falling back to the "old ways?"

ADVANTAGES OF THIS BOOK

- Wider scope than most books in covering implementation of change, ongoing change management, and prevention of reversion and deterioration.
- How to allocate employee and manager time between change efforts and regular work.
- How to develop an effective change objective and strategy and relate it to business vision, mission, and objectives.
- Address multiple change efforts so that effectiveness is increased on a cumulative basis.
- How to deal with over 100 issues and problems that arise during your change effort.
- How to address political and cultural factors at the department, organization, and country level.
- How to identify Quick Hit changes as well as long-term change.
- Develop a winning change implementation strategy and roadmap.
- Construct a pro-change structure for lasting improvements.
- How to use politics and resistance to change to help your change effort.
- Step-by-step approach for implementation of change.

Part I

Select Your Change Management Strategy and Approach

Chapter 1

Introduction

BACKGROUND OF CHANGE

From childhood we are exposed to change. Most of us are taught that change is often good—reflecting a positive religious, political, and cultural outlook. As we all age, we tend to get more comfortable in patterns that do not change much from day-to-day. People may jokingly remark that they "live in a rut," but when you offer people the opportunity to change, many decline. There is a lot behind this.

There is the fear of change and what might happen.
There is the potential loss of power due to the change.
There is the effort, sometimes, great to react to the change.

Psychologists indicate that the leading changes that cause real stress are divorce, changing jobs, moving, a death in the family, and marriage.

For centuries people have tried to make improvements to their lives through innovation, invention, government, automation, and other means. Things that we take for granted today were highly resisted when they were introduced. Several examples will help put change management in perspective.

You cannot assume that change markets and sells itself.

Edison created many inventions. When he demonstrated that electricity could be harnessed through electric lighting, many people were fearful and thought, "If God had meant for people to read and see in the dark, he would not have had night." He showed that you could read books at night in the dark. To many this was irrelevant—they had no books. Some could not read. So for many years, electricity was resisted because there were few perceived useful applications. Edison spent much of his working life attempting to invent devices that could use electricity. The lesson learned here is that:

If there are no guidelines as to what to do after the change, then there will be issues and problems.

You cannot assume that people will automatically do other useful things.

An overall lesson learned from this example is that change must be managed and directed. You cannot just expose something new and expect that everyone will adopt it with wild enthusiasm.

Even when the change is obvious and life hangs in the balance, people resist change. Consider the Roman army. Based mostly on foot, the Roman cavalry did not use stirrups that allow the rider to fire a bow and arrow while guiding the horse with his legs. The Dacians and other enemies used stirrups to great advantage against Romans—Rome was too late in adopting the change. People must see the need for change.

Another example occurred with the early invention of the facsimile machine. The fax machine was demonstrated in New York in the early days of the telephone. A manager was shown how he could send and receive the image of a page with someone in another building. When he found out that the cost would be a nickel (a lot of money in those days), he replied, "No, thanks. I can use this errand boy to take the message over for less than one penny." The fax machine languished for some years. The lesson learned here is that:

Timing is critical for successful change.

A fourth example occurred in the 1920s when industrial engineering and work measurement were born. Engineers went out and measured what people did at their workstations and workbenches. They considered detailed hand and body movements. They then instituted changes in procedures to improve production and efficiency. The engineers observed the workers doing the functions the new way and noted the improvements. They then left. It should be no surprise that when they returned some time later, people had reverted back to working the old way. Efficiency was lost.

There is another basic lesson learned here.

When you successfully implement change, you cannot assume that it will continue. Processes and work are subjected to continuous pressure that can lead to reversion.

Here are some factors to watch for:

- A new type of work can arrive. People don't know what to do so they revert.
- New employees are brought in without proper training in the work so they employ what they knew from before—the methods for doing the work have just been subverted.
- Somebody comes up with some new idea and unplanned change occurs— maybe good or bad.

- Lack of oversight of the work
- No method to deal with new types of work or activities
- Feeling of time pressure
- Lack of support of change by the supervisors
- Gaps and holes in the work exist in the changed process and were not addressed during the change, causing people to fall back
- Loss of key employee(s) who supported change
- Arrival of new supervisor or manager who changes things again
- Multiple shift operation where change was not carried on later shifts
- The benefits of change to the employee were not explained so that the employee is not motivated to keep the change in place
- No one is paying attention to the process anymore

Figure 1.1 Factors Contributing to Dilution or Reversion of the Change

Keeping these in mind, you can see that it is important to follow these guidelines.

- Very few processes or work patterns are stable—there is always pressure and factors that challenge the current methods.
- The effects of change and the work must be measured on an ongoing basis to detect reversion and to look for further improvement.
- There must be something in the change for the employee or person doing the work—self-interest is critical in change.
- The change and new ways must be protected from new situations that arise that can pervert or cause stress to the new process.

A list of factors that can cause work to revert back to an earlier state or to deteriorate is given in Figure 1.1.

MOTIVATION AND TRIGGERS FOR CHANGE

In order to understand change, it is important to understand what the trigger or impetus is or was for the change. From experience it is common that change results from multiple trigger factors. These can be a combination of external and internal pressures. Figure 1.2 gives a list of specific factors along with comments.

It is important to understand these triggers before you embark on planning and implementing change since they affect the dimensions of change differently. Looking at the list again in Figure 1.2, you can discern that there are identifiable categories that include the triggers. These include:

- Upper management, organization change, mergers
- Competition
- Regulation
- Customers/suppliers (change in the work)
- Failure of the current methods in the work
- Technology

- Internal factors
  - — Management change
  - — Change of management priorities
  - — Internal problems in the work
  - — High employee turnover
  - — Loss of key staff
  - — New products or services
  - — Implementation of new technology
  - — Merger or acquisitions
  - — Organization change

- External factors
  - — Sales increase or drop
  - — Competition heats up, forcing changes in processes
  - — New technology has emerged that is very compelling to use
  - — Government policies and regulations change
  - — Union contracts change
  - — Consultants recommend changes to the work

Figure 1.2   Potential Triggers for Change

Look at this and you see that most of these are uncontrollable and are also external to the process and work. What does this say? Well, the employees involved in the work will still feel that their existing methods will work since they may not be aware or pay much attention to external factors. This fact fuels the fires of resistance to change. Thus, whatever the other triggers are for change, it is important that:

Failure of the current methods in the work must be one of the triggers for change.

Here is a lesson learned. If the current methods work for the old situation still, then you would show the employees that they fail in the new situation.

There is another observation on these triggers for change related to the number of triggers. If there are too many triggers for change, the design and implementation of change become more difficult and complex.

DIMENSIONS OF CHANGE

Let's move from the triggers to the change itself. What are you going to change overall? Answering this is important for planning and success. Here are some of the major dimensions for change.

- Management (how work is directed)
- The work itself (what work is performed—scope)
- Procedures (how work will be done)

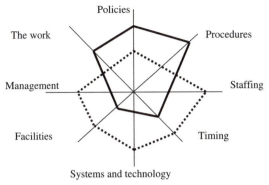

Figure 1.3 Dimensions of Change

Note: Change in the solid line characterizes traditional workflow and procedure change. The dotted line version is more representative or more radical change through automation.

- Systems and technology (how work is to be done)
- Staffing and organization (who does the work and its supervision)
- Policies (how work is governed)
- Facilities, location, and infrastructure (where the work is done)
- Timing (when the work is done)

You can now construct a spider chart or radar chart using each item in the list as a dimension. An example is given in Figure 1.3. Here there are two versions of change. In the solid version there are changes in procedures and policies, but the technology and other elements are basically retained. The dotted version corresponds to more radical change in E-Business where automation replaces traditional transactions. In any spider chart, where the lines are actually placed on the dimensions is subjective. The purpose of using these types of charts is to generate discussion in planning for change and to achieve consensus on the actions and approach to be taken.

BENEFITS OF CHANGE

Most people think of benefits in terms of cost or headcount reduction. However, real life is more complex. There are many other tangible benefits. Some key ones are listed below. Intangible benefits will be covered in Chapter 4.

- Elimination and/or simplification of work (reduced labor, training, supervision)
- Increased efficiency (higher productivity, volume and/or reduced labor)
- Improved management of the work (better planning and less labor)

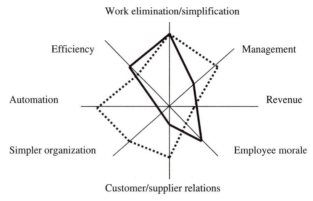

Figure 1.4   Dimensions of Benefits

Note: The two sets of lines correspond to the alternatives in Figure 1.3.

- Increased automation (more structure of work, less rework)
- Increased revenue
- Simpler organization (management, staffing)
- Improved customer/supplier relations
- Improved employee morale (reduced turnover, improved productivity)

You can draw another spider chart for these benefits (see Figure 1.4) so that you can now perform trade-offs between the scope of change and the benefits. The same two examples of Figure 1.3 are shown here. Of course, each situation is unique. In the solid line case, the benefits tend to lie in simplification and efficiency. Morale may be improved as well. In the dotted line case, the benefits for a business-to-business E-Business implementation are shown.

How do you use this? In your planning for change, you will be examining alternatives for objectives, areas of change, and impacts. Thus, you can define an alternative for change using Figure 1.3. Then, after analyzing the impact you can fill in Figure 1.4 so as to link the two.

EXPECTATIONS FOR CHANGE

One might think that expectations for change are the same as benefits from change. However, because change is often political and cultural, this may often not be true. Why is this important to you? Here are some answers.

- High expectations of management tend to push more radical change to get the results.
- Low expectations can lead to no change.

To understand this, you have to see how expectations are created and treated. Expectations are often created before there has been any analysis of the work. You say, "This doesn't make sense. How can you determine what will happen without information?" Well, management wants to have some idea of impact before they kick off a change or improvement effort.

How do expectations get created? Here are some examples from experience.

- Consultants want to get work so they overpromise results—raising expectations.
- Vendors of software, hardware, etc. desire to sell more of their products so they emphasize benefits—raising expectations.
- Internal managers want to get promoted or move the company ahead so they support change, and to get approval raise expectations.

WHAT IS CHANGE MANAGEMENT?

Formally, *change management* is the approach to plan, design, implement, manage, measure, and sustain changes in business processes and work. Some of the activities that are involved in change management include:

- Review the triggers and expectations of change
- Identify potential areas for change
- Market the change and change management throughout
- Define objectives and scope for change
- Select the activities for change
- Define how the work will be performed after the change
- Determine the implementation strategy for change
- Manage and direct the change
- Measure the work before, during, and after the change
- Ensure that the change is lasting and persistent
- Maintain the momentum of change

Perhaps, the items in the list that are overlooked most often are the last two. Many people and methods deal with change, but they address only the initial change. Making the effort and incurring the cost and time to implement change is basically worthless if the change is not persistent.

THE NEED AND IMPORTANCE FOR MANAGING CHANGE

What if some of the things listed above are not done? Let's consider these one by one. Figure 1.5 gives both the need and the impact of each management

Element	Need	Impact, if not addressed
Review of triggers, expectations	Understand where managers are coming from	Misjudge what is behind change
Identification of areas of potential change	Need to be able to understand alternatives for trade-offs	Missed opportunities
Define objectives	Realistic and attainable objectives	Lack of focus
Define the scope	Trade-off between activities, resources, schedule	Scope creep and expansion
Market change and change management	Marketing is required to compensate for inertia, resistance, and political/ cultural factors	Support for change will wane
Select activities for change	Get management behind the selection	Without active trade-offs, the the whole effort is in danger
Determine how work will be done after change	Need for vision of the change	No common vision of change effect leads to confusion, misunderstanding
Create the implementation strategy	Organized approach for phasing in change	Lack of direction of the change
Manage the change	Need for multiple levels of management	Problems remain unresolved for too long
Measure the work	Essential for benefits, morale, and momentum	Lack of confidence in change without measurement
Ensure lasting change	Essential in order to get benefits	Lower morale; more inefficient work
Maintain change momentum	Build cumulative effect	Change results may later be undone

Figure 1.5   Elements of Change Management

change element. In reviewing the table you can see that the need for each of the elements of change management is compelling.

The term "management" implies that there is structure, organization, planning, and control. Methods and techniques are in place along with guidelines for change. Because of the politics, culture, and actual and potential resistance to change, change management requires more planning and thought than other types of management. For example, reengineering attempts to carry out major change through a project. In reality, change management is beyond a project—it is an ongoing program.

Overall, if all of the elements of change management are not implemented and then carried out effectively, from experience you may face some or all of the following:

- The people who resist change win so future change becomes even more daunting and difficult.

- Processes, activities, and work tend to sink back into greater inefficiency.
- Automation and systems efforts tend to become more narrowly focused—leading to costs being incurred without the benefits.
- Management in its desire for savings resorts to more drastic measures of outsourcing and downsizing.
- The best junior people in departments become demoralized and often leave the organization.
- The organization is not perceived to be innovative from the outside—impacting supplier and customer relationships as well as the opinions of the investment market.

Not a pretty picture. In fact, out of fear some managers seek to avoid change management and concentrate on small changes and automation, hoping that systems and technology will somehow magically and automatically implement change. Given industry experience, this is not likely to happen at all.

A COMMON SENSE APPROACH TO CHANGE MANAGEMENT

Our approach to change management is based upon the following themes:

- *Grassroots participation.* If you have any hopes of lasting change, the will to continue the policies, procedures, and work rules that were put in place through change will have to be supported and sustained through the employees in departments who are doing the work on a day-to-day basis. You cannot rely on supervisory and managerial support.
- *Upper level management support, but only limited involvement.* Many people think that management must be heavily involved in change and change management. This is not realistic. Managers at all levels have many other issues and subjects to deal with everyday. Besides, you don't want heavy management involvement as it can interfere and impede the change. Employees become intimidated by managers and their power and so acquiesce and agree to anything a manager says—even if it wrong.

  You must have management support at the start. But after that it is a different matter. You really only want management support in dealing with specific key issues and problems. This is reasonable given the scope of what managers must do. Also, managers who are effective are good problem solvers. So the approach fits with their roles.

- *Collaboration.* You cannot carry out change alone. Also, a project team cannot hope to carry out change. Change requires a joint effort involving many people. The more people that get involved in all aspects of change, the better.

- *Implementation of change in terms of discrete waves.* While this has been discussed somewhat, there are some additional key ideas. First, change implementation can be very draining and tiring. The people and the organization become very tired of change. After some changes have been put in place, you have to take a rest. But it is not a true rest since you are measuring the results, gathering lessons learned, preventing reversion, and preparing for the next wave.
- *Measurement of the work.* Unless you measure the work and activities, how will you ever know if the change is effective? How will you know what methods work? Therefore, measurement is a key activity in change management—all the way through.
- *Development of a strategy for the processes and work.* You must have two strategies. One is the overall approach. The second is a winning strategy for implementation. These strategies are part of your planning and help you to achieve several important political objectives. First, they are evidence of an organized approach. Second, they are flexible to accommodate events. Essential ingredients for your success in the political arena.
- *Recognition and exploitation of the fact that change is often highly political.* Treating change as a technical or business subject is like saying the world is two dimensional. Politics is a fact of life. Organizations and people engage in politics. Much of the power that people have in organizations derives from the activities and work. Thus, any change to the work affects the political structure.
- *Cultural sensitivity.* While the principles of change apply anywhere in the world, the actual detailed methods, the sequencing and organization of actions related to change and the organization of change all relate to the specific culture. There are basically three levels of culture that must be addressed. One is the culture of the country. The second is that of the organization as a whole. The third is the specific culture in the individual business unit or department. Failure to take any of these into account can wreak havoc with any change effort.

ORGANIZATION OF THE BOOK

The book is structured in parts to support the above themes. In the first part you will first examine characteristics of change and resistance to change. These subjects provide the basis for developing your objectives and strategy for implementing change. Of key importance here is the emphasis on strategy. An effective change strategy for change is essential to overcome cultural barriers and political resistance. This is followed by an examination of change management approaches.

Part I provides the basis to begin the change process. Part II begins with selecting the activities to be changed. This is tricky because you must make your selection in such a way as to gain short-term wins as well as longer term persistent change. Guidelines are then presented for gathering information quickly and simultaneously gaining political support for change. The analysis of the information provides the basis for two things—long-term change and short-term quick hits. But defining what to do is not enough; you also must determine how to implement the change— the change implementation strategy. The strategy is then supported by a detailed implementation plan.

Part III addresses the actual implementation of both quick hits and long-term change. Measuring results and generating enthusiasm for change are important elements of implementation. There are two chapters on maintaining change momentum and preventing reversion.

The last part of the book, Part IV, addresses specific situations and serves to unify the guidelines presented in the earlier chapters. Two common types of change are addressed—systems and technology and E-Business.

Each chapter is designed in a similar way. After an introduction, the key topics are covered. This is followed by the following sections:

- *Examples*. The same examples are followed throughout most of the book. This gives the material more structure and makes the reading more interesting.
- *Potential issues and risks*. In each step there are always substantial risks. Issues lurk. Unless you are ready for these, your change management effort can be derailed from its inception.
- *Lessons learned*. These are more detailed guidelines on how to use the methods in the specific chapter.
- *Summary*. A short recap of the themes of the specific chapter.

In addition to the Index there are three appendices. One gives references, another lists some specific useful web sites, and the third is called the Magic Cross Reference. It is called "magic" because it provides a more rapid way of accessing key ideas in the book without using the Index.

EXAMPLES

In the last two chapters you will be examining two common areas of change through technology and process improvement. However, you need to see some additional examples of what went right with change management and what went horribly wrong. For the "wrong" results you will see a variety of organizations. For the "right" results, two organizations will be used.

Rockwood County is a major local government that has all of the problems of any government agency. Departments do not trust each other; they fight for money and power. Bureaucracy and autocracy reign. Yet, Rockwood was able to carry out change in over 60% of its agencies. These changes are in place today.

Legend Manufacturing is a producer of electrical motors as well as higher end integrated structures. Legend had tried several attempts at change, but the results were not encouraging. The computer and manufacturing systems at Legend are in need of modernization. The management is almost desperate in its desire to ensure that there will be a change this time. If it fails again, there is a real fear that there will not be another chance.

POTENTIAL ISSUES AND RISKS

Because of politics, culture, and other factors, at each step of the way toward change, there are issues to be faced and risks to be addressed. Let's pause for a moment and talk about risk. Risk is an extremely fuzzy and political term. It typically means something different to everyone. So you need a workable definition of risk. Here *risk* in a situation is present if there is one or more significant unresolved issue. The more issues that are present, the greater the risk.

Risk has two components: likelihood of a problem and impact of the problem (*exposure*). In the definition of risk here, the impact of the issues constitutes the exposure. The likelihood and time importance of the issues is the likelihood of the exposure occurring.

Here are some general risks to change management:

- Management wants change but is unwilling to be involved and assumes some of the risk as players in change implementation. Lip service is paid to change, but there is no supporting action. As you will see, you will want to test management resolve early.
- The scope of what is to be changed is not correct or suited to the politics or culture. This is a very common problem and has to be faced head-on. If the scope is too small, there are few benefits. Change management becomes "ho-hum" management. If the scope is too vast, then change takes too long to accomplish. Nothing is changed; there are no results or benefits. As they say in fairy tales and movies, "choose wisely or else..."
- There is too much enthusiasm at the start. Change management is a program. The situation is similar to that in running. Enthusiasm is great for a 100-meter dash. It is deadly in a marathon race. Implementing change is a marathon. Enthusiasm is great, but it must be measured and sustained by results.

LESSONS LEARNED

Lessons learned in this book are detailed guidelines that relate to using the methods of the chapter. Here are some lessons learned for this chapter:

- Any adoption of a change management approach should be viewed as tentative—regardless of how loudly and frequently managers support change and the approach. Everyone wants short-term proof that the approach yields tangible results.

- It is easy to get caught up in near-term Quick Hits of change. After all, they increase morale. Results are good. However, you have to keep your eye on the long-term change.
- Once you have implemented change in one activity, do not rush away and leave it. If you do, you are making the false assumption that the change will last on its own. Changes have to be tuned over time. People have to become comfortable with the new ways.
- Do not get caught up in high-level aspects of change. Otherwise, you will never get down to the details of change.
- By the same token, do not get trapped in the details of a specific change at the bottom of the organization. Otherwise, you will never be able to move on to other areas. Thus, you have to carefully steer a middle course between general and specific changes.
- People can get so caught up in carrying out change that they fail to learn from their actions. Then you will likely find that the same mistakes made in the past are committed again.

SUMMARY

The overall canvas of change management has been laid out before you. In addition to definitions you have been alerted to potential problems and have been given some proven guidelines. It is now time to pick up your tools and plan your painting of change.

Chapter 2

Dynamics of Change and Work

INTRODUCTION

With change management defined, some of the lessons learned about change and change management can be explored to provide a better understanding of what lies ahead. Change involves considering how the following elements relate to each other.

- Business processes and activities
- Procedures and business rules
- Business policies
- The business organization
- Information Technology (IT) and systems

A *business process* is a set of organized activities and work to carry out specific defined functions. Not only are such things as payroll, sales, production, and marketing included as processes, but so are supporting and analytical activities such as market research, IT support, facilities maintenance, etc. Some observations about processes are:

- Processes are often really composed of groups of smaller processes.
- It is difficult to consider just one process since processes are intertwined through the work.

The individual pieces of work may be just tasks or they may be transactions. A *transaction* consists of a defined set of steps that are performed within the process with specified inputs and results. Transactions can be performed many times a day or minute, or they may be only carried out infrequently based on the characteristics of the information input to the process.

The business process and its transactions are governed by informal and formal rules and guidelines, including:

- *Business rules* are formal, defined directions for what to do with the input to the process.
- *Procedures* are detailed methods that describe step by step how the transaction or work is to be handled.
- A *business policy* is a regulation imposed by the organization internally or externally through government, union, or other agreements and relationships.
- *Guidelines* are recommended methods and techniques on how to do the work.

How these are related is shown in Figure 2.1. In this diagram you can see that the different transactions and work are represented by the third dimension. In change management, you may elect to alter only a few transactions, leaving many or most of the work intact.

You really need all of the above elements to make up a business process and to govern the transactions. Why go through all of this now? Because you will have to decide when you are planning change and what will be changed. You can change the work by changing any or all of all these ingredients. Your change efforts may fail if you don't think about all of these elements together.

The work and transactions in the business process are carried out by people and through systems and technology. In modern processes, some or all of the work may be done by customers, suppliers, or by vendors through outsourcing. The *organization* provides the structure and management for the internal employees doing work in the process. Thus, the organization is one step removed from the business process. This is a key fact that will be employed several times in terms of your planning and implementation of change. Organizations are composed of divisions, departments, and other business units. The organization also establishes

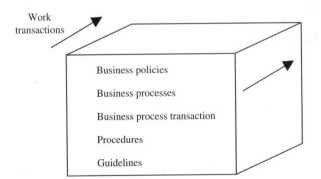

Figure 2.1   Elements of Business Processes

relationship principles that govern what suppliers, customers, and vendors can do in a business process.

CULTURE AND CHANGE

Culture and cultural factors play a strong role in influencing business processes. Some examples are:

- Culture can restrict or affect how customers and suppliers interrelate.
- Culture can impact the extent to which rules, procedures, and policies are formalized or left unspoken.

When you undertake and manage change, you have to be sensitive to three layers of culture.

- *Country or area culture.* This is the most commonly thought of by most people. It includes the mores, ethics, and habits of a geographic area.
- *Organization culture.* Any organization develops and evolves a culture over time. Typically, the roots of the organization culture were put in place by the founders and early experiences of the organization.
- *Department culture.* Within any organization there are many different units or departments. Each department can have its own unique cultural attributes.

Realize that these are intertwined so that if you institute change in one location, you may still be dealing with country culture, organization culture, and several different department cultures. This makes changes more complex and political.

POLITICS, POWER, AND CHANGE

In and around a business process swirl political currents. First, there is the direct power structure as seen in an organization chart. A fundamental mistake made in change management is to think that this is the extent of the power structure and political framework. Because change gets into the detail of the work, there are many more complex elements of politics to be considered. Some of these that will have to be considered are:

- Informal politics and power relationships among people doing the work.
- Politics between departments and business units.

In an established business process, there are people who have been doing the same work for many years. Over time these people have gathered knowledge and experience that gives them power. In this book these people will be referred to as the "king bees" and "queen bees." These people derive power from the following:

- They know the business rules for handling exceptional and unusual work.
- They know how to "work the system" to get things done.

As such, the junior employees rely on them for guidance. The king and queen bees then have power from those around them. These people can actually be very junior in terms of the formal organization structure, but are at the apex of power within the group. The king and queen bees also derive power from supervisors and middle level managers who are removed from the work and so often depend on the "bees" to maintain basic efficiency of the process.

In most cases, the king and queen bees represent the greatest political threat to change and sustaining lasting change. With change their power is eroded. If informal procedures are made formal, their power is eroded. Here is the bottomline lesson learned.

King a id queen bees can act as a blessing or a curse
to change management.

The bees are often a greater political threat to change than middle level managers and supervisors who may feel threatened, but are not involved directly in the work. To carry out change you often have to use the bees as sources of information for the business process and work. However, beware that they can be the greatest enemies and impediments to change.

CHANGE AND INFORMATION TECHNOLOGY

The relationship between IT and change has become more complex as the technology and systems have improved. In the early days of computerization, systems did not operate within the business process. Instead, they worked beside the business process. Typically, people performed tasks and then entered the results into a computer system. It is no wonder that many computer systems failed to generate savings in the business processes since they represented additional work.

On-line systems and networks produced profound changes in business processes. It became possible for customers and suppliers to do some or all of the work through electronic commerce or E-Business. Workflow tracking and automation have allowed software systems to track and monitor the performance of a business process down to the individual step of a transaction.

Now step back from this level of detail and what do you see? Here is one basic truth.

IT has acted to formalize business processes.

This is good and bad in its impact.

- Knowledge of business rules in the process often shifts to the IT group since the programmers there must be acutely aware of these to automate procedures.
- Automation makes a business process inflexible. That automation increases flexibility is a myth perpetuated by vendors and advocates of technology. In the real world when you commit rules and procedures to COBOL, Java, or ASP code, you now make changes more complex, time consuming, and expensive.
- Automation fosters additional shadow systems in departments and business units. If a business unit is faced with performing new work and the IT group cannot respond in time according to tight deadlines, the department may feel that it has no choice, but to invent a new system or process to handle this additional work.
- Automation is most successful in well-defined, stable processes where there is ample time to plan and implement changes to the software.

The situation has not and will not change with data management, object-oriented tools, etc., since these still must be used by technical people and require substantial time for making changes.

Yet, automation is also a key ally in change management.

- When you automate some work, you make it more formal and established and so remove a certain amount of the politics from the group doing the process work.
- Automation of work also makes it harder for the people doing the work to revert back to the old process and methods.
- Systems can provide for automated measurement of the process—extremely valuable on an ongoing basis.

THE IMPORTANCE OF INTERFACES

From experience we have observed and learned the basic truth that:

Change management is more about interfaces than it is about work in a small group or unit.

Look around at any process and what do you see? Interfaces. Figure 2.2 gives some of the critical interfaces and provides some comments about each one.

Interfaces play a critical role in change management. Here are some examples.

- If you change the work perfectly, the results can be nothing or worse than nothing because some of the interfaces were negatively impacted.
- Many of the best opportunities for change involve multiple processes, organizations, and systems.

Interface	Comments
The process and the organization	How effective and committed the people are to the work in the process
The process and the systems	The extent to which the system supports the work in the process
The process and other processes	How processes interface with information and controls
The organization supporting the process and that supporting another process	How two organizations collaborate and fight impacting the work performance
The process and the long-range business plan	The importance of the process to achieving the business objectives, mission, and vision
The process and the IT strategic plan	The priority of systems work for the process in the future
Transactions and work within the process	How one piece or type of work impacts another in the process
The process and facilities	How conducive and supportive the office, factory, or warehouse is for the process
The process and the culture	How the work is structured and impacted by the culture

Figure 2.2   Important Interfaces Involving Business Processes

- In trying to become more efficient and effective, processes are becoming more integrated. This is true in almost all industries and government agencies.

In a way,

Change management is concerned about processes, systems, and organization interfaces.

CHANGE AND BUSINESS PLANNING AND CONTROL

Change is also related to these elements of planning and management:

- Long-range business plan
- IT strategic plan
- Project management
- Process improvement

It is remarkable to us that so much effort is expended by companies on developing strategic business and IT plans. These are organizational plans. But the organization and IT only support the business process. They are *not* the business process. This indicates that there is a missing element in planning in many organizations —the development of plans for the key business processes. Thus, in a later chapter you will be defining and determining the direction of the business process through the process plan.

It is also very difficult to relate a business long-range plan with an IT strategic plan. The business long-range plan speaks of profit and sales targets, customer and supplier relations, and other general ideas. In contrast the IT strategic plan defines specific actions, projects, and strategies. These go together like oil and water. However, there is one thing they have in common.

The long-range business objectives and strategies can only come true through the business processes.

and

IT systems and strategies exist solely to affect the work and business processes.

Thus, it makes common sense to relate the business and IT plans through the process plans. Figure 2.3 provides a simplified view of the situation. Note that you will later be relating the fuzzy things like mission, vision, objectives, and strategies to concrete business processes through the process plans. In this diagram there are interfaces to and from all three elements. Formally, the *IT infrastructure* includes the hardware, system software, network, communications, and support that make the operation of the application systems and software tools such as groupware, intranets, e-mail, etc., possible.

Now let's turn to projects and programs. A *project* is a defined set of tasks and milestones intended to accomplish a specific objective in a limited, defined time

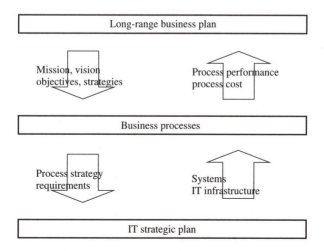

Figure 2.3   Business Processes and Business and IT Planning

with a set of resources. A *program* is an ongoing effort to achieve a series of longer term objectives. You can see the differences in the following table.

Characteristic	Project	Program
Time span	Limited	Extended
Methods	Defined	Variable
Focus	Very short term	Long term
Benefits	End with completion of project	Lasting

Turn now to efforts to carry out change and improvement. Many process improvement efforts are projects. Reengineering is typically a project. Six Sigma is often treated as a project. By contrast,

Change management is a program.

Once you embark on change management and you get results, it is like something you cannot get enough of. Change management continues.

THE PROCESS OF CHANGE

Figure 2.4 gives an overall figure of change and change management. Let's tear into this diagram one step at a time because it is important for you to grasp what is going on with change management. Look at the box on the left. This is a box showing processes and the ingredients of the processes. The third dimension of the box is to allow for multiple processes.

The purpose of change and change management is to move the situation and processes from the box on the left to the box on the right. This takes time and as you can see, the diagram is really a simplification since there will be many discrete changes over a period of time.

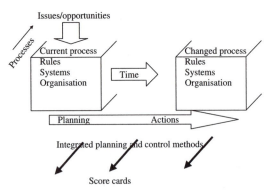

Figure 2.4   An Overview of Change in Processes

Now look at the upper left of the diagram. You can see issues and opportunities coming down on the processes. These represent *triggers for change*. A trigger for change is really a combination of factors that are compelling the organization to undertake change. You will need to understand the potential and actual triggers because

The nature of the triggers for change shape change management.

Now consider the large arrow from the left to the right below the boxes. You must first undertake planning to carry out the change. Then you will take a variety of actions to make the changes come true.

But you are not finished yet. What good is all of this work if there is no real change and an *acknowledgement of the change*? Thus, change must be measured, controlled, and planned through change management. The actual measurements will be accomplished through score cards. *Score cards* are a collaborative approach to more completely assess the performance and state of the business processes.

REVERSION DURING AND AFTER CHANGE

Most books and approaches stop with the last section. This is not effective. You have to be concerned with what happens after the change has been carried out. In the last chapter, reversion of the process to a previous or worse state was defined. Let's discuss it further.

People get in to habits regarding their individual and professional lives. Habits make work bearable and create efficiency since performing something out of habit or through "second nature," makes you more efficient. You don't have to think about it much. When you implement change, you often change people's habits. What they did before does not work now and may not even be relevant. Moreover, if they do the work the old way, the situation actually deteriorates.

Many people are also uncomfortable with change. They stay in poor personal relationships, bad geographic areas, undemanding jobs because they are uncomfortable. Change is threatening to this comfort zone.

Reversion and resistance to change don't just occur after the change has been taken; they can surface during the efforts to instill change. Thus, you have the following basic lesson learned.

Change management is about dealing with reversion
of the process from the very start.

Reversion can take many forms. The procedures may change, but the old policies governing the process remain. The king and queen bees may push for reversion to retain their power and influence, and the old power structure. People are pressured to keep process performance up during change. This often requires them to follow the old process rules and procedures until the final turnover to the new process.

10 COMMON MYTHS OF CHANGE

It is amazing in a way to think that with efforts to effect change over thousands of years, there still persist common myths related to change. Let's examine some of these.

- *Change is a one-time effort.* In the past this might have been possible. However, typically today changes have ripple effects through interfaces and integration.
- *You have to change the organization first to carry out change.* How do you know how to change the organization when you have not changed the work? What requirements do you know and can be certain of before the change?
- *You need systems and technology to carry out effective change.* Systems and technology can help and may be appropriate, but it depends upon the situation.
- *If management sees the need for change, then it is evident to everyone.* Generally, it is only evident to the managers.
- *If you know what you want to change, you can just go ahead and do it.* Because processes and work are more integrated and interfaces are more widespread, carrying out change in isolation by plunging in can be devastating.
- *You should carry out all of the changes at one time to avoid disruption.* This can result in a disaster.
- *The purpose of change is to implement a new stable business process.* This is too narrow a goal. You want to instill a new positive culture and attitude toward change.
- *If you failed in undertaking change in the past, then this is an indicator that change is too difficult to do.* While you can learn from the past, it is not a predictor of what will happen with other methods.
- *Change is positive and so it should be widely supported.* Change is often seen as negative and not positive. People look at the triggers for change and say to themselves, "If we need to change, it must be because the organization is in trouble." This is a natural feeling.
- *You only need to involve a limited number of key employees to implement change.* Nothing could be further from the truth. If you only involve the king and queen bees, you are likely to never have change or only very minor change that preserves their power.

21 REASONS WHY CHANGE FAILS

Let's pull together from the discussion so far and from experience a number of reasons why change efforts fail. Keep these in mind as a checklist when you are deeply involved in a change effort. It will help you retain the big picture of change in your mind's eye.

- *Change is not thought through or planned carefully.* In some cases, companies make an intensive initial effort to find improvements. Then they rush to implement. This has occurred, for example, in some quality improvement efforts. Later, to their chagrin, they find that the changes must be undone.
- *Management starts a change initiative, but does not follow through.* Some managers adopt some method with enthusiasm and then proceed to move on to something else. The organization is then littered with the debris of half attempted methods. After a few of these, the employees start to question the sanity of managers.
- *The company depends upon an external consulting firm to do too much of the work.* The consulting firm has made a glowing presentation promising major benefits. They cite past efforts and extensive experience. Management buys into this thinking that if they throw money at change, it will magically happen. Guess what? The consulting firm will likely exploit the company's employees and take credit for their ideas. Then they will embed themselves in the organization. The bill is increasing exponentially while the expected results are declining linearly.
- *The change effort becomes bogged down in exceptions and workarounds.* You have a few king and queen bees involved in the effort. They start mentioning exceptions and issues. The change leaders respect these people and so take all of this seriously. The change effort is now mired in a morass of meaningless detail.
- *The change effort fails to address critical shadow systems.* The change team and leaders become convinced that they have the right recipe for change. They ignore the shadow systems and fail to answer the question, "Why were these created and why are they still in use?"
- *Automation and technology are viewed as the golden weapons for change.* If technology becomes the driver for change, then almost all requirements are viewed in the context of the systems. Therefore, any new requirement means that the systems have to be changed to address the requirement. The change effort becomes one big IT project—likely to flounder and die a horrible death.
- *Change is instituted and driven top-down.* Management wants to get changes made—now. Generalized processes and workflows are defined. But when they finally reach earth, it is discovered that they do not work. Panic ensues. People just resort to simple changes to the current processes.
- *The change effort is dependent upon one leader who gets burned out.* Change management is not for the faint hearted or for the inexperienced person. Moreover, the political, managerial, and technical demands on the leader can become overwhelming—resulting in burn-out.

- *People are pulled from their normal jobs to implement the change.* When people are removed from their normal work, the relationship with their old colleagues still doing the process becomes strained. There is often mistrust. Wait! It often gets worse. The individuals who are now devoted to change see no need to complete the work quickly since they will just return to their normal work—rather boring considering the management's attention they are getting in the change effort.
- *Change is implemented in different business units and locations without regard to culture.* This often occurs in multinational firms where the same service or product is being offered in different countries. After all, except for packaging and marketing, it is the same stuff. In one case, the change effort antagonized customers in a country so much that the firm had to withdraw from this very profitable market.
- *Change is attempted without addressing the problems of existing, old computer systems.* The change effort is started and work progresses. Some enhancements to the current systems are identified. But there is no follow-up. Then when the change effort is ready for the systems with the changes, there is nothing there. Surprise.
- *Resistance to change during the process of change halts the effort.* This occurs frequently in organizations with weak middle management. Managers become intimidated by employees who say such things as, "If you want us to do the work, then we cannot change things now."
- *Management sees some early benefits and decides to stop.* The change effort gets off to a good start. There are some good initial results. Then people get tired as management loses interest. This happens all the time in weight loss programs where the individual loses some weight (mostly water) and gets on a high. The weight returns.
- *The scope of the change effort is too large so that there are no interim positive results.* This is characteristic of the large-scale change methods which focus overly on the long-term changes—viewing interim change as not worth the effort or trouble and taking resources away from the longer term effort.
- *There is no effort to measure the business process and work prior to implementing the change.* In survey after survey this has shown to be the case. In many IT projects there is no real effort to measure where you start.
- *Issues and problems that surface during the change effort are not addressed quickly enough.* Change requires a great deal of work to be done by a limited number of people so that it is easy to ignore or push aside some issue to be addressed later. Later may never come.
- *Political issues and the power structure are not considered as major parts of the change effort.* Change management and change itself are viewed by many in technical or management terms. This is to get a rigorous

approach. However, as you have seen politics can make or break the change effort.

- *People who do the work in the process are not heavily involved in the effort.* There are several factors that contribute to this. First, management may see these people as not having any good ideas. Second, they do not wish to disturb the current work. Yet, it is these people who are the core of the change.
- *Fuzzy measurements are employed to determine success or failure.* The world of change management is littered with intangible benefits. Our point is this—if you are going to go to all this effort, don't you want tangible benefits?
- *The change effort is managed as an IT project.* If you think that IT is to be involved in the change effort, then it is natural to think that IT should manage the change effort. However, the psychology of IT and background make it often ill-suited to change management. They can be involved in the management of change with business managers.
- *The organization attempts to utilize a method that is not suited to the organization and its culture.* Look at Six Sigma and the other methods of process improvement and you see major costs. People are pulled out of their jobs for intensive and extensive training. Can your organization make the sacrifices in the business and incur the risk in order to follow such an approach? Remember if you make the wrong decision, you could be betting the future of the company.

16 CRITICAL SUCCESS FACTORS FOR EFFECTIVE CHANGE

Let's move from the negative to the positive. There have been many successful change management efforts. These are not in just the decade, but span time. Here are some key lessons learned that can be employed as critical success factors to guide you in achieving success in change implementation.

- *Involve many people at the lower levels of the organization.* When you involve more people in change up to a point, then you gather support and participation in the change effort. It is the same as that of all the organized religions of the world. After all, the prophets of these religions did not preach to two guys in a tent.
- *Implement change in orderly waves.* This is discussed more in the next section. Here, you are going to consider making changes in different areas at discrete times and then measuring the results while continuing to prepare for future changes.

- *Try to limit involvement of upper management.* Management can kick off the change effort and give initial support. However, after that their involvement should be limited to key issues.
- *Restrict the roles and responsibilities of the king and queen bees.* These people can be sources of information for specific business rules. There is generally no need to have them involved in the project more than that.
- *Proactively identify and manage issues and problems as they arise.* You should retain and manage an issues database. Management reporting and communications should be heavily linked to issues. Analyzing issues makes the change leaders more in charge of what is going on.
- *Except for a core change team, ensure that all other team members and participants keep doing their existing jobs.* As you will see, if the team members are still involved in their work, they can take ideas back to their groups and get even more participation.
- *Measure almost on a continuous basis.* Measuring using a comprehensive score card is essential so that you will see the larger view of how progress is going.
- *Assume that after and during change reversion will surface.* You should always assume that danger lurks. People who support change must not be relied upon until they prove that they are for change with their actions.
- *Plan ahead for resistance to change.* This will be discussed in the next chapter in detail.
- *Have specific tasks in the change effort jointly performed by several people.* Collaboration is a critical factor in getting lasting change. You can talk teamwork and collaboration all you want, but if you don't back it up with actions, it is meaningless.
- *Utilize two managers to head up the change effort.* There are many benefits to having several people involved including backup, dealing with difficult situations, and getting new ideas.
- *Establish a two-tier steering committee approach to oversee change.* This will be discussed in depth later. Management of a high level steering committee is often too involved to get into the details.
- *Identify longer term IT and other actions and get them started early.* Given the lead time, this only makes sense.
- *Focus on marketing of the change effort continuously from inception to after completion.* Change does not sell itself—even when you show results. Change requires ongoing marketing and sales.
- *Gather lessons learned from the work as you go.* As you undertake change, you will experience many new situations. If you fail to gather knowledge from this, you will not have wisdom later when you need it for major change.
- *Give credit to the people who do the process work.* The people who perform the work are the key players who have to be nurtured.

CHANGE IN ORGANIZED WAVES

The previous chapter indicated the problems with the extremes of continuous change and the "big bang" change. In between are discrete waves of change. You plan and implement some changes in different areas. Then while you are planning for the later waves, you are also marketing and measuring the results.

This approach is definitely not the same as that of the large IT project where there are phases. In these projects typically, the end user department does not get any benefits until phase 23. In the approach here, each wave of change generates tangible benefits.

The trick that you will have to understand is how to organize the changes in a particular wave of change so that they are interrelated with each other, yield positive results, and are consistent with longer term change.

EXAMPLES

ROCKWOOD COUNTY

Rockwood County did not really take the need for change seriously until there was a major budget crunch. The managers were faced with some stark choices— either drastically cut services or streamline and change how government services were delivered. Rockwood had some initial success at making a few services available on the web, but that was a very limited effort. Rockwood lacked funds to hire consultants. So they initially housed the change management in the IT organization. The IT manager appointed a senior systems analyst. This failed almost immediately because the person lacked knowledge and sensitivity toward business processes and believed that the project was an IT effort. A business manager was named to be the joint change leader and the situation improved.

LEGEND MANUFACTURING

As was stated in Chapter 1, Legend had experienced several failed efforts. Fortunately, an effort was made before the next attempt to gather lessons learned from the past. The following factors were uncovered as major contributors to failure.

- Inconsistent direction from management. Management "blew hot and cold" on change management—disrupting the effort.
- Attempts at either small changes or the big change. They had never tried anything in between.
- Dependence on a small team to do all of the work. The team members become locked in process. Moreover, they did not get along with each other.

POTENTIAL ISSUES AND RISKS

- Companies often adopt a change management approach without looking at different alternatives. By considering a wide range of alternative methods, they begin to appreciate more of what lies ahead.
- There is also the fear and risk of being wrong when you undertake change. This is somewhat akin to the fear experienced by soldiers prior to combat. However, you want to also bear in mind the fear of doing nothing and keeping status quo.
- A potential issue at the start of a change effort is that people will become overly enthusiastic about change. This is bad because it is difficult to sustain.

LESSONS LEARNED

- You should review what efforts have been made to carry out change in the past. Often, this was not called change management. Ask yourself the following questions:
  — What was the outcome of the change attempt?
  — Were there measurements undertaken before, during, and after?
  — How was resistance addressed?
  — How were issues managed?
  — How many people were involved in the change?
  — What is the condition of the work and the process today?

- Look around at some of the key processes. Make a list of these. Determine if there has been any major change over the past two years. Identify potential barriers to change. This will help you later in doing assessments of groups of processes.

SUMMARY

Change management is complex when you consider the interfaces and politics involved. However, also remember that it is just making alterations in how everyday people do their everyday work. Keep the myths, failure sources, and critical success factors in mind as you progress through implementing change.

Chapter 3

Politics and the Resistance to Change

INTRODUCTION

Politics can be defined as the science centering on guiding and influencing policies and the conduct of work. Politics can play such a leading role in change management that it and resistance to change warrant a chapter of their own prior to starting to plan for change. After all, it is useful to know what you could potentially be in for before you start walking down the road to change. Politics and self-interest often dictate how people feel about change to their work or the work that they control.

Resistance is the active or passive opposition to change and the management of change. As you will see resistance can take many forms. Individuals and groups can also express or feel degrees of opposition. You must keep in mind that resistance is dynamic and changes depending on the specific situation. Why do people resist change?

- They feel that their jobs will be threatened.
- They will not be viewed with the same importance as they were after the change.
- The management structure above them will change.
- They will have to learn new software and systems.
- They will have to work in a different facility further from home.
- Friends and colleagues will become separated due to new organization of work.
- Their work will be scrutinized in more detail.
- Work performance goals will be increased.

As a result of resistance, individuals may take active steps to protect their positions. At Langley Aerospace (not a real firm), a group of employees was subjected to a reengineering effort. They felt threatened over their jobs. The future jobs they were promised were far less appealing than what they had had for years. The entire knowledge of the engineering process was in two places—their minds and documentation. The group gradually took the documentation home and eventually burned all copies without management having a clue. When management got around to completing change, they found that they could not change the process because the individuals in the group were the only ones who knew how the work was performed.

THE ROLE OF POLITICS

So you cannot ignore politics. It is present in every change situation. Up until now politics have been viewed in a negative light. This was done intentionally to raise your awareness and concern about political factors. This will now be altered here to a neutral state. Politics can be good or bad. A key lesson learned is that:

Change leaders must exploit political factors and use them for the advantage of implementing change.

What does the term, "exploit" mean? You want to first recognize that politics is a fact of life. No matter what you say or do, political factors do not disappear. So another critical success factor in change management is:

You have to understand the specific political situation in a business unit and then attempt to employ this knowledge in getting support for lasting change.

HOW TO DEAL WITH POLITICAL FACTORS

You can see that there are steps in understanding and working with political factors. If you have an organized method for coping with politics, your change efforts will be more successful. Here are some specific steps that have proven useful in past change programs.

- Recognize that individuals and groups act out of self-interest.
- Understand the political self-interest of employees and their supervisors through direct observation and casual conversation.
- Test your understanding by trying out small suggestions for change. Watch people's reactions. This will indicate where people are "coming from" and help you to comprehend their self-interest.

- Start to define the areas and activities in which they potentially feel threatened.
- Define approaches to ameliorate and ease their concerns. You may have to test some ideas out on them.
- Find out what they would like to do. Determine what changes they would make for themselves.
- Construct in your mind trade-offs between the necessary changes and what additional changes you can take that will please them.

Look at this list carefully. You are not trying to fully please people. If you did, the work would probably not change at all. But as was said in Chapter 1, there are many dimensions of change. You might change procedures and policies for the advantage of change, but you could also alter facilities or the working environment to make it a more pleasant place to work, for example. A key lesson learned is understanding that:

Change at its most fundamental level involves trade-offs
in order to be lasting.

Change can be imposed, but such change is often the most fleeting and short-lived.

Let's examine people and their work more. In almost every process there are things that people do not like. But they learn to accept them. As in human relationships, there are trade-offs. After a time an individual will stop thinking about these unpleasant things since they feel that nothing can be done. The thoughts are often suppressed. Now the change leaders and team come on the scene. If they are proceed carefully, they will listen to what the people who do the work have to say. They can then draw out what has been troubling the individuals for so long. This is, perhaps, a turning point toward success in change management. The lesson learned here is:

Success in getting lasting change is to have the employees doing the
work to admit that there are problems and issues with the way and
manner in which the work is performed.

When you have the admission that the current methods don't work well, then you open the door to having them accept change and even to invent potential changes. This will be a central theme as the book proceeds.

TYPES OF RESISTANCES

There are a number of ways to categorize resistance. This is useful for the change team and change management because it helps to understand, discuss, and counter the resistance. One way is by passive and active resistance.

- *Active resistance.* This is rarer in most societies due to culture. In active resistance, some employees will openly question the changes and indicate a lack of support for change. Active resistance is easier to cope with since it is out in the open. You can work with the problems that they raise. In the worst case you can even work around the person.
- *Passive resistance.* This may be difficult to detect. It takes time for you to uncover signs of this in people. People may actually express support for change, but when change is getting closer to being implemented, the resistance starts to come through.

A second related perspective is to consider open versus underground resistance. Underground resistance is more difficult to cope with than passive resistance, because it is active resistance but not evident. In fact, you can create a chart such as that in Figure 3.1. Here one axis is active and passive. The other is open and underground. You can place people's initials in the chart. In Figure 3.1, xyz is a person who actively resists change and openly does so. This is typically a king or queen bee. Person abc is someone who actively resists but does not do so out in the open. Person abc is a real threat to change management since you may not detect that abc feels this way early in the change effort. Person def is someone who is passively resistant to change and who now and then openly admits his/her concern. This is more unusual, but can often be addressed through logical argument. Finally, person ghi is someone whose resistance is passive and underground. These people are many in number since they have natural doubts about the change and whether it will really work. Oftentimes, these individuals can be brought along as the change effort proceeds. The change team may wish to identify individuals in this chart. However, it is obvious that this must be kept confidential.

Another way to view resistance is in terms of the source of the resistance. Already discussed have been emotional sources such as fear of loss of job and fear of power loss. Another source is that of dread of learning something new. Civilization has always had problems with getting new methods and technology

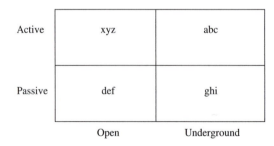

Figure 3.1   Categorization of Resistance

into widespread use—even after the new has been proven and demonstrated to be more effective than the old. This is particularly true with changes in business processes that involve automation. It is important to show the new system and, hence, the new process and procedures are simpler to use.

20 FACTORS BEHIND RESISTANCE

Several factors behind the resistance have been discussed. It is now time to examine a wider range of factors that give rise to resistance to change.

- *Fear of change is contagious.* People around you are afraid of change and transfer this to you. This is most frequently done by relating the worse case impacts of change. A cause of this is often that management did not clearly and convincingly spell out what would happen after the change.
- *Management emphasizes cost savings over productivity and satisfaction of employees.* The employees begin to look around and see that cost savings can only really come about in staff cuts. Junior employees become worried since they may feel that the last hired are the first terminated. Senior employees feel that their positions will be diminished.
- *In some situations people were not properly trained in their current jobs so that they have more resistance to change.* In many business units if, during the interview, it is found that they have done the same or similar work for another firm, they are hired and placed in a department. It is assumed that they do not need training since they know how of doing the work. However, this creates problems since there could be several different ways to do the work. This lack of standardization then leads to more problems when change is attempted.
- *Previous attempts at change in their business unit failed.* Employees may then think that this will be another failed attempt. They see no reason to support the change.
- *Change in another department resulted in job cutbacks.* The writing is on the wall. No matter what the management or the change team says, the real approach is perceived to be aimed at job cutback.
- *In carrying out the change, the change team does not value the knowledge and experience of the employees.* Their sense of worth is diminished so that they are more likely to resist change. Employees often sense this when they are asked what they do, but are not asked about how they do the work. They perceive that the change team does not care.
- *Fear of demotion or loss of position.* This has been discussed. It is interesting to note that the more management says that there will be no layoffs, the more the employees feel that there will be.

- *There has been a history of problems with management so that there is a lack of trust and faith.* Some managers in the past have gone hot and cold on change. They may have tried in a half-hearted way some exotic change method or something related to change. These initiatives then disrupted the work.
- *People are unwilling to participate in change because management views the additional work as part of the job and does not value it.* Management priorities are not clear. Moreover, the employees think that management feels that they must not do much work since they are insisting that the change can be carried out on top of existing work.
- *Employees receive different signals and messages from management and various members of the change team.* This leads not only to confusion, but also resistance. Different signals can be characterized by giving different directions, various and conflicting goals of change, and contradictory procedures or policies.
- *Employees participate and volunteer information at the start of the change effort, but they see that other people take credit for their work.* Some employees have embraced change and have come up with ideas of their own to the change team. Often, the employees had to really think about the change for a long time since they were not trained or have experience in change. Now they see members of the change team taking credit for their ideas. They rightly feel ripped off.
- *The employees are not told what is expected of them. There is a lack of planning with them.* They are just told how to change their work. There is no discussion of impact or what the benefits are to be. This fuzziness leads to confusion and then to resistance.
- *Resistance worked before in the past, it might work again.* This is human nature. What worked in the past is often what is perceived to work well in the current situation.
- *There is substantial management change and turnover.* Current management has directed that change be carried out. Yet, similar things have occurred in the past. Then the managers moved on to other jobs. The employees feel that if they can hold out longer, these managers will disappear.
- *The change is not addressing major needs.* The changes that are defined by the change team are good and perceived as such by the employees. However, there is no effort to address the major problems that the employees perceive to exist.
- *People are being pulled away from their work, but are still held accountable for the same performance.* The employees are involved in the change effort during working hours. However, their normal work is not done by anyone else. So they have to work over their breaks and lunch time to make up for the time lost in the change effort. What does this tell them about how management values their work?

- *The change leaders and team do not address issues raised by the employees.* The employees may raise legitimate issues and questions. The change team or leaders acknowledge the concerns, but nothing is done. The employees almost have no alternative, but to feel that (1) the change team does not care or value their opinions; (2) the change team is following their own agenda without regard to the employees.
- *There are major work pressures, such as year-end closing, right at the time when change is being attempted.* This is obviously poor timing and planning. However, you can still undertake change if you carefully work with these additional pressures.
- *After the change has been defined, middle managers and the change team tinker with the details of the change.* Specific directions have been given on how the work is to be done. A short time later a manager or supervisor arrives and sees what is going on and starts to insist on changes in details. The employees become confused and complain that they don't know what to do.
- *The change team does not make clear in detail how the new procedures are to work.* There are gaps between what directions they are given and what they must do. This is like being given a recipe for a food dish that is incomplete. You have to invent steps to fill the gaps, or you revert back to what you know works.

Now scan this list and what do you see? You see that the common sources of the problems were:

- Lack of coordination and training in carrying out change for the change team.
- Poor leadership by the change managers.
- Lack of coordination among managers and between managers and the change team.

When these problems occur, it should not surprise you that people resist change.

MOTIVATION FOR CHANGE

A person has to be motivated to change. This can be accomplished by accentuating both the positive and negative aspects of the situation.

You should assume that you will meet some resistance to change as this is only natural and a part of life. However, this does not mean that you should wait until resistance surfaces. You should be more proactive in trying to head off change. Part of this is to motivate people for change. How do you motivate employees toward change?

SIGNS OF RESISTANCE

Factors behind resistance have been covered so now it is time for you to examine the symptoms or signs of resistance to change. You will want to use the following list with the change team so that they become more aware of this as well.

- *Tone of voice.* As you present change management to employees and supervisors, look for their reaction in terms of what they say. Make sure that there are two people from the change leaders and the change team at such a presentation. Why? It is difficult to pick up signs when you are doing the talking.
- *Body language.* As you discuss change, watch how the people in the audience move. If they squirm in their chairs, then they are uncomfortable with what you are saying.
- *What employees discuss in your presence.* How carefully do they phrase and choose their words? This will be a sign of lack of familiarity at first. However, if it continues after initial contact, then there could be a problem.
- *What employees discuss in their breaks and lunch time.* Try to sit down at a table near them and read a magazine. See if you can overhear what they are saying. You will have to do this repeatedly to get them to feel comfortable with you there so that they will be more open with each other. You will find that the employees will begin to ask you questions about the effort. This is a good opportunity to detect problems and also to allay their concerns.

ADDRESS AND OVERCOME RESISTANCE

Don't wait for a major problem involving resistance to surface. Addressing resistance begins when you kick off the change effort with the employees of the business departments involved. In the kickoff meeting you will be discussing the approach to change, goals, benefits, and the organization of the effort. More on these later. You will also be stressing the following points (worded toward the employees).

- It is natural to feel most comfortable with the way things are since you have been doing this work for some time. Therefore, it is also natural to feel uneasy with change. The change team hopes to make the change easier for you. That is what we seek—your participation.
- To some of you change may be threatening. However, in most change efforts that begin with improving the work, change results in positive things for you. After all, management has begun with change and not downsizing.
- We are also aware of things that are cultural or political that affect change. That is also natural. So we will work with you on these as well.

Note that you are openly acknowledging in a soft manner that politics and resistance exist.

Once you have some symptoms of resistance or negative political factors, there is a tendency to want to go in and address these head-on. This is a bad idea in almost all situations. For:

> *Taking immediate action when you detect resistance will tend to drive the resistance underground instead of eliminating it.*

Remember too that you are only aware of the symptoms—not the causes of their concerns. Another basic idea from experience is that you should just observe and note the politics and resistance. Why? Because you act, you want to be decisive. If you act too soon, you reveal that you are aware of their resistance and the politics. They will now be strongly on their guard.

You really should have a resistance strategy. This is your approach to the timing and actions that you will take. A fundamental part of your resistance strategy should be:

> *Take action on resistance only to accomplish a positive goal—not to quash the resistance.*

What is a positive goal? Here are some examples. Implement a round of quick hits. Prepare the infrastructure for change. Implement a new policy or procedure. If you just try to crush resistance, it will likely just instill negative feelings and engender greater resistance. What do you do then? Couple the change or action with the positive benefits of the change.

Now we come to tactics. Without directly attacking the resistance, what can you do to overcome it? Here are some suggestions:

- Focus on detailed transactions and work. Politics becomes less relevant the closer you get to the actual work. This is because people are so busy doing the work that they have little time for politics.
- Center your attention on standard, non-exception transactions. These do not require much knowledge or involvement of king bees or queen bees.
- Isolate and deal with exceptions in a group. In that way you can give all of your effort at the exceptions, workarounds, and shadow systems –and the king and queen bees—without being distracted.
- As you work at the detailed level, you can allude to concerns of employees. They will start to see that there will still be jobs since the transactions and work cannot usually be totally automated.
- Volunteer to involve supervisors after you get started in the detailed analysis and change effort with the employees. However, keep out the king and queen bees. How do you do this? Indicate to the king and queen bees that they are too important in the other work (exceptions, workarounds, etc.) to be involved in the general work.

In general, the more time you spend with the people doing the work, the more you gain their confidence. The more you gain their confidence and trust, the less they feel concerned or threatened. Then it becomes harder for the king and queen bees, and the supervisors to interfere.

What are the signs of your progress? One sign is that employees become more open and relaxed around the change team. A second sign is that the king and queen bees become more resigned to change. Another sign is that the supervisors back off and leave you alone.

HOW TO USE POLITICS TO SUPPORT CHANGE

More generally, let's now move back and consider how you can exploit politics and political factors to reinforce your change effort. The first thing to remember is that everyone is aware of politics, but in most organizations it is not discussed openly. It is the hidden agenda. In order for management, the business unit employees, and the change team to deal with any political issue or symptom of a problem, it has to be discussed. One lesson learned here is:

> *If you wait until a political issue becomes critical, it is probably going to be too late.*

Why is this? Because previously there was no discussion of politics. Now you have to have the discussion with no preparation. Not a good idea.

A better approach is to start asking about business relationships when you are out collecting information on the work. This is a more subtle approach to starting a political discussion with business unit employees. As you work with these people more and more, there should be a feeling of trust so that you will begin to pick up political information. What information might be useful to the change team? Here are some examples.

- Relationships between managers, supervisors, and employees. Whom do the employees respect the most?
- The existing power structure within the department.
- Identification of king and queen bees.
- Relationship between departments.

You also want to have a session with the change team in which you devote almost the entire meeting to the importance of politics and culture, why it cannot be ignored, and how early obtained information can aid in change management. You also have some action items for the team members. When they go out into departments, they are to be sensitive to political factors and to report what they learn verbally to you. It is not a good idea to use a memo or e-mail here. Telephone or in-person communications are best.

USE A SCORE CARD FOR YOUR PERFORMANCE

Figure 3.2 provides a score card to assess your knowledge, skills, and progress with respect to politics and resistance. Some discussion of each of the points is useful here.

- Elapsed time between when the change effort started and resistance was first detected. Here the longer the time period generally means that you are less in touch with what is going on. If this time is short, then give yourself a high grade since you are becoming sensitive to people's feelings.
- Number of times that you were surprised when political issues surfaced. Obviously, the lower the number, the better. However, this is never likely to be zero since there is always something new that will surface.
- Number of political issues that surfaced that were new to you. This is similar to the previous one. A large number raises a concern that you are not paying sufficient attention to political factors.
- After several weeks in a department, the percentage of employees that you cannot determine if they are resistors to change. This is the great unknown in change management. If this percentage remains high, it may mean that the change team is not being sufficiently sensitive to the politics and resistance.

Element	Rating	Comment
Elapsed time between when the change effort started and resistance was first detected		
Number of times that you were surprised when political issues surfaced		
Number of political issues that surfaced that were new to you		
After several weeks in a department, the percentage of employees that you cannot determine if they are resistors to change		
Number of political issues as a percentage of the total number of issues surfaced		
List of symptoms of resistance that the team has encountered		
Reaction of the change team to discussions of politics and resistance		
Average time to resolve a political issue		
Attitude of the employees to the change effort at the start of the effort		
Attitude of the employees to the change effort now		
Involvement of the employees in the change effort		
Extent of new ideas and issues related to work that were surfaced by employees		

Figure 3.2 A Score Card to Assess your Knowledge, Skills, and Progress

- Number of political issues as a percentage of the total number of issues surfaced. This is a measure that will be used throughout the change effort. Initially, the percentage should be relatively high. Then it should diminish as work and technical issues surface and, hopefully, overwhelm the political issues.
- List of symptoms of resistance that the team has encountered. This list should grow quickly at the start of the change effort in a department. It should then taper off. If it continues to grow, then there could more problems and deeper problems than you originally thought.
- Reaction of the change team to discussions of politics and resistance. The team at first should be slightly nervous in participating in this discussion. Then they should feel more comfortable.
- Average time to resolve a political issue. This is the start of measuring the elapsed time between when an issue surfaces and when it is resolved. Remember too that an issue that is resolved can resurface in different symptoms. So be careful when you analyze symptoms.
- Attitude of the employees to the change effort at the start of the effort. This should be a mixed picture. Assessing yourself here makes you more aware of what people think when you start the change effort in a department.
- Attitude of the employees to the change effort now. Hopefully, this is improved. However, it can be the case (and it has happened to us) that employees become polarized. That is, they become either avid supporters or resistors to change.
- Involvement of the employees in the change effort. Over time employees should become more involved by volunteering issues in the work and ideas for change.
- Extent of new ideas and issues related to work that were surfaced by employees. This is a measure of what new ideas and issues were defined by the employees. Value issues as much as ideas since ideas often arise from issues.

You should administer this score card for yourself on a regular basis. Initially, this should be every two weeks to force yourself to be more sensitive to politics and resistance. Another suggestion is for you to have the change team members do the same.

MARKET CHANGE MANAGEMENT

As you will see in each chapter, marketing of change management is essential for success. Marketing forces you to think about how people view the change effort. By giving attention to marketing you avoid becoming complacent and internally focused. A main concept in marketing to overcome resistance and deal with politics is to be soft. That is, you do not want to be heavy handed and appear to be forcing change upon the employees. Here is your basic approach to marketing here.

Focus on change by indicating and drawing attention to what
will happen if change is not undertaken.

This is a repeated theme in change management—stressing the downside of the status quo. What you are doing is employing techniques used by automobile sales-people and doctors. A car salesman wants to see your car and ensure that you are aware of the age and problems with your car. In that way you will want a new car. In medicine no one wants to have an operation. It is expensive and takes you away from your family and work. Moreover, there is the risk involved. So how do doctors deal with this and get you to agree to have the operation? Through fear. They raise fear by indicating what will happen to you if you do not have the operation.

EXAMPLES

ROCKWOOD COUNTY

As was indicated in Chapter 1, politics abound at Rockwood. The place simply oozes with politics and infighting. Recognizing the political factors is very simple. What to do about this and exploit it to help your change effort is another matter. Our approach was to find the departments that favored change and had some political power. Then we used these departments to support change. Rather than deal with single employees who resisted change, we were dealing with almost entire departments who dreaded change. By leveraging off of the support-ive departments, we were able to get Quick Hits. Then we used these to get into the departments that resisted change. Our next step was to approach the lower level employees in departments who resisted change. Then we established teams across departments so that the ideas of change and issues of these junior employ-ees could be supported. This approach will be examined in more detail as we get into implementation.

LEGEND MANUFACTURING

At first the picture at Legend is almost the opposite of the Rockwood situation. But as we got into the firm, we discovered that while there were differences, there were departments who resisted change and who had derailed the previous change efforts. By asking about what had happened in the past, we were able to uncover the informal political structure at the middle level and supervisory level of

Legend. We then used this information to pursue change employing the methods discussed in this chapter.

POTENTIAL ISSUES AND RISKS

- When a change team lacks experience in undertaking change, there is often a tendency to overreact to resistance and politics. Then the team may commit the major mistake of trying to correct the situation and attitude on the spot. This is generally not a good idea since it may instill even more resistance. Moreover, it will drive resistance underground.
- You and the change team can get carried away with politics. It can be addictive because in an organization it resembles a soap opera. To overcome this potential issue, the change leaders must put the politics and resistance into perspective.
- It can happen that middle level managers will openly support change in front of their own management. Then when you move to implement change, they raise many issues. They want to study the potential of change more. How do you address this issue? Do not wait until it happens. Raise this as a potential issue to upper management before any presentation. Indicate in the meeting that paying lip service to change is not enough— they must participate. So you should have some immediate actions.

LESSONS LEARNED

- In order to detect passive resistance consider proposing some small changes to the work and see how individuals reacts. Ask them what they would to see done with the process. If you get nothing back, then there is likely to be passive resistance.
- When you have detected passive resistance, the question is what to do about it. A natural inclination is to try to change their minds directly and immediately. This often does not work well. It is better to take time and try to understand the emotional and psychological source of the resistance.
- How do you show people that a new process and way of doing of work is easier? By having the most junior people who are eager to get ahead do it first. Then it is evident to more senior people that it can be done with a limited learning curve. Patience and a sense of humor are also keys here.
- People often can state their problems and issues with their work. It is harder for them to think of changes and improvements since they have often learned to accept their situations. Your strategy should be to treat and value issues as much as new ideas. Then you want to turn the issue into a solution or opportunity by analyzing the issue with the employees.

SUMMARY

An important thing to remember from this chapter is that politics and resistance can be employed by the change management team in positive ways to facilitate change. You cannot expect to bring everyone along to support change. However, as you can implement Quick Hits and people see results, the morale and support for change should increase. Several other significant points raised were:

- The change team will be involved in the politics whether you like it or not. So it is better to orient them in the beginning and then to discuss it rather openly as the work progresses.
- You should use the score card defined in this chapter on an ongoing basis to ensure that you are aware of the political factors affecting the change effort.

Chapter 4

Develop Your Change Goals and Strategy

INTRODUCTION

In order to think about and then to carry out change, you have to understand the business goals and direction. Then you can start formulating alternative change goals. After the objectives of change management are defined, you can move on to the strategy for change. At the general business level, there are many fuzzy words. People think of mission, vision, etc., differently. So it is necessary to have some definitions first.

- *Stakeholders*. These are internal and external entities that are interested or involved in the activities of the organization.
- *Vision*. The vision of an organization is where it wants to be in 3–5 years. The vision is where you want to go—not how to get there.
- *Mission*. The mission of an organization is how in general terms it will try to reach the vision.
- *Business objectives*. Business objectives are more specific goals that support the mission.
- *Business issues*. These are problems and opportunities that impede or impair the attainment of the business objectives and, hence, the mission and the attainment of the vision.
- *Business strategy*. The business strategy is how you will attain the business objectives while handling the business issues.

How do these interrelate? Figure 4.1 gives a schematic picture. You can see the stakeholders over all planning elements. The mission is the largest general arrow toward the vision. The business objectives support the mission, but are impeded by the business issues. The business strategy is the approach to deal with or get

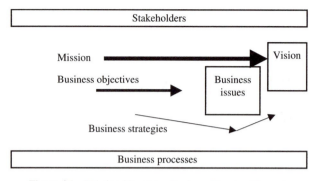

Figure 4.1   Relationship among Business Planning Elements

around the issues to achieve the strategy. All of this is carried out over the business processes.

Let's take an example. As you recall, Rockwood County was to embark on substantial change to business processes and then to its organization. One stakeholder is the public who are served by the county departments. The vision is to ensure that the public can have access to as much information as possible without having to visit county offices. The mission is to maximize the use of the web and Internet to serve the public. The business objective is to implement new web-based processes—not just systems. Several business issues are: (1) the department employees want to retain their power over their processes and so are reluctant to change; (2) the current systems and processes are not "Internet friendly." The business strategy is to implement several key web-based systems and processes in two departments and then to expand this to other departments.

From this simple example, you can see the importance of considering the business planning factors in change management. You can also see that if you do not consider them, the change management effort could get into real trouble. Here are some problems:

- The change management effort is not addressing critical areas identified in the vision, mission, and objectives of the organization.
- Management fails to support the change management effort since they do not see its relevance and importance.

As you are analyzing the planning factors, you will also want to observe some of the business processes. At this point it is assumed that you don't know where change will occur. This is discussed later in Chapter 6. However, you can develop your overall change goal and the strategy for change. Both will then be localized to the specific work in Chapter 6.

ASSESS THE BUSINESS PLANNING FACTORS

From real world experience, it is difficult to deal with fuzzy statements related to vision and mission. Therefore, you want to have a systematic approach for moving ahead. If you stick to the fuzzy language and paragraphs, then it will be very difficult, if not impossible, to develop the proper change management goals.

Let's start with stakeholders. You should make a list of stakeholders that are relevant to the vision and mission. Figure 4.2 is a sample list. Note that there are several interesting entries that you might not expect here. One is business processes. This is obviously critical to change management and so you want to start including it in your analysis. The second is information technology (IT) and technology. This is important since much of the change that is done involves systems and technology.

Next, you need to examine the vision statement. Let's take an example. Here is a vision statement extracted from a real company.

XXX is a government agency that is committed to providing high-quality, personalized experience to the public that provides superior service that exceeds expectations. We provide streamlined delivery of information and services on a cost-effective basis. We support high morale among our employees. We enhance the working and home environment of our residents.

If you examine each sentence and phrase, you can extract the elements of the vision given in Figure 4.3. Note that the company probably had not done this before. So you may find some strange entries and determine that there are gaps. This is a side benefit of defining your change management objectives— completeness and validation of business planning elements.

You may feel uncomfortable about having a fuzzy vision statement since it is very difficult to know when you have achieved success. An alternative is to

- Upper management
- Employees
- IT and technology
- Business processes
- Customers
- Suppliers
- Investors

Figure 4.2   Sample List of Stakeholders

- High quality service
- Personalized service
- Streamlined service delivery
- Cost-effective operations
- High employee morale

Figure 4.3   Sample Vision Elements

establish measurable vision elements. Here are some examples that relate to specific areas:

- Services provided
    — Range of services provided at a future date versus current services
    — Percentage of services provided that are personalized
- Performance/workload related
    — Number of customers/calls/transactions handled per person per time period
    — Number of customer complaints per person per time period
    — Total volume of work/total number of employee hours
    — Average time per customer call
- Cost/revenue related
    — Total revenue at a particular future date
    — Total profitability at a future date
    — Average cost per transaction for a time period
    — Average revenue generated per customer prospect for a time period
    — Average revenue generated per customer
    — Percentage of operating costs in labor hours
- Technology related
    — Percentage of the work and transactions that are automated
    — Percentage of work in a transaction that is manual for specific transactions
- Customer related
    — Customer/client/patient retention
    — Average number of visits per patient per time period
    — Level of customer satisfaction as revealed by surveys
- Quality and biotechnology related
    — Number of patents filed per unit time
    — Number of drugs and new treatments per unit time
- Employee related
    — Turnover of employees per time period
    — Total revenue divided by total number of employees
    — Total costs divided by the total number of employees

Now turn to the mission statement. Remember that the mission indicates how generally the vision will be attained.

XXX seeks to provide a full range of government services through both in-person service and automation based networks and systems. Service performance is actively measured and tracked along with extensive problem follow-up. Employee input and participation in service activities are valued and encouraged.

Doing the same with these sentences, you can develop the mission elements listed in Figure 4.4.

- Full range of IT supported services
- Measurement of customer satisfaction
- Employee participation

Figure 4.4   Sample Mission Elements

Next, you can make a list of critical business processes. Space does not allow us to make a complete list for Rockwood County. Instead, the following three processes will be considered as examples.

- Birth and death records
- Change of name
- Voter rolls and registration

Another list is that of major business units and departments. Here we will include only the recorder office, the elections office, and IT. In a real situation like business processes, you will have many more.

Another element of business planning is that of business objectives. You often have to read annual reports or presentations made by upper management to glean the objectives. Here are several that will be used as an example.

- Increase investment in systems and technology to serve the public better
- Reduce clerical workload and activity
- Control cost of services

But the business objectives, and hence the vision and mission, cannot be achieved quickly or immediately due to business issues. Here are some relevant business issues.

- Employees have political power through their union organization
- Some of the existing computer systems are quite old, impeding change
- A past previous effort at modernization of processes failed

With these issues, the problem is how to work toward the objectives. This is where business strategies come into play. Here are several business strategies:

- Implement new technology in departments that support change
- Use established methods and technology
- Involve employees in the work associated with change

ANALYSIS TABLES FOR BUSINESS PLANNING

Now sit back and see what lists you have defined. Here they are:

- Stakeholders
- Business processes

- Vision
- Mission
- Business objectives
- Business issues
- Business strategies

These elements serve as the basis for creating a number of valuable tables. Space does not permit the analysis of all 28 combinations, so let's discuss some of the more important ones.

- *Organization versus business processes.* The entry is the extent of involvement of the business unit in the process. Figure 4.5 tells you which organizations you will likely be dealing with for specific processes.
- *Business processes versus business issues.* The entry is the impact of the issue on the process. This and the next two help you to select which processes or activities to go after later either in terms of problems (issues) or goals (objectives and strategies). This is shown in Figure 4.6 for the example.
- *Business processes versus business objectives.* The entry is the importance of the process to the objective. Figure 4.7 contains an example.
- *Business processes versus business strategies.* The entry is the importance of the process to the strategy. See Figure 4.8.

Processes

Organization	Birth/death	Name change	Voting
Recorder	Ownership	Ownership	—
Election	—	Indirect user	Ownership
IT	Support	Support	Support

Figure 4.5   Organization versus Business Processes

Business issues

Process	Employee power	Old systems	Previous failure
Birth/death	Medium	Middle aged	No
Name change	Medium	Middle aged	No
Voting	Medium/high	Yes	High

Figure 4.6   Business Processes versus Business Issues

Business objectives

Process	Systems/technology	Reduce clerical	Cost control
Birth/death	Suitable	Suitable	Moderate impact
Name change	Suitable	Suitable	Limited impact
Voting	May not fit	Limited effect	Little impact

Figure 4.7   Business Processes versus Business Objectives

Business strategies

Process	New technology	Established methods	Employee involvement
Birth/death	Suitable	Suitable	Moderate
Name change	Suitable	Suitable	Moderate
Voting	Cannot justify much due to infrequent elections	Suitable	Good

Figure 4.8   Business Processes versus Business Strategies

Vision elements

Process	High quality	Personalized	Streamlined delivery	Cost-effective	Morale
Birth/death	Possible	Yes	Possible	Yes	Yes
Name change	Possible	Yes	Possible	Yes	Yes
Voting	Difficult due to volume, peaks	No	Not suitable	No	No

Figure 4.9   Business Processes versus Vision

Stakeholders

Process	Public	Employees	Management
Birth/death	Moderate	Moderate	Some
Name change	Moderate	Moderate	Some
Voting	Infrequent benefits	Limited number of employees	Some

Figure 4.10   Business Processes versus Stakeholders

- *Business processes versus vision.* The entry is the role of the process in the mission. This is often the volume of work performed that carries out the vision. See Figure 4.9.
- *Business processes versus stakeholders.* The entry is the value of business process to the specific stakeholder. See Figure 4.10.

As you read this list, you see the importance of business processes. That is natural given your focus on change management. From these figures you could create others by combining them (e.g., business objectives versus business issues). From reading the examples in Figures 4.4–4.10 you can see that the election process is not really a good candidate while the other two processes are.

How you develop these lists and tables? Well, you don't sit in a cubicle to do it. Make an initial set of lists and circulate these among managers. This will accomplish two things. First, it shows that a start is being made on change management. Second, you get them involved in the work—showing them that you are pursuing a collaborative method.

Once you have the lists, you can proceed to the tables. If you give people blank tables, they are not likely to know what to do and it will waste too much time. From experience it is a good idea to fill in a sample row and column for each table. Then hold a meeting to discuss the tables and fill in the other entries. Circulate the partially filled tables in advance.

SURVEY THE BUSINESS PROCESSES AND WORK

While you don't exactly know what work you will change, the effort involved in creating the tables along with comments from management will tend to identify some good candidates for change. A lesson learned is to go out into these potential processes and activities and observe them briefly. Do not do interviews or take a lot of notes. This could raise fears as well as expectations. Instead, indicate that you are just observing briefly.

What are you looking for? Here are some ideas.

- Whether the general workplace is organized. Do the people look busy or effective?
- Try to observe their faces and facial expressions.
- Do there appear to be established methods that people are following?
- How active are the supervisors in the work?

Information in these areas will help later in sifting through potential activities for change. Here you are just getting a general idea of the extent of potential improvement and problems. In our example, you would just go to several county offices and observe the work.

DEVELOP A GENERAL LONG-TERM SCENARIO FOR THE WORK

While it is correct that you have not selected the activities for change, you now have a better idea of what you will face based on the tables and observation. This is a good time to sit down and think about how a sample activity might work if the vision was fulfilled. This is not detailed. You are just developing a general idea. Why do this? Because you can use this as part of the basis for shaping your change objectives. Also, you can discuss with managers at least some general way that the work might be performed.

Let's take an example. For change of name, a person must go to a county office and obtain a form. Typically, the person does not have the information required so he/she has to return home and find the documents as well as fill out the form. Then he/she must return to the county office with the documents and the form completed. The clerk reviews this information and may or may not approve the work. Then in most counties the name change has to be approved by a judge. Today, there are more steps because the county does not want to abet a person changing his/her name for illegal purposes. The person is now up to three visits. There is fourth visit to obtain certified copies of the name change. Is it any wonder that people become upset with this bureaucracy?

The issue is how to define a process that provides improved service and yet protects the public at large. In the long-term scenario, secure transactions over the Internet are assumed so that someone cannot masquerade as someone else. In this scenario, a person would access a secure web site and view the form and instructions. The form would be completed on-line. The person is directed as to what documents to bring to the office. The form is transmitted on-line and reviewed in terms of checking against various data bases. If everything checks out, an appointment time is set so that there is no waiting. The person does a first visit to present the documentation. The judicial review is scheduled in the system at the same time the appointment is set so that delay is minimized. Certified copies could then be issued immediately. The number of visits is greatly reduced as is the staff time to handle the work.

There are several things to note in this example. First, the amount of detail is very limited. Only the general flow of the work is addressed. None of the details are. That would come later. Second, the roles of the various parties in the transaction are laid out so that people can visualize what is happening.

DETERMINE YOUR GOALS FOR CHANGE

Now you are at the point of defining the goals for change management. Many change efforts run into trouble because people do not take the time to formulate and gain consensus and support for the objectives of change. Then later when problems come up, there is less support for the change effort. It is useful to develop these goals in a collaborative way to gain support, but also to gain a widespread understanding of why all of this effort is being expended.

To help you a list of potential goals is listed in Figure 4.11 along with identification as to type and comments. Examine now the types or dimensions of the goals listed. Here are some comments on each.

- *Technical.* This is often to improve the productivity, reduce the error rate or rework of the process.
- *Business.* These goals focus on attaining certain financial objectives such as reduced cost or increased revenue.
- *Political.* Goals here to change the power structure in the organization, to address organizational issues that are impacting work, or to gain a higher degree of control.
- *Cultural.* This is not often voiced, but cultural goals are important to attain lasting change and enduring support for change.

Potential goal	Type	Comments
Reduce the cost of the work	Financial	Traditional, most common goal; often results in downsizing
Increase sales by providing new services, products	Financial	Often cited for E-Business
Reduce the number of employees doing the work	Financial	Urgent version employed by companies in place of the first goal
Streamline and simplify the work	Technical	Often one of the best technical goals
Improve employee productivity	Technical	Seen many times as threatening and ambiguous
Reduce the error rate and improve quality	Technical	Cited in Six Sigma and other reengineering methods
Streamline the organization; realign the organization to meet a new mission	Political	Used when organization change is to precede process change; interpreted by many as downsizing
Empower employees to be more involved in their work	Political	An excellent positive change goal
Reduce the degree of politics and disharmony among departments	Political	Often not a stated goal
Instill a greater degree of collaboration within departments	Cultural	Suitable for narrow-based change efforts
Instill greater collaboration among employees of different departments	Cultural	An excellent positive change goal for work that spans several departments or locations
Create a new value structure toward the work	Cultural	Difficult to achieve, but a good long-term goal

Figure 4.11   Potential Goals for Change Management

At the start of this book, you probably thought of the first two categories of goals. However, experience indicates that the political goals help you achieve initial change success while the cultural goals help you to ensure that the change is persistent. Achieving political goals combined with the technical goals will gain you the support of the people who do the work. Reaching business goals help keep the change effort alive. Building a new culture through the change effort tends to encourage people to have a more positive attitude toward change over the long term. Also, keep in mind that some managers have tried to implement a two pronged set of goals. There is the stated goal for employee consumption and then there is real agenda that only a few managers are in on. Beware that this backfires most of the time and the employees pick up on the real agenda. They become more angry and disenchanted since they think that managers view them as dummies.

In general, you want to pursue several objectives at one time in change management. However, it is also true that you will dominate goals at the start of the effort that will often change over time. You see—goals are related to time. At the start of a change management effort, people tend to either have very modest or very lofty goals. Then their experience in the early part of the effort makes people adjust their goals to be more realistic—up or down. That is why the Quick Hits are so important in change management. They help to provide optimism to people, but the effort that was required is more down-to-earth.

Our experience indicates that:

> *Your change effort has the greatest chance of success if you have*
> *at least one goal in each dimension.*

Having multiple goals allows you to do trade-offs when management is thinking about altering the direction of change management.

INVOLVE MANAGERS AND EMPLOYEES

How should you develop the change objectives and strategies? Through involvement of managers and, if possible, employees. The more people that get involved in setting goals, the more support you will engender for change. Alternatively, if someone in upper management imposes change objectives, they are likely to be satisfactory to that person, but do nothing for the people doing the work. Such change efforts often run into trouble and fail.

Here are some more specific guidelines in developing your change goals.

- Sit down with managers and some employees and identify specific problems and issues. After all, this is what bothers people most of the time. If the goal cannot address some of these issues, then there may be a problem in getting support for the change effort.
- Use the lists that were created earlier to build new tables (discussed later) involving candidates for the change objectives.
- Present the tables to management first as a discussion starting point. Use the approach that was followed in defining the earlier tables by giving them partially completed tables.
- For employees you might want to show them the tables related to change objectives to business processes and issues.
- Use the questions and table in Figure 4.12 to further analyze the potential change objectives.
- Once you have the feedback and performed the analysis, you can use this and the tables to tentatively select the winning change objectives. You will refine these as you determine your change strategy so don't treat it as final.

You can follow the same approach a short time later when you develop your change strategy.

Here are some of the tables of interest for change objectives.

- *Change objectives versus business processes.* This table is important because it relates to the work. The entry of the table is impact of the

Alternative change objectives

Questions			
Is the alternative too risky in terms of what management can support?			
Can the alternative be achieved in the overall time span available?			
With this objective can interim changes be obtained?			
Is there adequate staffing to support the work to attain the objective?			
What are the risks to the business if the objective is selected?			
Are there change managers in place who can address the objective?			

Figure 4.12   Questions Related to Alternative Change Objectives

objective on the process. The purpose of the table is to aid in selecting the objectives that yield the most positive benefit to the process. The table is also used in selecting the activities to change later in Chapter 6.

- *Change objectives versus business issues.* The purpose of the table is to assess how attaining change objectives take care or alleviate specific business issues. The entry is the extent to which achievement of an objective resolves an issue. This table is also useful in selecting which objectives you want for change.
- *Change objectives versus business objectives.* The aim of this table is to analyze alignment. The entry is the extent to which a change objective fits in with a business objective.
- *Change objectives versus mission.* This is a significant table in that the mission is how you will achieve your vision. The change objective is what you are seeking with your change effort. The entry is the degree to which attaining the objective supports the mission.
- *Change objectives versus vision.* Both of these are objectives. The table entry is the extent to which attaining the change objective brings the element of the vision closer to reality.
- *Change objectives versus stakeholders.* This table reveals how the change objectives impact the stakeholders. The entry is the involvement of the stakeholder in achieving the specific objective of change.

- *Change objectives versus business strategies.* The purpose of this table is to ensure that the change objectives are consistent with the business strategies. As such, it is most useful for your own analysis. The entry is the degree of agreement of the specific objective with the individual business strategy.

An additional tool to evaluate your potential change objectives is to answer the questions posed in Figure 4.12. This is given in the form of a table in which the rows are the questions and the columns are the alternative change objectives. The table entry is the degree to which the alternative objective answers the question. Let's explore each of these questions in more detail.

- *Is the alternative too risky in terms of what management can support?* If you select a broad objective that portends many changes, you may find that management support will evaporate.
- *Can the alternative be achieved in the overall time span available?* If the change objective is too broad, then it may be impossible to complete the change in the time frame allowed by management.
- *With this objective can interim changes be obtained?* Some change objectives require extreme, major changes so that making interim changes becomes very difficult.
- *Is there adequate staffing to support the work to attain the objective?* The wider the objective, the more people that will have to be committed (not just involved) in change management.
- *What are the risks to the business if the objective is selected?* When you undertake large-scale change, you may have to divert resources from their regular work to the change effort—potentially damaging the work and, hence, the business.
- *Are there change managers in place who can address the objective?* If there are few experienced managers who can direct the change effort, your change objective may have to be more modest.

The choice of the objectives for change resolved itself into: reduce the cost of the work and redirect employees to more productive work, simplify the work and involve employees more in processes, simplify relations among departments, and improve collaboration across departments.

DEFINE ALTERNATIVE CHANGE STRATEGIES

What is a change strategy? The change strategy is the approach you will use to try to achieve your change objectives at a general level. There are two parts of the change strategy that have to be defined. One is the "what." That is, what is the scope of the change? Figure 4.13 gives a list of areas you might consider. Use this as a starting checklist. This checklist also contains examples for the areas.

- Technology infrastructure (network, hardware, system software)
- Application systems (inventory, payroll, sales, accounting, finance)
- Organization structure (the hierarchy of the organization)
- Staffing of the work (change of people, increased training, different assignments)
- Management of the work (managers, supervisors)
- Policies governing the work
- Procedures affecting the work (methods, training materials, guidelines)
- Business rules impacting the work (detailed rules used in carrying out transactions and work)
- The work itself (regular work, exceptions, workarounds, shadow systems)
- Facilities and location of the work (where the work is performed, buildings, office layout)

Figure 4.13   List of Potential Areas of Scope of Change

Potential change strategy	Comments
Gradual change	This is continuous improvement
Major, sudden change	This is represented by downsizing and reengineering
Consistent changes in discrete waves	This is the approach followed in the book

Figure 4.14   Examples of "How" Change Strategies

The second part of your change strategy is "how." What is the general method that you will follow in carrying out change? Figure 4.14 gives examples of change strategies for the "how" part of the strategy. Your "how" change strategy is closely related to the method that you will be using to implement change.

With the change objectives defined along with the analysis of business planning elements that you performed, you will find that there are not many alternative change strategies. Why? Because the scope of change in the change strategy must be consistent with the objectives that you selected for change.

SELECT A WINNING CHANGE STRATEGY

Just as in the change objectives, there are trade-offs involved here. If you pick too many areas for change, then this can restrict your methods for "how" to perform the change. What if there is a seemingly obvious choice of a change strategy? You still want to define several alternatives in order to work with managers to obtain consensus. If you put forward only one choice and the management approves it, then if something goes wrong, there could be many problems for the change effort and for you.

Now let's turn to relevant tables for the change strategy candidates.

- *Change strategies versus change objectives.* The columns consist of elements of the change objectives (technical, business, political, cultural). The entry is the degree to which the individual strategy supports the change objective. The purpose of this table is to determine which strategy candidates are aligned to the business objective elements.

- *Change strategies versus business processes.* The entry is the potential impact of the strategy on the key business processes. The purpose of this table is to help select a strategy that is realistic in terms of the business processes.
- *Change strategies versus business strategies.* The entry is the degree to which the change strategy supports the business strategy. Like the one above, this table supports alignment.

Here are some questions that you should also try to answer.

- Is the change strategy really feasible given the overall business situation and funding available in the company?
- Does the change strategy fit with the culture of the organization and the departments?
- Is there adequate staffing to implement the change strategy?
- What is the risk to the business processes and business if the specific change strategy is selected?
- Is there leadership capable of directing the change strategy?

For Rockwood County the choice was to be comprehensive on the scope of change except for the organization. The other choice was to implement major discrete change.

APPLY THE CHANGE GOALS AND STRATEGY SCORE CARD

Figure 4.15 gives a score card that you can employ as a starting point. Note that most of these factors are subjective. That is OK since you are trying to assess

Factor	Score	Comment
Extent of participation by managers		
Number of managers involved in the work		
Amount of time spent as a group in reviewing and agreeing on change objectives		
Extent of resistance to change		
Extent of resistance to the change strategies		
Extent of employee involvement		
Contribution of employees toward the objectives and strategy		

Figure 4.15 Change Objectives and Strategies Score Card

the extent of involvement and participation. After all, you judge success as much by the extent of participation and involvement as you do by the end results. This is a key difference between the approach here and others in that there is a stress on the process of getting the specific action accomplished as well as the accomplishment itself. The lesson learned in change management here is that:

> *Because of the need for consensus and support, how you undertake actions in change management is often as important as the end results.*

This is particularly true in these early planning stages. During implementation of change, the focus shifts toward getting results.

MARKET THE CHANGE GOALS AND STRATEGY

You not only have to market the results of the planning for change, but you also often have to sell the method of selecting the objectives and strategy. Change and especially planning change does not sell itself. Notice that the method starts softly in that you do not plunge and get objectives. You first arrive at a common view of the business. This is extremely important because without this early agreement, there can be widespread disagreement on the need for change and the objectives for change. By considering the vision, mission, and especially business issues, the importance of change can be developed. This is consistent with people seeing the need for change before they tackle what changes they wish to perform.

Another thing to consider is that the change objectives are easier to talk about and deal with than the change strategy. This is because the change strategy centers on how to do something. This can be more threatening so that in terms of marketing the actions here, you want to spend most of the time and effort in the change objectives that are more positive. You may want to use the change strategy to politically validate that management is really in support of change.

EXAMPLES

ROCKWOOD COUNTY

Rockwood County has served as the example in this chapter. It is interesting to note in retrospect some of the attitudes of the management and employees when change objectives and strategies were considered. At the start of the discussion, the managers almost universally supported very limited change. Change was threatening as was seen in the preceding chapter. Meetings and the development of the tables helped to widen the horizon of change objectives. This was useful to create an atmosphere more positive toward change. Less time and effort was then required for the change strategy.

LEGEND MANUFACTURING

Let's consider Legend's failed attempt for change. Management wanted to implement change to reduce costs. In some departments this was addressed by downsizing first. This was a disaster as it often is. Downsizing should follow, not precede, change. In downsizing you force people out. Because you give more money to people with expertise and experience in the firm, these people tend to be the first out of the door along with younger workers who have energy. What was Legend left with? Older employees who were less competent and who would have a harder time finding jobs. Another group consisted of individuals who were not very interested in the work or who were not creative. This is definitely not a good starting point to then change the process or work.

POTENTIAL ISSUES AND RISKS

- A risk is that managers will lose interest in the change objectives as they appear too general. Here it is useful to focus on the questions and the tables. If worse comes to worse, you may have to start discussing the change strategies.
- An issue is that many of the business items are too vague. In this case, you may want to volunteer more specific elements.

LESSONS LEARNED

- Consider the change objectives and strategies separately. If you combine the work to define these to speed it up, it will likely just confuse things.
- It will take some elapsed time to get a wide consensus on the objectives. This is natural. If you force the pace too much, it will encourage resentment and resistance later. If you have to spend several extra days or a week here, you can gain it back later in implementation.
- Work with managers one at a time to gain involvement. Don't assume that enthusiasm means support. It may mean that they want to demonstrate surface level support.
- Be very selective on which employees you want to involve. Many employees by nature feel uncomfortable about general topics such as objectives and strategies.

SUMMARY

This is the chapter where change management begins—setting the goals and strategy for change. There is often a tendency to want to bypass this step and to think that the objectives are obvious and that since change is straightforward, there is no need for a change strategy. Hopefully, the discussion has revealed to you the many benefits of developing both the change objectives and strategy in a collaborative way. You are starting to construct support for change.

Chapter 5

Prepare Your Change Management Framework

INTRODUCTION

In many reengineering, quality management, and Six Sigma approaches, the emphasis is on a very formal method in which many employees are trained to varying degrees. The problem with this is that in many organizations the impact on the work and the company is to drain resources and impact the work. Thus, it is not just the cost of the approach, but also the negative impact on the firm. In one large garment manufacturing firm, the reengineering effort brought the firm to the edge of bankruptcy.

There are some basic lessons learned here.

- A change approach should limit its impact on the day-to-day performance of the work.
- The change method should be as common sense as possible to reduce the time required for training.

This is what the goals of the change management technique are that has been defined. Before going further it is important to make distinctions between what is going on in the work or business process and what is going on in the change management effort. From here on out, the following definitions will be used.

- *Issue*. An issue is a problem that arises in change management. It can relate to management, the change management team, the change action items, the methods and tools used for change, the business units, or external factors.
- *Opportunity*. An opportunity is a situation in the business process or work where improvement and positive change are possible.

Please keep these definitions in mind as we progress. It is sometimes easy to confuse what is going on in the work with that in the change effort.

Change management requires support in the following areas:

- *Organization.* How the change effort will be organized and structured.
- *Tracking and control.* How issues, opportunities, and lessons learned are gathered, organized, and maintained.
- *Project management.* How the change effort will be managed.

After exploring these areas in detail, specific guidelines will be provided that will help you minimize the administrative overhead. This is important because it is too easy to get caught up in the bureaucracy of change management. You must have an efficient way of organizing and managing the change effort.

From experience, the critical factors in effective management of lasting change are:

- *Collaboration.* Getting people involved in both the work and the management of the work so as to reduce the administrative burden on the change management leaders.
- *Templates.* High level project plans that can be reused and can expand with lessons learned.
- *Lessons learned.* Knowledge gained from doing change management is captured, organized, and linked to the templates for later use.
- *Issues.* Issues here are problems that arise in doing change management. Experience shows that the same issues recur again and again so that you need to have issues organized.

These things provide and support cumulative improvement in your change management effort. There are specific tools that can provide support for the above factors. These include:

- Project management software to track the change management effort.
- Groupware to support collaboration.
- Databases to organize and structure issues and lessons learned.

YOUR CHANGE MANAGEMENT FRAMEWORK

Let's consider now the framework for change management. Figure 5.1 gives an overall picture. The components are:

- *Executive change steering committee.* This is the committee of upper managers, who provide direction and approve major actions related to change management. The committee meets infrequently.
- *Operational change steering committee.* This committee is composed of several high level managers who are interested in change as well as members

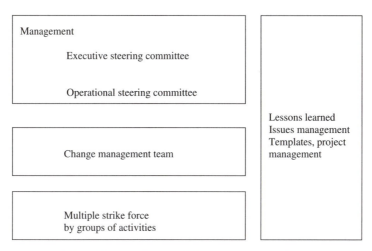

Figure 5.1 Overall Change Management Framework

of the change management team and the strike forces. This committee meets as needed to review the work of the strike forces related to change.

- *Change management team.* This is the core team for change headed by two change leaders.
- *Strike forces.* These are teams composed of department employees who evaluate current work and develop ideas for change. The members also support change implementation later. The number of strike forces depends upon the number of areas to be investigated for change.

The size of the strike force team varies depending on the situation. Typically, the change management team which is dedicated to change and, hence, full-time is 4–5 people, including the two change leaders. The strike forces are composed of 4–6 people from different departments.

The change management team acts to coordinate the work of change. They *do not* carry out the change. Otherwise, you will not achieve lasting change. More specific duties include:

- Maintain the infrastructure of change management.
- Track down, manage, and coordinate the resolution of issues.
- Report to management on issues, progress, and other elements of change management.
- Plan for change management.
- Communicate with employees, management, and vendors/consultants.
- Build lessons learned to improve future change management efforts.
- Direct the change management effort.
- Step in to help employees in designing and implementing change.

The composition of the strike forces must be carried out with planning and thoughtfulness. Otherwise, you might end up with a group that just validates the way the work is performed now. Assume that a strike force is going to examine accounting related work. An accounting employee acts as a resource for the work of the strike force. Most importantly,

The leader of each strike force comes from a department that often is in disagreement with the subject department of the strike force.

This is absolutely crucial. This person will press for changes. He or she may have very specific and precise complaints and concerns. This brings many benefits to the change effort. First, major issues are going to be surfaced. Second, there are likely to be more than cosmetic changes proposed. Third, this approach ensures that multiple department views are brought to bear.

The remainder of the strike force comes from other departments. A key idea is that:

The strike force members still perform their regular work in addition to the strike force.

This means that they can only allocate limited time for the effort. This ensures faster results. This is feasible because they are tasked with developing and examining ideas. Implementation of change will come later.

How does a strike force do its work? The strike force often will meet at lunch time. A member of the change management team helps to organize and coordinate the work of each strike force. There will not be many meetings. There is a kick-off meeting followed by specific meetings to discuss and vote on opportunities and the business cases of approved opportunities for change. Later, some strike force members may participate in the implementation of the change.

Now turn to the change management team. Its major role is coordinating and facilitating the change effort. Members of the change management team and leaders perform the following roles:

- Coach the change steering committees and strike forces in the change management method.
- Coordinate and review the work of the strike forces.
- Step into a strike force when needed to handle disputes or to sustain progress.
- Maintain the templates, lessons learned, and issues databases.
- Coordinate and act upon issues and decisions related to change management.

Why is the team size so limited? The above list gives the answer. It is because the roles and responsibilities are in coordination, not coming with the change ideas and implementation. If the change management team were to implement, the size of the team would be much larger. Also, the likelihood of failure would be higher since the people in departments would neither be involved nor committed to change.

Note that there are political undertones to this structure. There are two change steering committees because of the following factors:

- You want to have the upper level committee so that senior managers will not meddle in the change effort.
- The operational change steering committee provides a link between upper level management and the change team.
- Strike forces provide participation in change activities for many employees. This allows for the negation of impacts of queen and king bees.

On the side you can see that there are the critical methods of templates, lessons learned, and issues management. How do these elements relate to each other? Look at the diagram in Figure 5.2. The change templates appear in the upper level of this figure. The change leaders and team will take the templates and create the project plan for the change effort, resulting in the project plan in the lower left of the diagram. As the change effort goes on and individual change projects are completed, the experience can be employed to improve the change templates. As the change project plan is established, issues are identified for the work and can be derived from the issues database. Lessons learned can be gleaned from the lessons learned database that is related to the change templates. The experience in resolving issues helps to create more lessons learned. Conversely, the lessons learned are applied to resolve issues. Experiences from both are used to update the databases.

Figure 5.3 indicates how the change effort will work. There are basically two sets of phases here. The first set deals with the setup of the change effort. The second consists of steps to carry out the change (covered in later chapters). Here are some guidelines for the initial phases.

- The first phase is to ensure that upper management is behind the change effort. They need to have a role defined for them at the start. Otherwise, a senior manager may feel uneasy about change management.
- The change objectives and strategy are defined in this first phase as well using the techniques of Chapter 4. The change leaders are typically in place.
- Once the first phase is complete, the strike forces are formed. This is accomplished by the change leaders working with department managers.

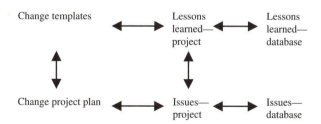

Figure 5.2 Diagram of Templates, Lessons Learned, and Issues

Establish change management infrastructure

Phase I
- Assess business planning factors
- Develop the change objectives and change strategy

Phase II
- Establish executive change steering committee
- Appoint the change management leaders

Phase III
- Form strike forces for the potential areas of change
- Create the operational change steering committee
- Form the change management team

Phase IV
- Establish the change management framework
- Conduct change familiarization sessions with strike forces
- Present change management framework to change steering committees

Change management work

- Identify and select your areas of change (Chapter 6)
- Collect detailed work information (Chapter 7)
- Define your long-term change and Quick Hits (Chapter 8)
- Determine your change implementation strategy (Chapter 9)
- Develop your change implementation project plan (Chapter 10)
- Implement Quick Hits (Chapter 11)
- Measure results (Chapter 12)
- Undertake major changes (Chapter 13)
- Build momentum for change (Chapter 14) and prevent reversion (Chapter 15)

Figure 5.3   Method for Change Management

Strike force members are often younger employees who show initiative and energy, are unhappy with the way the work is performed, and who lack political power in the department.

Why pick people who lack power? Because these are the ones who typically want change. If you pick the people with the knowledge and existing power, you often end up endorsing the status quo.

More guidelines are:

- After strike forces are formed, the change leaders identify those that would be most suitable for being in the change management team.
- The Operational Change Steering Committee is then formed from managers and from members of the strike forces. This ensures that there will be communications between management and the strike forces.
- In the next phase, the change management leaders and team create the change management framework. This framework is presented to the change steering committees. The benefit here is that the committee members understand their roles and responsibilities.

- Meetings are conducted with the strike forces to explain how the change management work will be organized and performed.

CHANGE TEMPLATES

If you had to start with a blank piece of paper to plan out the tasks for the change effort, you would spend most of your time in planning and not in doing! Therefore, you want to start with as much as you can. Having a project template for a change effort can save a great deal of time. What is a change template? It is a collection of high level tasks. To create your specific change plan, you and the change management team members will fill in detailed tasks as you progress. Figure 5.4 gives a list of tasks and milestones for the template. Note that Figure 5.4 contains a single list of tasks and milestones. In reality you will want to break this up into smaller chunks. This can be done by the major headings. How do you employ this? Don't accept it as is. It is just a starting point. It is critical that the change management team and then the change steering committees understand all of the tasks and milestones and that they buy into the list. Otherwise, there can be misunderstandings later. Why not use a work breakdown structure? Because it is too restrictive. A template provides greater flexibility since you can define the tasks under the template to be anything you want them to be.

When you implement the change template, you will likely be employing project management software, such as Microsoft Project. Here are some guidelines for using this software.

- Number all tasks so that you easily discuss and track them
- Define customized data elements for the following:
  - Indicator of whether the task has an associated change issue
  - Numbers of the change issues that apply to the tasks
  - Numbers of the lessons learned that apply to the tasks
- Customize the GANTT chart view in the palette so that you can highlight the tasks that have change issues

When one is doing change management, the subject of risk arises. The term "risk" is often so fuzzy because it means something different to everyone. Here a task has *risk* if it has one or more associated active change issues. This is a precise definition that can be easily and widely understood. This approach also offers you the advantage of verifying the completeness of the tasks and the change issues. Here is what you do.

- Go down the issues in the general database of issue. As you find an applicable issue, look for the corresponding tasks in the change plan. If there is no task, then you have a missing task.
- Review each task to see if you think it has risk or an issue. Go to the general database of issues and look for the issue. If the issue is not there, then you have found a missing issue.

1000 Change goals and strategy
      1100 Understand the business planning elements
      1200 Structure the vision, mission, business objectives, business strategies, and business issues
      1300 Identify the business processes and activities
      1400 Develop alternative business objectives
      1500 Evaluate the business objectives
      1600 Create the change management planning tables
      1700 Document and present the change objectives
      1800 Define alternative change strategies
      1900 Develop change strategy tables and evaluation
      2000 Select the change strategy
      Milestones: business planning tables, change objectives, change strategies

3000 Implement the change organization
      3100 Define the general change approach
      3200 Identify members of the executive change steering committee
      3300 Identify the necessary strike forces
      3400 Determine the strike force leaders
      3500 Set the membership of the strike forces
      3600 Identify members of the operational change steering committee
      3700 Identify members of the change team
      3800 Familiarize all players with the change methods
      Milestones: change steering committees, strike forces, change team in place

4000 Install the change framework and infrastructure
      4100 Review and modify the change management template
      4200 Create the change issues databases
      4300 Establish the lessons learned databases
      4400 Create the opportunities tracking databases
      4500 Review the use of the template and databases with change team, strike forces
      Milestones: change template and related databases in place

5000 Select the work for the change effort
      5100 Identify key potential areas
      5200 Define evaluation criteria
      5300 Perform evaluation of areas
      5400 Make selection of work for change
      5500 Gain approval for selection
      Milestones: areas of change; strategy for other areas

6000 Collect information on current work
      6100 Perform initial data collection
      6200 Detailed observation and data collection
      6300 Analyze information collected
      6400 Identify problems and opportunities in work
      6500 Gain consensus on impact of problems
      6600 Develop ideas for potential improvements
      6700 Gain approval for what has been developed
      Milestones: detailed information on work, problems with work, potential solutions

Figure 5.4 *Continued*

7000 Develop Quick Hits and long-term change solution
    7100 Sort and vote on opportunities into Quick Hits and long term
    7200 Gain approval for opportunities from management
    7300 Develop business cases for opportunities
    7400 Review and approve business cases
    Milestones: approved opportunities, business cases

8000 Determine the change implementation strategy
    8100 Define areas of change
    8200 Determine performance measures
    8300 Define phases of change
    8400 Score the current situation
    8500 Develop alternative models for implementation
    8600 Evaluate alternatives
    8700 Make selection
    Milestones: acceptable change implementation strategy and roadmap

9000 Construct the change implementation plan
    9100 Examine the change implementation template
    9200 Adapt template to the change effort
    9300 Assemble the change implementation team
    9400 Develop the change implementation plan
    9500 Gain acceptance of the plan
    Milestones: approved change implementation plan; change implementation team

10000 Implement Quick Wins
    10100 Organize for Quick Wins
    10200 Carry out Quick Wins
    10300 Deal with resistance and political factors
    Milestones: Implemented Quick Wins

11000 Measure Quick Hit results
    11100 Establish measurement approach for Quick Hits
    11200 Collect information for measurements
    11300 Perform assessment of Quick Hits
    11400 Review Quick Hit evaluation and measurement
    11500 Market Quick Hit results to employees and management
    11600 Adjust future Quick Hit approach based upon experience
    Milestones: Quick Hits implemented; measurements completed

12000 Implement long-term change
    12100 Prepare infrastructure for long-term change
    12200 Implement systems and technology changes
    12300 Implement changes
    Milestones: Implemented infrastructure, systems, technology, and work changes

13000 Measure results of overall change
    13100 Define measurement criteria
    13200 Collect information for measurement
    13300 Carry out measurements
    13400 Verify results
    Milestones: approved and verified results

Figure 5.4 Tasks and Milestones of the Change Management Template

Change templates do not stop here. You will be making presentations to management. Typically, the most common involve status, issues or problems, benefits of change, and explanation of change. Use outlines here so that management does not have to deal with a different structure each time. Remember that people must first understand structure before content. If they take too long in understanding the structure, there is little time left for content. With the same structure for each type of presentation, you and the managers spend more time on the content of the message.

ISSUES DATABASES AND MANAGEMENT

Issues are so important that a chapter has been created to discuss commonly encountered issues in change management (Chapter 18). After reading this section, you may want to scan the issues in that chapter. There are three related databases for issues. The first is that for issues in general. The data elements are given in Figure 5.5. An issue is then found to apply to a specific change effort. This is a second database whose elements appear in Figure 5.6. Then you will assign an issue to be investigated. Eventually decisions and actions will be taken. This is the third database on actions for issues (Figure 5.7). The databases are linked through the identifier of the issue.

Some comments on the data elements are useful here.

- *Type of issue*. This pertains to whether it is related to the change team, strike forces, business unit/department, management, the change work, the business process, technology, or external factors
- *Status*. An issue in a change effort can be open, closed, pending (no action), merged with another issue.

- Change issue identifier
- Issue title
- Date issue was created
- Who created the issue
- Description
- Type of issue
- General impact if the issue is not addressed
- Related change issues
- Related lessons learned
- Activities to which the issue usually applies (work affected)
- Comments

Figure 5.5   Data Elements for the General Issues Database

- Change issue identifier
- Change effort identifier
- Tasks identifiers
- Status
- Priority
- Date issue was associated with this change effort
- Who created the issue for this change effort
- Related issues
- Activities to which the change issue applies
- Impact on these activities if the issue is not addressed
- Date that the issue was resolved
- How the issue was resolved (decisions)
- Benefits of resolution
- Outcomes or results of resolution
- Lessons learned from issue resolution
- Comments

Figure 5.6   Data Elements for the Specific Change Effort Issues

- Issue identifier
- Date of action
- Who took the action
- Action taken
- Results achieved
- Comments

Figure 5.7   Data Elements for Actions on Issues

- *Priority.* This can be on a numerical scale of 1–5 (1—low; 5—high).
- *Impact.* This is the impact on the change effort if the issue is not solved.
- *Work affected.* This is the process or activity that is impacted by the issue.

Let's consider now the management of issues. Issues are first identified and entered into the issues database. If the issue is new, it is entered in the general database first. Then it is added to the specific issues for the change effort. Note that the change issue is referenced to the specific change effort and tasks within the change plan. This is to ensure that you can map back and forth between the change template and plan and the change issues. The change issue is then associated with the change plan.

Once the issue has been identified, then someone will begin to take actions to address it. These can be entered in the third database of actions. After the issue is resolved, the flag for the task is lifted, how the issue was resolved is entered in the issues database at the individual change effort level.

LESSONS LEARNED DATABASES AND COORDINATION

Lessons learned from the change effort can pertain to techniques regarding the work being done in the change effort or to the business activity itself. Like the issues databases, you can establish three lessons learned databases. The first is given in Figure 5.8. This relates to the general lessons learned. The second database is a cross-reference to the tasks and specific change effort (Figure 5.9). Now when you attempt to apply a lesson learned to a specific piece of work, you will have some experience or result. These are recorded in the application database (Figure 5.10).

Let's see how this works. As you do planning and work in the change effort, the change team will gain experiences as will the strike forces and change steering committees. Now you will hold specific meetings to gather lessons learned.

- Lessons learned identifier
- Title
- Status
- Date created
- Who created
- Description
- Processes to which the lesson learned applies
- Situations to which the lesson learned applies
- Expected outcome when the lesson learned is applied
- Benefits of the lesson learned
- Guidelines to implement the lesson learned
- Related lessons learned
- Related change issues
- Comments

Figure 5.8   Data Elements of the Change Lessons Learned Database

- Lessons learned identifier
- Change effort identifier
- Tasks in change effort

Figure 5.9   Lessons Learned Cross-Reference to Tasks

- Lessons learned identifier
- Change effort identifier
- Date of application
- Who entered action
- Action taken
- Result achieved
- Suggestions for future application
- Comments

Figure 5.10   Application of Lesson Learned Data Elements

This has a number of benefits. First, it forces people to assess and rate how they are doing. Second, you are pulling together experience while it is fresh in their minds. Note that this is almost the opposite from the standard course in projects where you gather experience at the end. At the end people are gone. Whomever is left cannot remember details and is trying to get on with their other work.

After gathering some experience you now structure the information and input it into the lessons learned database. Then you can relate the new information to the change management template for future access and reference.

At the start of a particular activity in the change effort you sit down with the team and review what is to be done (the relevant tasks in your change plan). This is the best time to review the related lessons learned. Later, as you and the team apply these, you will gain new insights and can update the lessons learned through the lessons learned database.

OPPORTUNITIES TRACKING

An opportunity is a situation in the business unit or department in which a change would be beneficial. It is an issue in the business process. Typically, a strike force may identify over 25–30 opportunities. If there are 10 strike forces, then this means a potential over 250–300 opportunities. It is obvious that some structure is necessary to track these opportunities. For this reason the database in Figure 5.11 was created. It is similar to the issues database, but there are only two databases.

How should you track opportunities? The strike forces identify opportunities. The change team gives identifiers to them. Part of the identifier should be that of the department. The opportunity is then placed in the opportunity database. As work progresses, activities take place relative to the opportunity. Opportunities

- Opportunity identifier
- Title
- Status
- Date created
- Who created the opportunity
- Type
- Description
- Process/work to which it applies
- How you could address the problem or opportunity
- Impact if not carried out
- Benefits of the opportunity
- Urgency (time importance)
- Ease of implementation
- Related opportunities
- Comments

Figure 5.11   Data Elements for the Opportunity Tracking Database

- Opportunity identifier
- Date of action
- Who took action
- Action taken
- Result achieved
- Comments

Figure 5.12   Data Elements for Actions on Change Opportunities

get defined in more detail. Some may be combined. Some may be dropped. Others may make it all of the way through implementation. Tracking is key here.

Let's briefly look at the data elements for opportunities (Figure 5.12). When a strike force has identified an opportunity for change, often the first thing that comes into mind is the impact on the work if the opportunity is not addressed. This naturally leads to the priority and the time urgency of the opportunity. Since the strike force members are doing the actual work or are close to the work, they often can be coached by the change team into ideas for improvement of the work. But it does not stop there. You want the strike force to address implementation of the idea and ease of implementation.

What does "ease of implementation" mean? Well, implementation may often be a combination of the following:

- Procedure change (easy)
- Policy change (easy to moderate)
- System change (moderate to difficult)
- Overall management direction change (hard)
- Organization change (moderate to hard)
- Facilities change (easy to hard)

Once the opportunities have been documented, the strike forces vote on the opportunities in terms of the following:

- Benefit
- Ease of implementation
- Impact if not done
- Alignment with the mission, vision, and objectives of the business

Strike forces review each others work and also participate in voting across all opportunities.

The best opportunities and voting results now go to the operational change steering committee and then to the executive change steering committee. A list of opportunities has now been approved for further analysis.

The strike forces now construct more detailed business cases that detail the changes needed, the benefits, the measurement of the benefits, impacts if not addressed, related opportunities, and implementation steps. The business cases are voted upon and the same review process occurs.

Opportunities are identified and documented.

Opportunities are voted upon by the strike forces coordinated by the change team.

Results are reviewed by the two change steering committees.

Approved opportunities have more detailed business cases prepared by the strike forces.

Voting on business cases among strike forces occurs

Results are review by the two change steering committees.

The change management team prepares alternative change implementation strategies and reviews this with strike force members and the two change steering committees.

A change implementation plan is now prepared based upon the change implementation strategy.

Implementation of the first wave of changes.

Measurement of the results and preparation for the next wave of changes.

Figure 5.13   Steps in the Change Method

At this point there is an approved slate of business cases. Now they must be organized into groups and sequenced over time into phases of change. This is the change implementation strategy or roadmap. The change implementation plan and implementation follow. Results are measured. These steps are shown in Figure 5.13.

BENEFITS OF THE CHANGE MANAGEMENT FRAMEWORK

As you can see, there is quite a lot of structure to create. Is this necessary? Well, change management is a program. That is, you will likely do many change efforts over time as you are successful. Then you want to build the infrastructure to support a longer-term program versus a one time project.

Another way to look at the framework is to consider what happens if you don't implement a particular element of the framework. Let's consider each major component.

- *Two change steering committees.* If you have one change committee, there is no buffer between the committee and the strike forces. From experience, this often results in more interference with the strike forces. Politics is a bigger player. Two committees help to keep the politics from management out of the work.

- *Strike forces.* If you use a standard project team approach, you will likely pull too many people from their everyday work into the change effort—negatively impacting departmental work performance. A standard team approach will also employ fewer people so that there is less collaboration and support for change.
- *Change templates.* If you have no templates, then every time a presentation or plan has to be created, it must be done from scratch—eating up your most valuable asset—time.
- *Issues management.* If you do not have an organized approach for identifying, tracking, and addressing issues, then you will likely be doomed to repeat the same problems and issues. Issues management provides structure for addressing problems.
- *Issues database.* The issues database is a repository of issues and their history. Without this you are likely to see the same issues again and again. Moreover, the resolution of issues will most likely not be consistent—leading to more problems.
- *Lessons learned database and coordination.* Gathering experience in one change effort to be used in later ones is critical to getting cumulative benefit from change management. If you have no structure for this, then you are going to spend more time and repeat mistakes in the next effort.
- *Opportunities tracking.* Recall that opportunities are situations that can be improved in the work or business process. Since opportunities interrelate and there are many of these, tracking is critical. Without tracking you may find that some improvements conflict or are not consistent with each other.

There are several additional benefits. First, as you work on one change effort, you gather lessons learned that will be useful in the next effort. Second, experience in doing change will help you make the template more detailed and improved. Third, as you solve issues, you will find that the same issues recur repeatedly. With an issues database you can solve the same, recurring issues faster and more effectively.

MARKET THE CHANGE MANAGEMENT APPROACH

Let's pause here and consider that you have to sell the change management approach to not only the management, but also to the employees. Now a number of advantages and benefits have been listed and discussed. That is a starting point. You should consider each audience relevant to the change effort.

- *Upper management.* They may endorse the change approach generally, but they often want fast benefits—especially if they want to create a track record for themselves and then move on. They are not interested in long-term

programs. The word "cumulative" probably does not enter their vocabulary
often. For upper level managers, you should make the following points:
— The method provides for Quick Hits so that there will be useful and
measurable short-term results.
— The approach provides for widespread involvement of employees
so that there is low risk.
— The involvement of upper management in the executive change steering
committee is limited in terms of their time. Moreover, topics are filtered
through the team and the operational change steering committee first.
— The cost of the approach is limited since people are doing their own
jobs. There is no massive training effort in some jargon-laden method.

- *Middle level management.* This group may feel as threatened as the
employees. Their fears can be calmed by stressing the following points:
— The approach provides for extensive employee involvement. The Quick
Hits do not upset the organization structure. Thus, their positions are
secure up until the major change with the new process. Even then
organization change will, if it comes at all, follow this.
— There is the opportunity for manager involvement in the operational
change steering committee so that they can provide input.

- *Employees who will become strike force members.* These individuals
should have a number of concerns related to extent of involvement and
preparation to the work of the strike force. They may feel that the effort
has high risk to them. Here are some points to make.
— Strike force members have limited involvement in that they identify
opportunities and vote. They may also prepare business cases and
participate in presentations.
— They get an opportunity to gain some low risk visibility to management.
— Their work is coached and coordinated by the change team so that
there are opportunities for learning by doing.
— They can limit their involvement to the planning and specification of
changes so that they won't have to be involved in implementation.

- *Employees who will become members of the change management team.*
These individuals will have much more involvement in coordination.
They have the most to risk if the change effort flounders or fails. You
can employ the arguments listed above for the strike force members.
Next, you can indicate that they will obtain guidance from the change
leaders. You can also indicate that if they feel uncomfortable in the
effort, they can bail out before implementation of the Quick Hits and
major changes.
- *General employees.* They may fear the changes. However, if they have
input through members of their departments in the strike forces, they can
shape the opportunities and provide support to the strike force members.

Also, the early Quick Wins do not often result in lost jobs. They most often yield positive change in their own jobs so that their working lives are improved.

BUILD THE CHANGE MANAGEMENT TEAM

The change leaders will have to identify the members of the change management team. This is not performed in a vacuum. This is not a typical IT project where you just ask a department manager for some employee. Rather, you as a leader will work with the management to identify medium or junior level employees who show initiative and favor changes. You will identify other potential candidates out of the strike forces.

The change management team is not static. Its membership will change with implementation. The composition can also be modified depending on which opportunities are approved and staged for business cases.

How many should be on the team depending on the extent and scope of the change effort. However, you will want to keep the team size small. Even in large change efforts, we have found that up to five people is manageable. More than that and you start to run into coordination problems within the team.

TRAIN THE CHANGE TEAM

What skills are needed? Here is a list.

- *Problem solving ability*. This cannot be taught to most people. They either have it or they don't. In addition, you do not have the luxury of time to train them to be creative in problem solving.
- *Communication skills*. The same comments for problem solving apply here.
- *Knowledge of the business processes*. The team members have acquired this in their work so that they have in-depth knowledge of their own department's processes. They may have very limited knowledge of the work of other departments.
- *Ability to deal with issues in change management*. This needs to be developed.

How do you develop the skills of the change team? For the knowledge of the processes they can be educated through the strike forces. A member can be assigned to a coordination role for a strike force of an unfamiliar department.

In terms of issues, experience has shown that a suitable approach is to take some of the issues in Chapter 17 and have the team simulate and work through several issues in team meetings. This is very useful in that it gets the team to think the same way. In addition, the team members can become more aware of the political and resistance factors discussed in Chapter 3.

DEVELOP THE DETAILED CHANGE PROJECT PLAN

With the change template and team in place, you are now prepared to develop the project plan. Here are some guidelines.

- Each pair of team members is assigned an area of the change template. They define detailed tasks for this area. The change leaders review this. More issues will surface—which is good. This is performed for the first 3–4 months in detail.
- The team members then define dependencies, additional resources, and the schedule. This is done for the entire plan but at the template level for later tasks. There is another review.
- The change leaders then assemble the entire change plan. If it is too long, they can break up tasks to get more parallel effort. They can also address issues associated with the tasks. Finally, they can examine the critical path of the project.
- Team members will be updating their own tasks and creating new ones. The changes and updates are reviewed by the change leaders.

There are a number of advantages to this method. First, the team members are involved so that they will become more committed. Second, there are fewer misunderstandings since they did the definition themselves. Third, the method frees up some of the time of the change leaders.

EMPLOY THE CHANGE FRAMEWORK SCORE CARD

Figure 5.14 lists a series of elements for the score card. Note that most of these are subjective. This is by intent. You want to use the score card with the change management team as a method for assessing progress.

EXAMPLES

ROCKWOOD COUNTY

Establishing the change management framework initially resulted in too many strike forces. Almost every department wanted to have their processes examined. So the scope had to be narrowed and focused, thereby limiting the number of strike forces.

Element	Score	Comments
Change template in place		
Change template development was collaborative		
Management is supportive of the framework		
The right managers are on the steering committees		
The pace and speed at which the framework was established		
Team participation in project plan development		
Completeness of issues identified		
Extent of involvement of employees in the strike forces		
Percentage of employees who are serving on multiple strike forces		

Figure 5.14   Score Card for the Change Framework

LEGEND MANUFACTURING

Implementing the change management framework served as fresh air as compared to the previous efforts. These previous attempts were closed and had little employee involvement. The approach here is participative and open. Employees embraced the involvement—especially after complaining about the closed nature of the previous approach.

POTENTIAL ISSUES AND RISKS

- People feel that they are too busy to gather lessons learned. They may feel that they will never run into the situation that gave rise to the experience. How do they know that? They don't. So it is always a good idea to gather experience as you go.
- There is the general rush to get through the activities in this chapter. Why? Because it is overhead. It is not change itself. However, if you rush through this and omit some of the steps, then you will find that you will later have to back up and carry out the steps—wasting time and delaying change. It does not take that much time if you start with the lists, databases, and templates of this chapter.
- There is a danger that king and queen bees will be chosen for the strike forces. You already have seen how deadly this can be. You should get the right strike force leaders in place. Again, these are people who are not on good terms with the management of the department that is the subject of the strike force. Work with them to ensure that the king and queen bees are not included.

LESSONS LEARNED

- Members of the change management team should be rotated in and out so that employees do not get burned out with the effort. This also provides the benefit of raising more support for the change effort.
- When you go to a manager to identify strike force members, the manager has a tendency to either give you the most knowledgeable (often a king or queen bee) or someone who is not doing much or someone who is new to the department. You do not want any of these people. You want someone who is junior and very productive and busy. They are valuable, but not critical to the department.
- Do not assume that you can gather lessons learned in a casual manner. You must specify a meeting to deal just with lessons learned. That gives the lessons learned attention and importance.

SUMMARY

This chapter is significant because it is here that you lay the foundation and organization for your change effort. This structure is in several parts. First, you have the organization of the change effort into the change team, strike forces, and the change steering committees. Second, you have the framework of templates, issues, lessons learned, and opportunities. Note that the details here support the overall themes of collaboration and sustained and cumulative change. The goal of the organization part of the change is to ensure that the atmosphere for change is positive. The structure for the change aims at minimizing your effort as well as supporting cumulative ease of change.

Part II

Get Ready for Change

Chapter 6

Determine Activities for Change

INTRODUCTION

Let's step back and look at what you have accomplished so far. In Chapter 4 you defined your change objectives and strategy. In the preceding chapter you established the framework for undertaking the change effort. Now you are ready to select the activities that will be examined in detail and changed through Quick Wins and long-term change. The selection process is not only technical, but also managerial and political. After all, you could spend a great deal of time in selection only to find that management has already prejudged what is to be changed. For this and related reasons quite a bit of time will be dedicated to political concerns and factors.

The importance of this chapter is rather obvious. If you fail to select the best group of activities, do not succeed in marketing the choice, or do not involve the employees and managers outside of the change team, you risk:

- Designing and implementing change that results in marginal benefits.
- Dooming the change effort from the beginning because people did not have a say in the choice of activities for change.

IDENTIFY POTENTIAL AREAS OF CHANGE WITHIN THE GOALS

The first step is to review the change objectives and strategy that you developed in Chapter 4. That will give you an idea of where to start in terms of considering business processes. However, we strongly urge you to cast a wider net at the start.

There is no reason not to consider a wider range of processes. In terms of effort this just translates into a few more strike forces. What are the benefits of an expanded initial scope?

- You consider more processes so that you are less likely to miss good opportunities.
- You get more people interested and involved in the change effort.
- You are likely to uncover additional opportunities for later implementation.
- Management will get an idea of the scope of a change management program in terms of the range of activities, processes, and work.

What are some of the risks of doing this?

- You raise expectations of change. People think that if an area is studied, then changes will be made. This can be mitigated by setting the expectations for change and for this initial exploration early.
- There are so many opportunities for change that the change team is overwhelmed and becomes indecisive in recommending areas for change. This is actually very good, because it will reveal the potential scope of change.

Overall, experience indicates that the benefits of the wider scope outweigh the risks.

Let us now assume that the wider range of investigation has been selected. Using the structure of Chapter 5, the strike force members will be identified. The change leaders will go to the department managers and discuss the initial change effort. No commitments are made as to what areas will be changed. Point out to the manager that the activities in the department may not have sufficient benefits for change or that the change will require extensive IT or facilities or other work. In other words, don't overpromise. When you turn to the identification of the strike force members, indicate that you are looking for junior people who are ambitious and have some experience in the department. Tell the manager that the people that are selected will only have limited involvement so that they can do most, if not all, of their normal work. Strongly emphasize that you are not interested in new employees who lack department knowledge or the king or queen bees. Try to have the manager nominate more than one person so that you can talk to them and have some choice.

The manager will now go out into the work area and bring you to the nominees. Talk to them in terms of getting at the following questions:

- How long have they been in the department?
- Where did they work before?

Then explain briefly the purpose and approach of the change management effort. You will want to emphasize Quick Hits and the involvement of the department employees. If possible, you should try to give this same talk to all of the employees of the department to allay fears. We suggest that you address some concerns head-on. That is, indicate that most change efforts do not result in staff cuts. Clerical parts of work may get simplified or automated. These and other changes make working life easier.

COLLECT INFORMATION ON PROCESSES, WORK, AND ORGANIZATION

Now you have the strike forces, the change team, and the change steering committees in place. You are ready to collect information. In the standard traditional project or systems analysis, you would conduct interviews about problems and requirements. There are a number of difficulties with this method. For interviewing, the problems are:

- Often, the people being interviewed have been removed from the work for some time through promotions, etc. Hence, much of the information they can supply is second hand.
- Some managers may want to get rid of you as soon as possible so they will endeavor to tell you what they perceive you want to hear.
- Other managers may have an axe to grind, score to settle, or some other hidden agenda.

If you did conduct the interviews, you would then have to spend considerable time in weeding out useful information from garbage. Our experience is that this is not worth the trouble.

There are also problems with gathering requirements by asking people what problems they have and what they want.

- You often get a wide range of minor to major problems. There is no prioritization or thought.
- There is no vision of how the work should really be performed in the future so the requirements can point anywhere.
- Because of the method of data collection and its casual, ad hoc nature, any information you receive or glean out of raw data will likely be incomplete.

A better approach for data collection consists of the following steps:

- Collect information through observation and then through specific questions.
- Collect information during a number of visits—not just one. Employees will then be more willing to open up and tell you more.
- Using this information identify the problems with the current work.
- Get validation from the employees that these are the real problems. These are the opportunities for change. Have them talk about the impacts of the problems on them and their work.

- Talk with the employees and suggest potential solutions. Employees react to this and make changes. They suggest other ideas. They begin to have ownership over the ideas. These ideas serve as the basis for Quick Hits and for long-term change.
- After you have defined the short- and long-term changes, you can now work with the employees to determine the benefits of the change. You can also collaboratively develop requirements for getting from the current to the future situation.

There are several advantages of this approach, including:

- The information you collect can be validated right away since you are in the middle of where the work is being performed.
- Requirements are more precise and complete since there are specific changes and targets.
- Benefits are more tangible since you can relate the benefits to exact transactions.
- Through collaboration they do a substantial part of the work so that the employees become more interested and involved in change. Interest and involvement lead to commitment and support for initial and lasting change.
- By using the employees as part of the effort, your time is spent more effectively and efficiently.

Now let's take this approach and apply it to the strike forces.

- *Identify the processes and work.* The change team can have the strike force first identify the processes that are performed in the area to which they are assigned. The result is a list of processes for each area.
- *Determine problems and opportunities.* With the list of processes identified, the strike forces can collect information from the work and from employees doing the work to determine problems and opportunities for change and improvement.

The strike forces can then analyze these opportunities—coming right up in the next section.

OPPORTUNITY WRITEUP

For each opportunity the strike force members can define the following:

- Type of opportunity
- Description of the problem
- Impact on the process if the problem continues and is not solved or addressed
- Potential general solution

- Benefits to the work and people if the problem is solved
- Ease of implementing the change

Type of opportunity indicates if the opportunity is related to procedures, policies, information technology (IT), organization, structure of the work, etc. You may have several entries here. If you do, you may have a more complex opportunity so that, perhaps, you should split the opportunity so that each one of the resulting opportunities is of a single type.

Impact is the potential damage that continues to occur if the opportunity is not carried out. Examples of impacts to consider are:

- Lost productivity
- High error rate
- Rework
- Employee turnover
- Lost time from work
- Extended time to do a transaction or piece of work
- Difficulty in tracking and measuring the work

Benefits are tangible benefits. Thus, making a change that makes the work easier is not a benefit unless it translates into something more concrete. In this case, ease of use and doing work means that higher volumes are achieved with the same labor, costs are lower, etc. Examples of tangible benefits are:

- Lower amounts of labor to do a fixed amount of work
- Reduced overtime through handling more work
- Reduced training costs
- Lower system maintenance or operations costs
- Reduced supervisory positions
- Handling of new types of work without additional expense

Ease of implementation is a critical component of the analysis. A change is simple if it can be done by a modification to a procedure. Change to a policy may take management approval, but it is reasonable. Systems, facilities, organization, and other structural changes are more complex and difficult—not immediate Quick Hits. Notice that cost is not one of the factors. This is because cost is reflected in the ease of implementation. You should consider the following factors when you are developing the ease of implementation ratings with the strike forces.

- Procedure change
- Policy change
- Modification or simplification of business rules
- Systems changes
- Technology infrastructure changes
- Changes in supervision
- Organization change
- Alternations to facilities

How do strike forces and the change team estimate impacts, benefits, and ease of implementation without detailed information? First, note that the sheer volume of the opportunities does not allow this detailed data collection. Second, the team members arrive at these ratings and estimates through collaborative discussion and some analysis of the work. Finally, they are not coming up with numbers, but really orders of magnitude and comparative ratings.

You want to have the strike forces document the opportunities with the coordinating assistance of the change team. An example of a form to use for the writeup of opportunities appears in Figure 6.1.

Opportunity identifier: _____   Date: _____

Strike force: _____   Prepared by: _____

Process to which it applies: _____

Type: _____

Description of the opportunity: _____

_____

_____

Impact on the process if the opportunity is not addressed: _____

_____

_____

Potential solution: _____

_____

Tangible benefits: _____

_____

Ease of implementation: _____

_____

Comments: _____

_____

Figure 6.1 Opportunity Writeup Form

Next, the strike forces and change team can analyze and aggregate the opportunities. Here, as with the initial opportunities, you want to involve employees doing the work. You want their involvement to validate the analysis as well as to support it later with management.

ROLL-UP OF OPPORTUNITIES TO THE BUSINESS PROCESS

Your goal is to select the business processes or work that meets several goals, including the following:

- *Potential benefits.* For the work, activities, or processes selected, there are substantial potential benefits that justify the change effort.
- *Change objectives and strategy.* Change in the selected activities or processes support the change objectives and strategy.
- *Business importance.* The activities are important to the business. Obviously, carrying out change in marginal activities may provide training to the change team, but doesn't do much for management or the organization. This can be seen through the table of business objectives versus business processes developed in Chapter 4.
- *Manageability.* The range of activities that are selected can be successfully addressed and managed by the change team.

To start the evaluation, begin with a roll-up of the information on opportunities to the activity or process. Now if you review Figure 6.1 again, you will see that it is possible to read the text of each part and develop a rating scale of 1–5 where 1 is low and 5 is high. For example, for impacts a "1" means that the opportunity, if changed, will not impact the process performance. A "3" for benefits means that carrying out the change will yield at least moderate benefits. The rating of "5" for ease of implementation implies that the opportunity will be easy to implement. The table for a single process is shown in Figure 6.2. Here the opportunities are

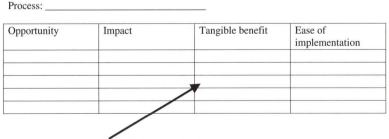

Figure 6.2 Summary Table for Specific Process or Activity

rows and the columns are, respectively, impact, benefit, and ease of implementation. The numerical rating appears as the table entry.

ANALYSIS TO POTENTIALLY GROUP PROCESSES AND WORK FOR CHANGE

It is seldom the case that an activity or process stands alone. Usually, it is tightly linked to a few other activities. Often, it is loosely linked to many others. It is useful to consider this linkage because you may wish to cluster the activities. Examples of types of linkage are:

- Both activities are performed by the same people.
- Both activities use the same system.
- Both activities are supported by the same department or location.
- The activities adhere to the same policies or rules.
- The activities serve the same customers.
- The activities are related to the suppliers.
- The activities are performed in the same facility.

Rather than dealing with this as fuzzy text, you should consider creating another table. Figure 6.3 contains a table of processes versus processes. The table entry can be the degree of linkage (H—high, M—medium, L—low). You could also enter the type of linkage. Note that since the same things are listed as rows and columns, you will only complete one-half of the table since the other half is redundant.

AGGREGATION OF ACTIVITIES AND PROCESSES INTO POTENTIAL CHANGE CANDIDATES

You are now prepared to combine the processes or activities that are tightly linked with each other. When you do this, you can combine the opportunities for the groups. Please note that a single activity can be part of more than one cluster or group of activities. You should also keep important activities or processes as separate entities as well. The result of this step is a list of single and combined activities with substantial overlap. We will call this list, *potential change candidates.*

Figure 6.3 Linkage between Activities or Processes

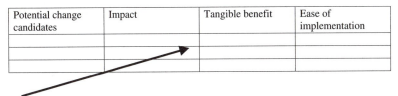

Potential change candidates	Impact	Tangible benefit	Ease of implementation

Average of ratings of individual opportunities

Figure 6.4   Roll-up of Opportunity Ratings for Potential Change Candidates

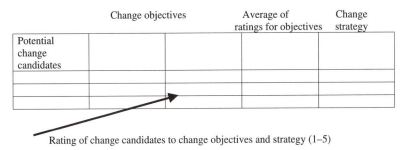

	Change objectives		Average of ratings for objectives	Change strategy
Potential change candidates				

Rating of change candidates to change objectives and strategy (1–5)

Figure 6.5   Potential Change Candidates versus Change Objectives and Strategy

It is now time to aggregate the opportunities for each potential change candidate. This is carried out by averaging the scores of opportunities pertaining to the activities in the potential change candidate. It is assumed that all opportunities are equally weighted. This makes sense since you are considering overall impact, benefit, and ease of implementation. The resulting table will be of the form that appears in Figure 6.4.

ANALYSIS OF POTENTIAL CHANGE CANDIDATES AND CHANGE OBJECTIVES AND STRATEGIES

From Chapter 4 you developed the change objectives and your change strategy. You can now employ these to create a new table shown in Figure 6.5. The rows of the table are the potential change candidates. The columns are the change objectives and the change strategy. The table entry is the extent to which carrying out change in the activities in the row will support the specific change objective or strategy on a scale of 1–5 (1—low, 5—high). This table is important because:

- The table validates the change objectives and strategy. If there is no high rating in a column, then you should question the objective.
- The table serves to indicate which groups of activities yield the greatest support for the objective or strategy.

Note that there is a column that averages the ratings for the individual objectives. This will be useful in the final evaluation and selection.

ANALYSIS OF POTENTIAL CHANGE CANDIDATES AND BUSINESS FACTORS

In theory you do not need to do this analysis since in Chapter 4 you related the change objectives and strategy to the business factors of mission, vision, business objectives, business strategies, and business issues. However, it often helps in communicating with the management and the employees to "close the loop" and create the following tables.

- *Potential change candidates versus mission elements.* The table contains a rating of how the group of activities supports or is critical to the elements of the mission.
- *Potential change candidates versus vision elements.* The table relates how a change candidate supports the vision of the organization.
- *Potential change candidates versus business objectives.* The table entry is a rating of how important the activities are in a row to each business objective.
- *Potential change candidates versus business issues.* The table entry relates the change candidates to the specific business issues in terms of relevance.
- *Potential change candidates versus business strategies.* This table indicates the importance of the processes in the row to the specific business strategy.

EMPLOY THE SCORE CARD FOR POTENTIAL CHANGE ACTIVITIES

With the preceding analysis you are ready to develop an overall score card for the potential change activities. The resulting table is shown in Figure 6.6. The rows are the potential change activities and the columns are:

- Impact if not carried out (from Figure 6.4).
- Tangible benefits (from Figure 6.4).
- Ease of implementation (from Figure 6.4).
- Averaged support for change objectives (from Figure 6.5).
- Support for change strategy (from Figure 6.5).

You will employ this table in the evaluation and selection of activities discussed in the next section.

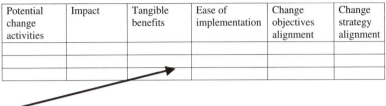

Potential change activities	Impact	Tangible benefits	Ease of implementation	Change objectives alignment	Change strategy alignment

Ratings from Figures 6.4 and 6.5

Figure 6.6   Score Card for Potential Change Activities

EVALUATE AND SELECT THE ACTIVITIES FOR CHANGE

As you may have many potential change candidates, it may often be necessary to filter out some as finalists before proceeding further with the evaluation. Here are some guidelines for doing this.

- Rank the candidates to get the top three activities in terms of impact if not implemented. This will reveal the ones where there will be the greatest easing of pain. In a way this is the negative internal benefit for change.
- Rank the candidates to get the top three activities for tangible benefits. These are ones that would likely yield the most benefits to the business overall.
- Order the candidates to find the ones that are the easiest to implement. Regardless of what else is approved, you may want to pursue these if they are simple. It will raise morale and support for change.
- Grade the activities to determine the top three that are aligned with the change objectives. This means that you will identify those that have the highest degree of alignment with the business factors.
- Rank the candidates to get the top three that support the change strategy. This is different from the change objectives since it focuses more on implementation.

While some candidates may emerge on several lists, it is usually the case that there will not be one that appears on almost all lists. For example, an activity may be in need change, but is not crucial to the business. Another example is that the activities that are critical to the business have no Quick Hits.

Now let's turn to a sample chart that you can create with the score card information. Figure 6.7 contains a spider chart in which each of the dimensions are one of the criteria in the potential change candidate score card. The group of activities, labeled A, is almost ideal. It scores high on all five criteria. Look at this one longingly as you may not see it again in real life often.

Group A ——————
Group B — — — —
Group C ············

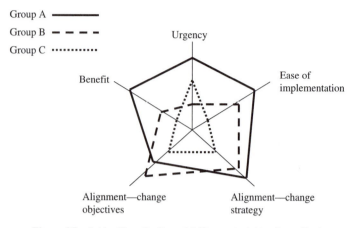

Figure 6.7   Spider Chart for Potential Change Activities Score Card

Now consider Group B. There is a problem here. It is rated fairly well in terms of all criteria except urgency. What is going on? It likely means that the activities in the group work fairly well internally in the department, but represent significant opportunities in terms of benefits, alignment, and ease of implementation. You might find some resistance to change for this one.

Finally, consider group C. It aligns with the change objectives and strategy, and has urgency. However, the benefits and ease of implementation are lower in ratings. This may mean that there are some problems that need to be addressed. However, making the change will not be easy and there may not be many benefits. You would probably pass on this group.

It is critical that you now begin to involve the two change steering committees and management. They will need to participate in order to get their later support. Moreover, involvement here will reveal to you where their real priorities lie. This is because what has gone before was quite general and nonspecific. Here they are going to determine exactly what activities the change management will deal with.

The score card and the other tables provide useful information for evaluation and selection, but they are not the entire story. There are additional factors to consider, including:

- *Availability of Quick Hits.* Ease of implementation helps to determine this, but you should also look at the highest rated finalists to see if there are sufficient Quick Hits.
- *Elapsed time required to achieve major long-term change.* You could have a set of activities that are a group of Quick Hits and very long-term change.

- *Measurability of benefits.* While tangibility of benefits has been covered, ease of measurement of the benefits has not been addressed.
- *Potential resistance to change.* This is the assessment of the strike force in terms of potential resistance to change.
- *Risk of failure.* Potential changes that involve outside, external entities typically have a higher risk of failure since so much is out of your direct control.
- *Number of organizations involved.* This is measured in part by ease of implementation, but it is useful here in that the change team could be spread very thin if the number is high.
- *Scope of changes.* Everything might be otherwise OK, but when you review what has to be changed, you find that no areas of potential change have been left out. This may indicate that the scope is too large.

Another chart can be generated by combining the above factors with those of the score card. The factors then become.

- Alignment with change objectives and strategy
- Ease of implementation; availability of Quick Hits
- Risk and resistance to change
- Benefits and their measurability
- Impact if not undertaken
- Urgency
- Elapsed time
- Scope of change

Using these factors you can create the chart in Figure 6.8. The chart shown is for an almost ideal group. It has benefits. The scope is limited. There is alignment

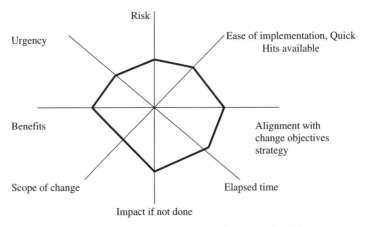

Figure 6.8 Combined Evaluation Chart for Change Candidates

Selection strategies

Criteria	Conservative	Aggressive	Ltd. Resources	Technology	Short term
Urgency	H	M	M	L	M
Risk	L	M–H	L–M	M	L
Benefits	M	H	M–H	H	H
Measurement of benefits	H	M–H	M	M–H	H
Availability of Quick Hits	H	M	M–H	L–M	H
Elapsed time	L–M	M	L–M	M–H	L
Potential resistance	L–M	M	L	M	L–M
Scope	L–M	M–H	L	M–H	L
No. organizations	L	M–H	L	M	L
Objectives alignment	M	H	L–M	H	L–M
Strategy alignment	M	H	L–M	H	L–M

Figure 6.9   Selection Strategies for Change Candidates

with the change objectives and scope. There is moderate urgency so that there is no panic. Risk is limited. Elapsed time is moderate. The impact, if not done, is moderate.

Now with this analysis you can work with the two change steering committees to move toward a selection. There is an additional table that should be created with the participation of the change operations steering committee. It is shown in Figure 6.9. Here the rows are specific criteria identified in this section and from the score card. The columns are general strategies for selection. These include:

- *Conservative*. This is characterized by moderation in almost all categories and high on ease of implementation and resistance to change. If management goes for this selection strategy, you may find that you have limited support when you are dealing with issues and resistance to change.
- *Aggressive*. Here the candidates that maximize benefits, ease of implementation, align to the change objectives and strategy, and have a limited elapsed time are favored. This is good, but if you don't show results in the Quick Hits, management may intervene or interfere in the change effort.
- *Limited resources*. This strategy favors those candidates that have limited scope and number of organizations. This strategy shows a more tentative commitment to the change effort by management.
- *Technology*. Under this strategy, longer term gains are favored over Quick Hits. Alignment with the change objectives, and, hence, the business

factors is crucial. Management feels that it is best to achieve more lasting automation than short-term changes. If the technology and systems don't deliver and there are few Quick Hits, the change effort could be in big trouble.

- *Short term.* This is the strategy of a firm that could be in financial trouble or in other difficulties. Management may need Quick Hits to demonstrate results to outside investors, for example.

The entry in the table is either high (H), medium (M), or low (L). This table is very interesting when you put it to use. It tends to put management to the acid test of commitment and direction of change. The table is a nice, non-confrontational way to do this. Thus, we strongly encourage you to use it. Remember that the table has the back-up of all of the analysis and meetings of the change team and strike forces.

WHAT TO DO WITH LOSING POTENTIAL CHANGE ACTIVITIES

Once the selection has been made, there is a tendency to move on to the next stage. Don't do that. You should revisit the losing potential change candidates and look for some that have Quick Hit potential, substantial benefits that are measurable, low risk, and low potential resistance. See if you can keep these going through to implementation. These represent the "low hanging fruit" of your change effort so far.

For the other ones, go to the department managers whose processes and activities were not selected. Discuss why the other ones were selected. Indicate that it is highly likely that change management will get to them. Also, indicate that their information and concerns are not wasted as the same information will be updated for the next round of changes.

UTILIZE THE ACTIVITIES SELECTION SCORE CARD

Figure 6.10 gives the score card for activities selection. Note as with other score cards, many of the factors are subjective. As with other score cards, you want to develop this with the change team so that you and they can gather lessons learned for the next time.

MARKET THE SELECTED ACTIVITIES

Marketing here is not just performed after the activities have been selected. You have to be marketing change all of the way. At the same time you cannot overpromise results—IT has made too many promises for IT projects and you can

Criteria	Score	Comments
Number of employees involved		
Percentage of total number of employees involved		
Number of managers involved		
Percentage of number of managers involved		
Number of finalist candidates		
Quality of writeups by strike forces		
Performance of the strike forces		
Performance of change team		
Quality of management review		
Number of opportunities surfaced		
Number of groups		
Extent of resistance encountered		

Figure 6.10   Activities Selection Score Card

see the lack of credibility that IT has in many organizations. Here is a possible marketing approach for you.

> *Indicate that there are a number of steps and substantial effort before changes are made. Stress that there are Quick Hits as well as long-term change coming. Also, point out that this is their chance to participate without being left out of the change effort.*

This is a positive, but realistic approach that stresses their participation and involvement.

Marketing for management is best done through the change steering committee members. Doing this provides several benefits. First, you reinforce the new process of change steering committees that have been established. Managers will, hopefully, be less willing to go outside of the committees. Second, you are getting early involvement of the managers after they have kicked off the change effort.

You can judge your marketing success through the score card and from the extent of their involvement and how they react to the final slate of change candidates. It is here that the "rubber meets the road." Hidden agendas and fears will be expressed indirectly through their opinions on which change candidate to pursue. For you this is critical information since it provides you with omens as to the future of change.

EXAMPLES

ROCKWOOD COUNTY

Rockwood departments were at first reluctant to get involved in this work. They were used to managers telling them what to do and what the priorities were. It took considerable time for the change team to get the strike force members and employees to open up about opportunities.

However, this barrier was easier to overcome than the one encountered when there were attempts at consensus in the strike forces. It was like energy had been bottled up for months or years and now was released. People wanted to plunge in and implement some changes to address items that were obvious and could be addressed quickly. It took the change leaders, the change team, and management to indicate that this would come later. A lesson learned here is that you can never assume that people are dumb or do not care. When it comes down to having an opportunity to voice their views without risk on topics related to their jobs, people really open up.

LEGEND MANUFACTURING

As you recall from Chapter 1, Legend Manufacturing had had several failed attempts at change. These were top-down. When this collaborative approach was introduced, the managers were resistant. Several wanted to name the activities for change right away. It then took some time to convince them that collaboration with employees and strike forces would provide additional, detailed information that they lacked.

POTENTIAL ISSUES AND RISKS

- Employees on the strike forces will often be reluctant to identify opportunities. They might feel that these make supervisors and managers look bad so that they might be punished. The change team should assume that this will happen and perform active coordination.
- A strike force may have difficulty deciding on a rating for a change candidate. There is not much information. So you must trust the experience of the strike force members in doing their work in the departments. You cannot afford to do detailed data collection here.

LESSONS LEARNED

- There is a tendency to want to go out and make many changes after so many good opportunities have been identified. Don't follow this path.

A leading garment manufacturer tried this approach with over 60 (yes, sixty) parallel change efforts. The firm almost went bankrupt.

- Developing the opportunities in a group environment such as the strike forces provides a degree of anonymity to the individuals who suggest the opportunities. If a person volunteers an opportunity in his or her own department, it is a good idea if someone else on the strike force writes it up. Otherwise, the opportunity could easily be traced to the person. Another way to protect an individual is to have another strike force member carry out an investigation to validate the opportunity.
- What if you run into a situation in which the strike force really lacks critical information? The coordinating change team member must decide how much effort would be required to collect the additional information.

SUMMARY

This is one of the most important early topics since it identifies where the change management will be focused. However, it is also important because it tests management's will and direction for change. You will learn about future management involvement and their willingness to take on issues and problems here. Overall, the step of determining which activities to pursue for change establishes a working pattern of behavior among the change team, strike forces, employees, and members of the change steering committees.

Chapter 7

Collect Information on Today's Work

INTRODUCTION

If you are thinking that this chapter is going to be a standard academic, boring discussion about esoteric data collection and statistics, forget it. When you are collecting information, you are deeply immersed in the politics of the departments and organization. Whatever you say or do may be used against you or misinterpreted for someone's political ends. No matter how you start the change effort with intense management support, things can go badly awry here—requiring a massive effort at damage control. Here is a basic lesson learned.

You have to plan and carry out information collection with great care to avoid causing problems and increasing risk to the change effort.

Notice how different the data collection is from the standard methods you learned in school. Figure 7.1 highlights some of the differences. We can elaborate on this table with the following comments.

- *Interviewing.* Interviewing is of little true value in many cases and especially in change management since people often tell you what you want to hear or just reinforce the current work methods.
- *Direct observation of work.* While this is viewed as one of the ways to collect information, in change management it is absolutely critical. You have to grasp the detail in order to define, validate, and implement change.
- *Focus of contacts.* To keep the effort limited, you are often told to interview the key supervisors and employees. These employees are often the king

Characteristic	Standard information collection	Change management information collection
Interviewing	Relied upon heavily	Not very important
Direct observation of work	Useful	Critical
Focus of contacts	Key managers and queen and king bees	As many lower level employees
Frequent goal	Define requirements	Gather information on how work is done and problems
Political goal	None	Major; get employees to see the problems and want change
Truth	Defined through the information and then accepted	Never really known since the work environment is changing and dynamic
Risk	Very low; not considered	Moderate to high

Figure 7.1 Comparison of Characteristics for Standard and Change Management Information Collection

and queen bees. However, as has been stated before, these people tend to have no interest in change since they desire to maintain their power.

- *Frequent goal.* The goal is often to gather requirements for process change or a new system. In change management you are not close to this stage yet. Requirements and benefits are defined later as you perform analysis.
- *Political goal.* In traditional data collection, there is no politics discussed. In change management there is the overriding political goal that you have to get the employees to desire change by seeing the problems with the current work.
- *Truth.* Traditionally, it is assumed that people are giving you the truth and that it is stable. In change management it is very different. Truth is relative and is different for each person. It is the same as the "X-Files." The truth is out there—somewhere.
- *Risk.* In change management there is great risk. You may raise people's dread of change. Alternatively, you may raise expectations for change that cannot be easily met. In your change effort in this stage, you are walking a tightrope because this is the first time you are out in the departments where the work is being done.

In addition to these factors, there is the question of time. The more time you spend in a department collecting information, the greater the risk and the higher the expectations. After all, if the people spend a lot of time with you, they expect something in return. A graphical view of this is given in Figure 7.2. Here you see several lines. First, you see a bell-shaped curve. This is the value of information. If you collect too much or too little, then there is little value. Another curve is the effort required to collect the data. It goes up exponentially as you collect more data. What is more data? Collecting information on all of the details of exceptions and workarounds. As you will see, don't get sucked into this black hole. Now look at the figure again and you see two dashed vertical lines. These

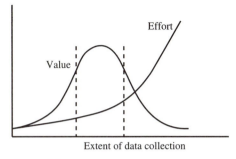

Figure 7.2   Trade-Offs in Information Collection

are the limits of what you should collect. However, there is no quantitative measure. A fundamental lesson learned is that:

> *You have to adapt your information collection as you go.*
> *There is no magic, predefined formula.*

So how do you use this figure? Be aware that you have to make trade-offs and be flexible as you go for technical, business, and political reasons.

DEFINE THE SCOPE FOR DATA COLLECTION

Let's first consider scope—the range of what you are going to collect. You have selected the group of activities or processes in the preceding chapter. So you might think that the scope should be all of the information about these activities. Forget it! You will never achieve this due to the exceptions, workarounds, and shadow systems. Moreover,

> *The more information you collect on exceptions, the more*
> *you give them credibility and importance.*

You now start to be influenced by the king and queen bees who have the most information on exceptions, etc. You pave the way for potential risk and failure by reinforcing these things.

> *If your change effort becomes focused or obsessed on exceptional work,*
> *then your changes to the work will likely be very limited.*

What should the scope consist of? Here are some general guidelines.

- Centerpost your work in standard, common transactions and work across and within departments.
- Focus on cross department work as you may find this to be an area where you can make the greatest improvement.

- Only consider a limited number of exceptions.
- Try to uncover as many shadow systems as you can, but avoid too much detail.
- Keep in mind that you are conveying as much information and impressions as you are getting.

There is also a management scope to this. You want to inform managers of what is going on and of some of the initial findings. Get their reactions. If they seem hesitant to support small changes or if they are disinterested, then you can almost certainly see potential problems ahead. It is better to know now.

By testing the strike forces, the change team, and management reaction, you are moving a major risk of failure, not implementing change, up in time.

Note that you are eliminating the risk. You are only becoming more aware of the dimensions of the risk and problems.

DETERMINE THE APPROACH

Here are some common sense steps that work.

- Collect initial information from managers and supervisors and move as quickly as possible down to where the work is being performed.
- Gather information at the lowest level through various means—being trained in the work, doing the work, observation, and casual conversation.
- Write up and analyze information as you go. This must be an interactive approach.
- Share with employees and elicit their concerns and problems.
- Work to define some potential solutions.
- Have the employees take ownership of the findings.
- Through the strike forces and work in this phase of change management, you want to validate management interest and commitment to change.

Note that you will not identify all of the problems or issues. Completeness is not a goal. Your political goal is to get them to recognize the problems and their impacts on their work. Next, the solutions you define with them will likely not be complete or comprehensive. They tell you what is possible and what has been tried before and failed.

ORGANIZE THE STRIKE FORCES FOR DATA COLLECTION

You cannot just turn the strike forces loose without providing guidance in line with the above discussion. How do you bring the strike force members along?

You could just relate the above. However, experience indicates that this has little practical impact.

A better approach is to carry out a simulation of data collection. Have members of the change team act as strike force members and as employees. Remember that the strike force members are employees too and so are probably aware of who to talk to and where some good information sources are. After all, they do their work with these people every day. Exploit this. This is a major benefit of the strike forces over consultants or outsiders.

It takes less time to gather and validate the information
with employees than outsiders.

The initial information collection should occur in a friendly department on one of the activities or processes of lesser importance. This has several important benefits.

- The risk is reduced during this learning curve
- The strike forces gain confidence

You can bring the change team members along in the same manner first.

Now let's get into the politics of real world data collection. The change team and strike forces have to have the same answers to the following questions.

- *Is this just another attempt at change? Other efforts have not resulted in anything good.* This is often a very valid point. Here is a common, acceptable answer. You really do not know. However, if you and the employees can identify some needed changes that improve the work in a tangible way, management will likely be behind it. But you never know for sure so you will find out soon through the initial work.
- *Is management really behind this or is it a fancy?* This relates to the above concern. The answer is again that you do not know for sure. Don't say management is 100% behind this since you cannot say that until some changes are begun to be made. Many people are behind change—up to the point of implementation of change—where the "rubber meets the road."
- *What will happen to us?* While this might not be stated openly, it is a basic concern. Indicate that while this could happen, it is not likely. Indicate that this occurs most often when downsizing is undertaken first. Here it is not.

So do you wait for people to ask these questions? We don't think so. It is far better to be proactive. You can say that, "You may have the concern that. ... Well, it is more likely that..."

PERFORM THE INITIAL DATA COLLECTION

Now you send the strike forces out with a member of the change team. What are they doing?

- They may be trained in how to do the common work as new employees. This is an excellent way to see the quality of training, the application of the business rules, and how the work is performed.
- The team members should try to do some of the work with some specific activities. Have the employees watch them and offer comments.
- When a problem is uncovered, talk with the employees about the effect of the problem. What do they do when the problem arises? How often does it occur?
- Ask people for ideas on how to fix the problem. You often will have to make some suggestions to get them to react. So we suggest that you offer some rather impossible or outlandish suggestions to get them to react. They will then reveal their intelligence and experience and suggest some better way to go. Voila!! They are starting to assume ownership.

After collecting some initial information, what next? Have them get together in a short meeting and cover the following items.

- What did they learn?
- If they had to do it over, what would they do differently?
- Did they pick up signs of resistance?
- What information and impressions did they convey to the employees?
- What guidelines do they have for future work tomorrow?

What is this? Gathering lessons learned as you go so that you can refine the application of the approach while it is in process. Gathering the lessons learned at the end is often too late. Any damage will have already been done and may not be undone.

ANALYZE INFORMATION ON ACTIVITIES

What information have you gathered? The general answer is that you have identified how the work is performed. Here are some specific items to organize.

- Identification of common transactions (the 20% of the types of work that cover over 50–60% of the volume of work).
- Steps in the transactions, who does them, what they do.
- Issues and problems at the level of steps.
- Impact of business rules and policies and how they are carried out.

How do you document this? There are two useful ways. Experience shows that it is valuable to do both. The first way is a simple table as shown in Figure 7.3. This explains the issues and comments for each step in the transaction. Why is this appealing? Because the first three columns are a summary of the current procedures and follow playscript—a technique that is 2500 years old—as old as the Greek plays.

Transaction: _____

Step	Who	What	Issues	Comments

Figure 7.3 Analysis Table for a Single Transaction

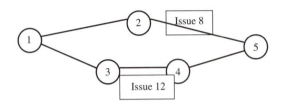

Figure 7.4 Flowchart Representation of the Transaction

Activity: _____

Other characteristics

Transaction	Issues			

Figure 7.5 Summary for a Group of Transactions

The second approach is to construct a simple information flowchart. An example is given in Figure 7.4. This is valuable to both the employees and the management because it graphically pinpoints where the issues are. In the example, there are two issues that impact this transaction and where the impact occurs is shown in the chart.

Can you do this for all transactions? Of course not. Impossible! You are only going to do for the common, non-exception work. That is more reasonable.

COLLECT FURTHER DATA

The data collection continues for various transactions or work. You can now aggregate this and get a summary table across multiple transactions. The format is shown in Figure 7.5. Note that there are blank columns. Here you can put some of the following:

- Volume of the work in this transaction
- Frequency of the transaction
- Error rates in the work
- Extent of automation of the work

Transactions

Issues				

Figure 7.6   Issues versus Transactions

Note that these are not going to be precise, but estimates gathered from the employees.

With this table you are now prepared to construct a new summary table as shown in Figure 7.6. Here the rows are the issues involved in the transactions. The columns are the transactions. The entry in the table is the impact of the specific issue on the individual transaction. You can also indicate the degree of impact. This table is useful in revealing the impact of an issue on multiple transactions. It begins to tell you which issues are most important.

What are some examples of issues in processes? Here is a partial list. You will build your own. However, you can use this as a checklist to start with.

- Existing business rules are getting in the way of the work
- There is a lack of consistency in how the step is performed
- There is often judgment required for specific steps
- The step is not necessary; the need has long since evaporated
- The current automation or system does not adequately support the step
- There is a high degree of errors made
- Excessive time is required to check the work

GAIN SUPPORT FOR CHANGE AND DISSATISFACTION WITH THE CURRENT SITUATION

All during the effort you are trying to make the employees aware of the problems. This is fine as a general statement, but how do you really do this without alienating the employees. Here are some guidelines.

- Point out that you are having a hard time understanding how to do the step.
- Ask why the step is being done in the way it is.
- Inquire if they don't feel frustrated because of the problem.

Don't label the problem as a problem at this point. It is too soon. It is just recognized and is hanging there. Now consider the impact of the problem before it is defined.

- What is the effect of the problem?
- If the problem was solved, what could they do?
- How would their working lives be made easier if the problem was solved?

Once you work through the impact of the problem, you can now encourage them to define and characterize the problem and its extent.

Go away and start to draw up the tables for specific transactions. Keep to the detailed level. Don't generalize. That will come later. Make the initial tables crude and even handwritten so that it is informal. If you throw down a professional table, they will most likely not accept it as their own. When you show it to them, point out some gaps or problems with the completeness. Incorporate their suggestions. You see—they are getting more involved and interested.

Then talk about how some of the issues seem to impact different transactions. They will likely agree. This leads to a discussion of overall impact and to the summary table. Again, reveal this table to them informally.

UNCOVER RESISTANCE TO CHANGE

As the teams are working on collection and analysis, they will interact with employees many times. Everyone should be sensitive to overt and covert signs of resistance. This will help later when you undertake implementation of the change. You may be able to identify individuals who, after all of the effort, still raise issues and problems with change. In addition, you can see how this resistance is manifested. This will indicate how resistance will likely occur later at the point or onset of change.

DEVELOP POSSIBLE APPROACHES FOR CHANGING ACTIVITIES

Now that you have raised the interest of the employees, you have to go farther. If you leave them here, they are just depressed because they see the problems and the substantial negative impacts.

You want the employees and strike force members to not only think of the changes, but also to embrace and to own them. But there is a problem. How do you do this? You need triggers to generate ideas for change. Here is a list that will be referred to in later chapters. It appears in Figure 7.7. We will call the resulting ideas for change as approaches for change.

Using this list you should be able to generate a number of alternatives. How do you document an alternative approach for change? Go back to the current work. Figure 7.8 is the table for the new transaction. The first three columns correspond to the step, who, and what—playscript again. The next column summarizes the differences between the step in the new approach of change and the current approach. Steps can be combined; new steps can be created.

- *Money.* If you could spend money to improve things, what would you do?
- *Control.* What if you change policies or business rules?
- *People.* What if you could add more people to do the work?
- *Time.* What if you had more time to do the work?
- *Procedures.* What if you could perform the work differently?
- *Automation.* What if you could automate more of the work?
- *Clerical and low level steps.* What if you could eliminate or simplify the clerical part of the work?
- *Departments.* What if you move part of the work from one department to another?
- *Customers or suppliers.* What if you could move some of the work out to customers or suppliers?
- *Management and supervision.* What if people were more empowered in doing the work?
- *Training and documentation.* What if the training and documentation were improved?

Figure 7.7   Potential Triggers to Think of Potential Changes

Transaction: _____

Trigger for change: _____

Step	Who	What	Difference	Benefits	Requirements

Figure 7.8   Table for a New Approach for a Transaction

The next two columns are very important. The first is the benefits that accrue if the change is carried out at the detailed step level. These can be benefits to any or all of the following:

- Individuals doing the work
- The department
- The organization
- Customers
- Suppliers
- Management

Now you have to consider what is required to take you from the current step to the future step. This is the last column. Requirements are defined in terms of changes to:

- Procedures
- Policies
- Facilities
- Automation and systems
- Management
- Business rules

An important fact here is that your requirements are on more solid ground because:

- The requirements are at the detailed step level.
- The requirements can be more easily understood and justified.
- The requirements are the difference between the current and potential new approach.

So you have the following lesson learned.

> *Requirements based on knowing where you are and where you are going are more valuable and valid than those that only stem from knowing the current situation.*

EVALUATE AND COMPARE THE POSSIBLE APPROACHES

The next step is to roll this information up to cover multiple transactions. Similar to Figure 7.5 you can construct the table in Figure 7.9. This summarizes the issues, differences, benefits, and requirements for multiple transactions based on a single trigger for change.

You are also in a position to develop additional analysis tables. The first applies to issues and appears in Figure 7.10. Here the rows are the issues and the columns are the possible approaches. The entry is the extent to which an issue is handled or addressed by the approach.

There is still more analysis that you can perform. In previous chapters you identified the objectives and strategy for change. You also analyzed the vision, mission, business objectives, and business issues. You can generate the

Trigger for change: _____

Transaction	Issues	Differences	Benefits	Requirements

Figure 7.9   Summary Table for Approaches Based on a Specific Trigger

Alternative approaches

Issues				

Figure 7.10   The Impact of Alternative Approaches on the Issues

following tables:

- *Change objectives versus approaches.* The support of a change objective by a specific approach.
- *Elements of the vision versus possible approaches.* The degree to which the approach supports the vision.
- *Elements of the mission versus possible approaches.* The extent to which an approach sustains a mission element.
- *Business objectives versus possible approaches.* The degree to which the approach carries out the business objective.
- *Business issues versus possible approaches.* The extent to which an approach takes care of a specific business issue for a group of transactions.

What do these all add up to? They show the comparative alignment of the approaches to the business and to change management. As a result of doing this work, you may begin to combine approaches to develop new ones. Notice that these are still referred to as approaches, not solutions. Solutions will be developed in the next chapter based upon the work here.

Keep in mind that this is an iterative process that must involve members of both the change team and strike forces. Selected employees who are interested in change can also be involved.

USE THE SCORE CARD FOR ACTIVITY DATA COLLECTION AND ANALYSIS

Figure 7.11 gives the elements of a score card for the data collection and analysis. These are self-explanatory. They pertain to the change team, strike forces, employees, and management. Almost universally, they are subjective. As with the other score cards, you should develop this in a collaborative manner involving team members. In fact, you should apply the score card multiple times during the work to assess how you are doing. Don't wait until the end.

MARKET THE ANALYSIS

Marketing to management begins long before the work is complete. You want to establish informal communications with managers who are supportive of change. This will validate their support and even increase it. When you approach a manager, go with these items.

- Status of the work
- Example of some of the analysis for a specific detailed transactions
- Observations on the attitude of employees and extent of their support for the change effort
- Examples of specific issues in the work
- Examples or anecdotes of specific work that highlights some of the issues

Element of score card	Score	Comment
Extent of political awareness of strike forces		
Extent of political awareness of change team		
Degree to which employees acknowledge problems in the current work		
Extent of participation of employees in the work		
Degree to which employees were involved in suggesting change		
Volume and extent of communications with management		
Extent of resistance to change uncovered		
Improvement of the strike forces over the course of the work		
Detection of resistance to change		
Scheduled versus actual time to do this work		
Extent of management and supervisory interference in the work		

Figure 7.11   Score Card for Data Collection on Activities

You risk getting them excited—so aroused that they want to make changes right away. Indicate that these findings are still preliminary.

As the work progresses, you can start showing some samples of the tables. This will prepare them for the format and content of the complete tables later.

When you have the tables and approaches ready, you should present the results top-down. That is, you begin with the summary tables for the current transactions and for the better approaches. Then drill down to a sample transaction. This will support and validate the general analysis. Indicate which approaches did not pan out. This will show them the completeness and thoroughness of the work.

EXAMPLES

ROCKWOOD COUNTY

The data collection was very instructive in that pockets of resistance were identified. These consisted largely of newer employees who were following the lead of the king and queen bees.

As you recall from Chapter 1, Rockwood had much infighting and problems between departments. The way this was addressed was to get people who were doing the work in several departments to analyze and discuss specific transactions. At that low level of detail there were fewer political factors. Politics did surface when the transactions were aggregated. However, by then there was grassroots support for change and for addressing some of the problems in the work so that the politics were mitigated somewhat. The politics still exists today, but they were put aside here.

LEGEND MANUFACTURING

Due to past problems and attempts at change, employees were very reluctant to participate in the work. The people at the bottom who did and do the work were the least affected by the past effort. Thus, an effort was made from the beginning to involve them.

The tables proved very useful to management because it validated and supported their faith in the collaborative approach. The tables also provided additional ideas for improvements in procedures in terms of lessons learned in how better to do the work. These resulted in some of the early Quick Hits.

POTENTIAL ISSUES AND RISKS

- You have to continually monitor what the strike forces are doing. There is sometimes a tendency to collect more information and detail. You will have to rein in this desire from the beginning. Otherwise, the schedule gets out of hand.
- Strike force or change team members give out false or misleading information. This is most often not by intent. They are trying to calm people down, but go overboard. That is why you need two people working in the same area so that this problem can be detected before it becomes a "cause celebre." You want to step in and correct wrong impressions before they spread.
- False information and impressions typically abound during the initial data collection. This can often be traced to king or queen bees. It is best dealt with proactively by indicating that some people (unspecified, of course) may oppose change, the real facts are...

LESSONS LEARNED

- Try to have two people of the opposite sex collect data in a department. There are several reasons for this. First, some employees may feel more comfortable talking to a woman (or man). Second, it gives you a second set of eyes.

- In collecting information have the strike force members work alone. If they work together, the employees may feel that they are being outnumbered and may "clam up."
- Do not ignore collecting data in restrooms. Here is a technique that works. Go into the bathroom and sit in a staff toilet. Listen to what people talk about as they come and go. This sounds gross, but it will uncover some gems of information.
- Go out where people smoke. People who smoke tend to talk more. They are relaxing and unwinding.
- Go to where people take their lunch or other breaks. Sit at a nearby table with a magazine or newspaper and pretend to read it. Listen to what the employees are talking about. A rule of thumb is that if they don't discuss their work at all, it must be pretty bad. Normally, employees will compare notes and share complaints—very useful to you.
- When team members are doing some work in the department, suggest that they make some simple mistakes. This has several benefits. First, it shows to the employees their value. Second, it reveals that the team members are human. Third, it provides a wider basis of conversation through common experiences.
- The strike force and change team members should not take notes in front of the employees. This makes people in general nervous. Do it right after the experience while it is fresh—away from them.
- When you begin to make management presentations, it is critical to involve employees in strike force in the presentations. They know the work first hand and so have infinite credibility compared to you and the rest of the change team who are seen to have a vested interest in change.

SUMMARY

A step-by-step approach has been laid out for you to collect and analyze information to not only understand the current work, but also to define potential individual changes. You have not analyzed these to select what should be done when. This is enough to do. Remember that you have three dominant political objectives in this data collection. The first is to get the employees to acknowledge the need for change and to embrace it. Second, you and the teams have identified potential resistance to actual change along with characteristics of the resistance. The third is to start testing management resolve to support specific changes.

Chapter 8

Define Your Long-Term Solution and Quick Hits

INTRODUCTION

Each time you start a new activity in change management, you should first review where you are. The business has been reviewed. The goals and strategy of change management have been defined. Processes have been selected for potential change. Information has been collected and analyzed for these activities. All of this has been undertaken in a collaborative way. So you have many opportunities for change along with specific alternatives or scenarios for change (future process). From the analysis of the preceding chapter you also have some idea of benefits and requirements at the detailed level.

With all of this completed, there is a tendency to want to go into some department and make changes. However, there are many risks that are present.

- Short-term changes that look good now may turn sour and be thrown out later. This jeopardizes the change effort and confuses the employees.
- Disorganized change takes more time and effort than following a strategy.
- Fragmented change tends to result in few major benefits.

If you were to start implementing, you would be close to following the Total Quality Management (TQM) approach of continuous change. Overall, it pays to carry out a few more steps. In this chapter you will organize potential changes into Quick Hits and longer-term change. Having completed this, your change implementation strategy will be created in Chapter 9 to be followed by project planning and implementation.

PERFORM IN-DEPTH ANALYSIS OF THE APPROACHES FOR CHANGE

Now recall from Chapter 7 that you have some good opportunities or scenarios for change that individually have benefits and can be implemented. This is the starting point for doing in-depth analysis. There are several key tasks to perform.

- Go through the results and see if some can be combined.
- Relate improvements in terms of sequencing.
- Determine requirements for implementation of the improvements.
- Decide on whether an improvement is a quick hit or is longer term.

SORT OUT QUICK HITS AND LONG-TERM CHANGES

What is the difference? Obviously, a key is the extent of preparation and effort required to implement the opportunity. Another parameter that is often over-looked, is the extent of management involvement and approval. If the change is substantial, then there will be more time required. Some characteristics to use in sorting the opportunities are given in Figure 8.1. Note that there are performance measures here such as time, cost, and risk as well as parameters that indicate the scope of the opportunity.

Characteristic	Quick Hits	Longer-term change
Time to implement	A month or less	Longer
Interdependency with other opportunities	Not critical	Multiple, complex dependencies
Policies	Minor policy changes in terms of parameters	Major policy shifts
Systems	Little or no work on systems	Potential major work
IT infrastructure	Little or nothing	Minor to major
Customer impact	Little or nothing	May be significant
Supplier impact	Little or nothing	May be significant
Procedures	Significant changes	Changes supportive of other changes
Concern about resistance to change	Low	Moderate to high
Cost of change	Low or nothing	Significant
Risk to process	Low, can be changed	Moderate to high

Figure 8.1   Characteristics of Quick Hits versus Longer-Term Change

IDENTIFY OPPORTUNITY DEPENDENCIES

After you have sorted out the opportunities in terms of Quick Hits and longer-term change, you seek to determine which opportunities are interrelated or interdependent. Let's first consider how two potential changes can be linked.

- *Time sequenced.* Opportunity B depends upon opportunity A being completed. An example might be that the new department (B) cannot be established until the facilities are ready (A).
- *Resource shared for implementation.* The opportunities could require the same people for implementation. This may create an excessive burden for these people so that the changes would have to be staggered.
- *Resource shared for operation.* The changes will affect the same group of employees. Here the question is always whether it is better to carry out several changes at the same time or to stage these over time.
- *Technology dependence.* The two opportunities depend on the same software changes or the same technology so that it is logical that the changes might be done together.
- *Facilities sharing.* If one change involved a facility change, that would probably impact other changes.
- *Same customer or supplier focus.* Both opportunities, if implemented, will impact the same group of customers or suppliers.
- *Same manager or management.* This will make life easier since you have the same people to work with for both opportunities. The two opportunities can be in different business departments, but under the same management.

If processes and people were independent, then there might be fewer combinations of dependencies possible. However, since they are dependent most of the time, you are likely to face a combination of dependencies that have to be sorted out. This is a useful exercise since it helps you set priorities. More importantly, it gets people to widen their thinking as to what is possible in terms of grouping.

There are some dangers here of which you should be aware. First, people tend to think that opportunities are more interdependent than they really are. This is often due to traditional thinking that favors sequential relationships that people accepted as true in the past. Some signs of this are: people want to include all opportunities that fall in one department or one location; all opportunities dependent upon the same technology.

From these comments it is best to construct a table in which the opportunities appear as both rows and columns (see Figure 8.2). The table entries are the types of dependencies between the specific opportunities. Otherwise, the table entry is blank. Use this table to initiate a discussion of how important dependencies are. The table is triangular in that only the upper right or lower left half of the table is completed.

Opportunity

Opportunity			

Figure 8.2   Dependencies between Opportunities. (Here the table entry is the nature of the dependency between one opportunity and another.)

DISCUSS DIFFERENT WAYS TO IMPLEMENT AN OPPORTUNITY

In discussing the relationship among opportunities, you are naturally bound to consider how the opportunities will be implemented. Now this was considered in previous chapters, but it is not final. Over the elapsed time people think more about the potential changes and may come up with new ideas. Allow people to be creative. Be flexible and don't become locked into some specific implementation approach. Here are some examples in the form of different dimensions.

- *Procedures and policies.* These are simplest to implement.
- *Technology and systems.* There are several things to consider here. They range from simple software changes to implementing new technology.
- *Range of the organization impacted.* This can range from one small group to an entire business unit.
- *Organization structure.* This is the most complex and we have stressed that this come after the change. However, there may be minor changes that can make implementing an opportunity easy. Changes in the roles of specific individuals are examples.

In discussing relationships and in grouping which is considered next, you should use the above list as a starting point and guideline in thinking about the opportunities. It will also help you achieve consensus in how people consider changes.

GROUP THE OPPORTUNITIES

The first part of grouping occurred above in the analysis of dependencies. Now you have to decide which opportunities will go in the first wave of change, the second, and so on. Usually, the last wave of change is the major process change in terms of changed organization and systems. Changing the organization should come later to avoid disruption. Also, you will have more information on the effects of the detailed changes in the work.

There are several methods for grouping. You should try all of these to generate different groupings.

- *The first round of Quick Hits.* What can you implement quickly without major preparation and prior opportunities? Here you can create a list of first round potential Quick Hits. Then you can work your way into the future in terms of time. You can next identify what can be done assuming that the first round of change was successful. This approach gives you short-term gains, but could delay longer-term change.
- *The long-term end changes and results.* This is the opposite of the previous method. Here you begin at the end in terms of longer-term change. Then you proceed backward in time to see what is necessary to precede the longer-term changes. The long-term change approach may not yield the best short-term gains.
- *Vision and mission.* Here you start with the end results in terms of benefits and how activities would function. You would then start backward to the long-term changes and proceed as in the previous method. This approach yields a much longer-term view of change.
- *Specific departments.* You would consider all of the opportunities for a specific department and sequence these. Then you would consider successive departments. The problem with this approach is that cross department opportunities are considered later in the work.
- *Systems and technology.* In this approach you would examine specific systems and technology and then project change. Then you would expand to other technology areas. The limitation with this approach is that non-information technology (IT), manual changes are given lower priority or are just included in IT-related changes.
- *Location.* You start with one location of the organization and identify and work through the changes to be made for that location. Then you consider the next location. The problem here is that this implicitly assumes that the sites are independent, which is often not the case.

Note that each of these alternatives has specific limitations. Why should you generate all of these alternatives? Because of the need to generate alternatives for trade-offs. You should end up with some identical groupings arrived at different ways. Here are some other benefits. Overall, part of your goal is not to achieve change, but lasting change. Lasting change only comes about if people understand and participate in the analysis and planning for selecting and sequencing the things to be changed.

- By looking at different forms of groupings, you can involve employees and managers in a more organized manner than casual discussion.
- People can start to understand the differences in sequencing.
- By discussing the relationships between opportunities, individuals tend to think of simpler and easier ways to implement changes. Otherwise, they will often stick with the first method of implementing the change.

Now that you have different groupings, you can start on evaluation of the groupings. Here is a list of criteria.

- Benefits and delivery of short-term results.
- Long-term benefits and attainment of long-term objectives.
- Risk to the business with the particular grouping. This includes business and technical risk.
- Number of departments involved in implementation. The fewer the departments, the easier the change. However, benefits might be smaller. The more departments the more involved the change.
- Elapsed time to implement the group.
- Importance of the processes or activities impacted to the business.
- Cost of implementation.
- Importance of processes not affected by the changes. This indicates the downside of not implementing change in other areas.

Obviously, some of these factors are subjective. How do you compare these? One approach is to use a spider or radar chart. An example is given in Figure 8.3. Each of the items in the above list is a dimension on the chart. You can take a group and, with managers or employees, start rating the group on the basis of these factors. Note that many of these are subjective. What are the benefits of doing this? First, you build consensus for groupings. Second, people are able to compare several groups on the basis of multiple criteria.

Now let's consider the examples in Figure 8.3. The solid line group has some attractive features. There are good, short-term Quick Hits. In addition, there is low risk and only a few departments are involved. Costs are lower and the elapsed time is shorter. However, this grouping does not address key processes. Yes, you get

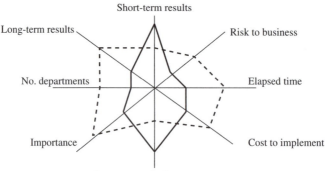

Figure 8.3   Example of Spider or Radar Chart for Evaluation of Groupings

benefits, but you divert resources and time to less important targets or processes. In the ideal world you would pick the dashed alternative group since it has more long-lasting benefits. However, if this is your first effort at affecting change, then it might be wise politically to go with the group in the solid line. Politically, it is very useful to walk through this type of chart with managers. There are a number of benefits. First, they become more involved in the selection of what is to be done—the scope and purpose. Second, you can determine the degree of risk and extent of time and money they are willing to invest in carrying out change.

DOCUMENT AND VOTE ON WHAT TO DO

In general there is a tendency to over document what is going on. One reason for this is political cover. People want to protect themselves from potential blame and criticism. Another reason is that benefits, risks, costs, and other factors have to be explained to people. However, many times the documentation fails. One reason is that the audience is management. The real audience consists of the employees doing the work. They have to support, implement, and sustain the change. Another reason is that people develop overly complex documents and diagrams. A number of Six Sigma and reengineering efforts have failed because of this.

Let's now turn to the document. Your audience is the employees doing the work. The purpose of the document is that they will understand and support the change. The scope of the document consists of the grouping of opportunities and activities. Another purpose is that you want to use this document later and update it to save yourself work later. We are not lazy, but if you can reuse documentation, you want to. It makes things easier to understand and accept since people have seen parts of it before.

The outline of the document consists of the following:

- Definition of the grouping of opportunities
- Why this grouping makes sense; reason or trigger factor for the grouping
- How the opportunities relate to each other in the group
- How the opportunities would be sequenced for change
- Overall cost estimate and schedule
- Elements of risk in change—technical, business, cultural, political
- For each opportunity you explain:
  - Importance of the activity
  - Impact if there is no change
  - Benefits of the change
  - How the change would be measured
  - Brief description of the change
  - Elapsed time estimate of change
  - Estimated cost and effort for the change

How should you develop this document? If you assign people to write this and they have never done it before, you will likely fail or run into too much elapsed time delaying the effort. If you have someone outside the work do the documentation, the employees will probably not buy into or support the change. Neither extreme is acceptable. So you have to find middle ground.

One proven method is to develop a list of bullet points under the above outline and then show this to the employees to get their comments. You would then incorporate their comments into a more detailed bulleted outline. They would then review it.

In traditional systems analysis this would be the end of it. But here you are dealing with politics and change management. So you want to ensure that you have the support of the teams. There is another step-voting. Employees on the teams vote on the groups and opportunities. The political purpose of voting is to ensure and establish consensus and common understanding.

There are several questions that have to be addressed here.

- What criteria should be employed for the voting?
- What is the scoring for the voting?
- How should the voting be conducted?
- How do you analyze the voting?

Let's examine each of these. For the criteria there are a number of alternatives.

- Use the list that appeared as dimensions for the spider chart above. This is immediate and has direct relevance.
- Use a list gathered from the mission, vision, and objectives statements of the organization. This has the benefit of indicating the degree of alignment of the grouping and opportunities to the firm's goals.
- Use a combined approach.

Figure 8.4 gives an example. In each column each person's votes would be listed. Here we have used the goals for Rockwood County along with the criteria above.

The next question is related to how scoring should be done. Here are two approaches that we have used. One is High, Medium, and Low. Another is a scale of 1–5. The first one is easier to do. The second requires more explanation since you have to indicate how "very high" differs from "high," etc.

The voting can be conducted in two stages. You first hold a short meeting of the team to explain the factors and answer questions. The employees are then given time to develop their opinions. Then there is a second meeting where each person explains his/her vote row by row. This approach supports your goal of ensuring widespread consensus and agreement.

In analyzing the voting you can average the scores across each row. You are looking for variance in scores. Hopefully, the variance is low since the meetings should have led to consensus. It is very important to ask individuals why they assigned a specific score to an item. That will surface potential unseen problems.

Criteria	Person A	Person F	Average
Cost	2	3	2.5
Risk	3	4	3.5
Elapsed time	3	4	3.5
Short-term benefits	5	3	4
Long-term benefits	2	4	3
No. of departments	3	3	3
Importance of group	4	4	4
Importance of other groups	2	2	2
Customer service	4	5	4.5
Quality of work	2	1	1.5
Productivity	3	3	3
Organization effectiveness	4	3	3.5
Overall	3.4	3.6	3.5

Figure 8.4   Example of Voting of a Group for Rockwood County

Note: In this example that the two people differ on the benefits (short or long term) the most. This would trigger a discussion to get at what is behind their views. In a real case you would have more columns. Comments would be added as bullets at the bottom of the table for presentation purposes. The average at the bottom is useful in that it helps to reveal people's individual attitudes toward the group.

It will also show areas where there are misunderstandings or disagreements. The tables can become part of a presentation to the steering committees.

HANDLE GOOD, BUT LOSING OPPORTUNITIES FOR CHANGE

As with many things there are winners and losers. In change management we are often concerned with opportunities that provide good, short-term results, but were not selected due to lack of alignment with overall goals, lower ranking of benefits, etc. What do you do with these? Do not ignore them. People who participated in the process and contributed are likely to be disheartened or resentful if their efforts come to nothing. So what do you do?

If the opportunities can be carried out as Quick Hits, then they can be considered separately and individually. Perhaps, they can be implemented right away after steering committee review. However, some may require more analysis or resources such as IT or systems work. Then they would have to wait for a later phase in the overall change effort.

How do you prevent the people who participated from losing faith and being "put out of the loop?" The answer is to involve them in implementation and measurement of the Quick Hits. There is, after all, a need to have people independently measure the results of the Quick Hits. The people who implement the Quick Hits are not exactly unbiased. Moreover, they are involved in the daily work of change. Monitors and observers can provide a more balanced and unbiased view.

In the role of the monitor an employee can be asked to look for answers to some of the following questions.

- What was done right?
- What could have been done better?
- What additional things or alternatives could have been taken to speed up the implementation of change?
- What were the results of the changes?
- What results were unforeseen?

These are just examples. You will want the employees to create their own list of questions so that they become more involved.

INVOLVE THE CHANGE STEERING COMMITTEES

As you recall, there are two steering committees. The lower level one, the operational steering committee, is composed of middle level managers and some employees from the teams. This committee is of critical importance because it is here that you gain validation and detailed support for the changes and voting.

What does the operational steering committee do? They first hear a presentation by the team members of the voting and results. This presentation should contain the following elements:

- A summary of the process of what was done; this shows that they understand and support the process.
- A summary of the major alternative groups and the voting results.
- Additional comments and examples that bring the change to life and convey a sense of enthusiasm for change.

The committee can then see the support for change. Some committee members were on teams and can add further support. This helps to convince upper and middle level managers on the steering committee that people are serious and that the change has been thought through.

The losing, but good, opportunities can be summarized as well along with recommended actions. This can show that all bases have been covered.

A summary of the presentation is then given to the executive change steering committee. This is mainly for information as business cases have not been prepared with more detailed analysis. Nor have Quick Hits been grouped. So the presentation is in the form of an update and status. The political goal is to show upper management that there is grassroots support for change and that there are likely to be significant benefits.

DEFINE MINI-BUSINESS CASES FOR QUICK HITS

Now with approval there is more work to be done. The group of activities and opportunities have been identified, voted upon, and presented. There are several steps that must be accomplished before seeking final approval for the changes.

* Prepare mini-business cases for change Quick Hits. The mini-business case goes into implementation, cost, schedule, resistance, and risk in more detail. It is called a mini-business case because there is no time or need to develop massive documents. The mini-business case will serve as the basis for implementation.
* Long-term change and Quick Hits have to be grouped and generally sequenced. Here order must be imposed since there are limited resources and the business operations of departments cannot be excessively disrupted.
* An implementation timeline is created wherein all of the changes are mapped into phases. Note that this is also general since more detailed analysis has to be done to get a detailed phasing. This will come in the next chapter when a change implementation strategy is defined and laid out.

What is the goal of the mini-business case? First, the work provides the basis for approval of specific opportunities. After this sequencing and implementation occur. But there is no more analysis. Second, this is another opportunity to get widespread grassroots for change among employees and middle level managers. This is a chance to overcome resistance. Didn't you handle resistance already? Ah, yes. However, resistance may not totally disappear. It can just go underground. So you want to use this work as an opportunity to ferret out pockets of resistance.

What are the ingredients of the mini-business case? Here is a list of elements.

* Opportunity title.
* Business process and transactions of work affected by the opportunity.
* Departments involved and affected by the opportunity.
* People involved in creating the mini-business case.
* Description of the current situation.
* Impact if the opportunity is not addressed. This points out the impact of both the current situation and deterioration if there is no action.
* How the change would be carried out.
* Who would be involved in the change effort.
* What would be the results of the change. This can be a side-by-side comparison with the current situation.
* Benefits of carrying out the change.
* How the benefit would be measured.
* The risks involved in the change and how these will be minimized.

- The schedule for carrying out the change.
- The resources and costs required for the change.

As you can see, some of this can be reused from the initial opportunity writeup. Other parts are new. You can have the teams create bullets under each item.

How do you go about building a mini-business case? In developing the mini-business case it is good to have the change management team work with the strike force members to develop the first mini-business case. Then people can work in pairs on developing the other cases using the first one as a model. This provides more parallel effort and reduces the overall elapsed time. It also provides for more widespread participation.

When developing the business case, it is most important that the strike force lay out a step-by-step approach for implementation. After all, this will be a roadmap for the implementation team. You don't want to encounter the situation where the implementation is left in the dark and then has to be implemented from scratch. This would entail too much risk in that the wrong changes might be implemented. Moreover, it would consume too much time.

After developing the mini-business cases, the strike force members can review their voting earlier to see if there are any significant issues or problems that have surfaced. Another important review is that of either finance or audit in reviewing the analysis of costs and benefits. You really do need to have independent validation. Without this you run the risk of repeating what happens in many IT projects. Benefits are not validated and so are not credible so that there is questioning of the entire effort.

GROUP QUICK HITS AND LONG-TERM CHANGES

Now you have a stack of mini-business cases for Quick Hits along with the long-term changes defined. These now need to be grouped in terms of which precede each other. Relationships and groupings can be on the basis of the following:

- Organizations involved
- Policies involved
- Systems changes needed
- IT infrastructure required
- Facilities changes needed
- Individuals involved in change
- Customers affected
- Suppliers impacted

This analysis helps you to understand what is possible to be implemented at the same time with the available resources and priorities. There is also a political reason for doing this. That is, to gain more support for change and to show

Area of change	Stages of change			

Figure 8.5 General Implementation Timeline for Quick Hits

employees that change is getting closer. You will find that additional resource issues will surface here. As implementation draws closer, there will be problems involving resource allocation of employee time between implementing change and performing their normal work. This is to be expected here since the realization that change is near is growing.

CREATE AN IMPLEMENTATION TIMELINE FOR QUICK HITS

With that analysis, there is one more step. That is to develop an initial timeline of changes. You can do this by creating a table such as that in Figure 8.5. In this table, the first column contains the areas of change. This can be either by department or by process. The other columns are phases of change for each row. However, at this point there is NO association of elements between the rows. At this time there is no relationship between the rows. That will come in the next chapter.

Here you are laying out each change area. Note that one opportunity may require changes in several areas. So, changes for specific opportunities may have entries in the same rows. That is why additional analysis is needed to determine what is a feasible implementation strategy. After all, you do not want to undertake so many changes in one area that standard work is excessively disrupted.

GAIN MANAGEMENT APPROVAL OF THE CHANGES

Now with this work you can return to the change steering committees. You first show the overall implementation timeline to the operational change committee. This shows that there is an understanding of what the overall changes add up to. Next, the detailed mini-business cases are summarized. What you want to achieve with the operational change steering committee is to get agreement with the results.

When you move up to the executive level change steering committee, you are not only providing status, but you are getting approval for the opportunities and that actions will be taken. This is, in a way, the last chance to question the changes and results of the analysis. However, since you had prepared both committees with the voting and earlier analysis of the grouping of opportunities, there should not be resistance. Questions will likely be raised about implementation. Congratulations, you have now reached a significant milestone in communications. You have turned the corner from "What will we do?" to "How will we do it?"

USE THE SCORE CARD FOR THE QUICK HITS AND LONG-TERM CHANGES

It is time to evaluate how you are doing. The score card for this chapter is given in Figure 8.6. Let's comment on each of these factors.

- Number of employees involved. This serves to illustrate the extent of participation.
- Elapsed time to do the analysis.
- Issues that arose that were unplanned in the development of the mini-business cases. This indicates how good and complete the earlier analysis was.

Factor	Score	Comment
Number of employees involved		
Elapsed time to do the analysis		
Issues that arose that were unplanned in the development of the mini-business cases		
Quality of the mini-business cases in terms of detail, etc.		
Acceptance and participation of the operational change steering committee		
Acceptance and participation of the executive change steering committee		
Extent of work performed by strike force members on their own		
Degree of consensus reached among strike force members		
Extent of resistance before and after the work		

Figure 8.6   Score Card for Quick Hits and Long-Term Change

- Quality of the mini-business cases in terms of detail, etc. This goes to the general quality of work.
- Acceptance and participation of the operational change steering committee. This will indicate the degree of support of the change effort.
- Acceptance and participation of the executive change steering committee. Same as above.
- Extent of work performed by strike force members on their own. This is another indicator of participation and commitment to change.
- Degree of consensus reached among strike force members. This serves to show how the team members work together and is an omen for implementation.
- Extent of resistance encountered before and after the work. This reveals how much additional resistance was uncovered and shows how it was addressed.

MARKET THE QUICK HITS AND LONG-TERM CHANGES

You would think at first that there is no marketing required. Not true. You have to market to employees to show that you are serious and that their thoughts and ideas are taken into account. Through their participation in the analysis, discussions, and voting, you gain support. The process is helping you do the marketing.

By having multiple reviews with the operational change steering committee you are getting their support. In addition to the formal presentations you want to have strike force team members make informal presentations to some of the steering committee members. This gives more detail and fleshes out what has to be general in the formal presentations. Moreover, it shows the dedication and commitment of the strike force members to change. It will also likely open the eyes of managers to the problems that exist in the work today—very valuable to get change.

The same comments generally apply to the executive level change steering committee. You are going to use the managers on the operational committee to help market to the executive level committee. You can also use the enthusiasm of the strike force members to your political advantage. You can indicate that if the changes are not approved or if management hesitates, then there will be many problems in morale and credibility. This helps to get any reluctant managers on your side.

EXAMPLES

ROCKWOOD COUNTY

As was indicated at the outset, Rockwood has deep political divisions and issues. We definitely cannot overcome these directly. Yet, if they are left isolated or ignored, then there will be more problems and the implementation may not be supported at all. What do you do? Well, in this case, you first realize that where the work is done and transactions are undertaken, there is less politics. People have to get work done and there is less time to be political. This factor was used in the work at Rockwood. The strike force members were involved in the work. Some were political, but they could address political issues more openly with the help of the coordination from the change management team. Eventually, political factors were even addressed openly at the operational change steering committee. It was agreed that political factors were important, but that they had to be put aside to get the work done.

LEGEND MANUFACTURING

With the experience of past failures, there was a general desire on the part of both employees and middle level managers to succeed. This resulted in an excessive number of opportunities—a number of which were marginal. They would have been suitable for Total Quality Management (TQM), but were just not sufficiently significant to warrant or justify action. To avoid morale problems, the people who proposed these changes were brought into the implementation and the development of the change implementation strategy as well as the measurement of the change effects.

POTENTIAL ISSUES AND RISKS

- There may surface substantial resistance to change. People on the strike forces may not want to participate. Here you can have one strike force serve as an example and lead the way. This can "shame" the other teams into participating more actively in the work.
- People on the strike forces do not have the time to participate in the work due to their regular commitments. What do you do? Do you replace them? No. This shows that you are giving in and that the change effort is not that important. Instead, you should work with them to help them do the work in less time. Part of this may be reluctance because they may think that they could fail. There is no failure here if people do the best they can.
- Steering committee members may want to slow down the change effort. Middle managers may resist change. Do not accept this. Anticipate that it will happen. Indicate to the committees that inaction can lower morale and torpedo the entire change effort.

LESSONS LEARNED

- It is important to have one strike force do initial work that can serve as an example to others. This also shows that the work level is reasonable. Do the same for each strike force with their first writeup and first mini-business case.
- Focus on informal communications with the managers on the steering committees. Here the change management team can act as a bridge between the strike forces and the managers. If you get them communicating, you will get more support.
- The change management team should provide coordination but should not do the work. There is often a tendency for the core team members to step in and do the work so that the overall schedule does not suffer. This must be avoided since you must have widespread participation.

SUMMARY

In this chapter, you saw the important analysis steps that must be undertaken. It is also here that you gather more widespread and deeper support for change. This chapter is also important because it is here that change management turns from what to do to how to do the change.

Chapter 9

Develop Your Change
Implementation Strategy

INTRODUCTION

Let's review where you are now. You took steps to understand the current business situation. You then defined your change management objectives. Then strike forces defined, documented, and voted upon opportunities for change and work improvement. After review by the change steering committees, mini-business cases were prepared, the opportunities organized and sequenced, and a table prepared that consisted of an implementation timeline. Up until the middle of the last chapter, focus was on analysis. Now it is on implementation. There is a fundamental lesson learned.

When attention moves from analysis of what to do to issues on how
to carry out change, you are on the road to success.

Now that you have a table of what to implement, can't you just go ahead and implement. It would be nice to think that, but in real life things are not that simple. You have to determine the sequencing and organization of the Quick Hits and long-term change. This is the subject of the change implementation strategy. With this in hand, you can develop a detailed project plan for change (Chapter 10). Then you can implement.

What happens if you rush into implementation?

- You encounter unanticipated problems. The solution of these diverts you from the change and slows down the change effort.
- You fail to overcome pockets of resistance. Queen and king bees may yet rise up to resist change.

- Management expectations are now raised to such a high level that it is impossible to satisfy them. Thus, management is let down and may not support the change effort to the extent necessary.

What is a change implementation strategy? The strategy is a roadmap for how change will be undertaken in stages. Some of the activities are preparation for the long-term change. As such, they have costs but no benefits. Other changes are procedural or policy related and so have benefits. You want to add up the benefits, costs, and risks of all of the activities in each phase of change. But there is more than one way to carry out the change sequencing based upon politics, technology, organization, and processes. That is why the change implementation strategy is so important.

The change implementation strategy forces people to think about how multiple changes in different areas will be undertaken and successfully carried out.

A major benefit of the change implementation strategy is that with success people gain confidence about the change. They feel that, indeed, more major changes are possible.

There is another basic point to keep in mind.

You can come up with wonderful ideas for change, but if you fail to determine how best to organize their implementation, you are very likely to fail.

Or, put another way,

Talk and analysis are cheap. The rubber meets the road when you reach the change implementation strategy.

WHAT ARE INGREDIENTS OF THE CHANGE IMPLEMENTATION STRATEGY?

Think of the change implementation strategy as a large table. The first column of the table consists of two groups of rows. The first group of rows consists of areas of change. The second group of rows focuses on performance measures. The second, third, and other columns refer to changes by phase. However, these are not just preparation phases as in information technology (IT) projects. These are substantial changes that lead to long-term change. The final column indicates the last stage of change. Figure 9.1 gives an overall schematic of the change implementation strategy or roadmap.

How do you complete the table to generate a potential change implementation strategy? Here are the first two steps that are shown in Figure 9.2.

Areas of change	Current	Phase 1		Phase N	Long-term change
Performance measures					

Figure 9.1   General Structure of the Change Implementation Strategy

Areas of change	Current	Phase 1		Phase N	Long-term change
1	2	3		4	
Performance measures					

Figure 9.2   Seqeuencing of the General Structure of the Change Implementation Strategy

- Identify the factors that will change (labeled 1 in the diagram). These can be processes, departments, policies, systems, IT infrastructure, customers, or suppliers. You want to be complete in terms of identifying what will change. Below the dark line you will need to list performance measures such as cost, schedule, risk, and benefits. You can also include perspectives. That is, what will employees, managers, customers, or suppliers get from the changes in the entries above the line.
- The columns are the row headings, the current situation, phases or waves of Quick Hits and the long-term solution or process.
- In the second column you have the current state or situation (labeled 2 in the diagram). Here you would indicate with some comments the issues that have surfaced in each area of change. Then below the line you indicate the overall impact of the current situation.

It is appropriate to make some observations now. First, you want to be complete in the row headings. Note that unlike IT projects or other work, change management has potentially a much broader scope. So it is difficult for people to understand the changes that will be taking place and their ramifications.

Second, you want to ensure that managers and employees are "on the same page" in that they have a common perspective of the current situation. That is the purpose of the second column. It shows the issues above the line and the impacts below the line.

Now let's move to the other steps.

- For each area of change (each row above the line) enter the changes in the appropriate columns (labeled 3 in the diagram). This is now an alternative change implementation strategy.
- But what does it mean? Now you must "add up" all of the changes in each column and determine the impacts below the line (labeled 4 in the diagram). This helps you to see the effects of the change. It will assist you in evaluating alternative change implementation strategies.

Figure 9.3 gives an example of a change implementation strategy for Rockwood County. This is for modifying the timekeeping process for county employees. In the current situation employees have to manually complete time-keeping sheets each day and then submit these for review. Payroll then reviews these and enters information into the payroll system. Thus, the situation is manual except for the last step. For simplicity we have only included one round of Quick Hits. In real life there would several phases of Quick Hits.

In the example, the categories of change are: county employees, payroll, and IT. The performance measures and perspectives are: cost, risk, benefits, schedule, and employee. In the current situation (column 2), all employees must complete a form every day. This is very labor intensive and subject to error and missing

Factor	Current situation	Quick Hits	Long-term change
Employees	Fill out forms manually	Move to exception forms	Complete forms on-line
Payroll	Manual review and audit	Only check exceptions	Review only rejected transactions
IT	Payroll system	New network infrastructure; modify payroll system	Intranet application
Management	Many problems and manual intervention	Concentration on exceptions	Review only rejected transactions
Cost	Labor to complete	IT cost; training	IT cost; training
Benefits	Habit	Reduced labor; improved productivity	Improved productivity; reduced labor
Risk	Manual errors	Payroll resistance	Employee acceptance
Schedule	N/A	1–3 months	6 months
Employees	Labor intensive	Reduced work	Self-help

Figure 9.3   Example of Change Implementation Strategy for Rockwood County

data. The correction rate is high. There is substantial dissatisfaction with the current process.

For Quick Hits, the current form will be replaced by an exception form. Work will begin on the new IT infrastructure to establish an intranet for employees. IT will also have to change the payroll system to handle the exception form. There are a number of impacts of the Quick Hits. First, the volume of forms completed by employees will dramatically decrease. Less than 10% of the employees have an exception each day. Second, the cost of the Quick Hits will be in the initial IT work as well as in the training and forms. But there is resistance that cannot be ignored in a bureaucratic organization. The payroll group will see 90% of their work disappear. This means that payroll management along with Human Resources must make plans for redeploying the employees to other work. The schedule for Quick Hits is 1–3 months because of the IT time and the time to deal with the payroll employees.

Now move to the last column. This is the long-term solution. Here a new intranet system will be put into place. Employees will enter exceptions on-line. These will then be evaluated and edited by the new system. The new intranet system will "front end" the payroll system. Employees will have to be trained in the new system. Payroll will see their duties and their role reduced further. The costs are the systems work and training. The benefits are further cost reductions in labor. Employees will have greater traceability and control over their information. Duplicate data entry will be eliminated.

Now you can sit back and evaluate this change implementation strategy. You can generate an alternative approach by viewing the entire effort as a standard IT project. In that case, you would obtain the change implementation strategy shown in Figure 9.4. In this example, the first two columns are similar to Figure 9.3.

Factor	Current situation	Long-term change
Employees	Fill out forms manually	Exceptions; complete forms on-line
Payroll	Manual review and audit	Review only rejected transactions
IT	Payroll system	Intranet application
Management	Many problems and manual intervention	Review role; better statistics
Cost	Labor to complete	IT cost; training
Benefits	Habit	Improved productivity; reduced labor
Risk	Manual errors	Employee acceptance; widespread resistance in payroll
Schedule	N/A	6 months
Employees	Labor intensive	Self-help

Figure 9.4 IT Oriented Change Implementation Strategy

However, now all of the change is occurring in one phase. This has many problems.

- Resistance by payroll is handled in Figure 9.3 prior to the new system being rolled out.
- The process is changed to an exception basis through policy modification. This paves the way for automation. So in Figure 9.3 you are implementing the policies and procedures for efficiency. Then in the long-term solution, the automation comes. The risk is spread out.
- By having the Quick Hits you can have the new process settle down and start to get grassroots support for automation. Once people accept the new process, they will more likely see the benefits of automation.
- If you attempt to do all of the change at one time like a reengineering or IT project, then you have much more resistance. With the Quick Hits, the major resistance is dealt with separate from the system.

This example is important since it reveals the benefits of Quick Hits in spreading out the risks and in phasing in the change.

GET TEAM, EMPLOYEE, AND MANAGEMENT INVOLVEMENT

Why is it important to obtain involvement now when people have already participated in the previous work? Well, consider how people have been involved. Strike force members have focused on individual changes and small groups of changes. Implementation has been considered to a lesser extent than have benefits, costs, risks, and other factors. Here is where both managers and employees see the entire scope of the change effort. This can be daunting in that when you consider all of the changes in one table along with standard work, the effort may appear overwhelming. That is just why they need to participate. Politically, you are not only reinforcing support for change, but also getting people to start thinking that they can do the change work along with thier normal work.

Now that the change implementation strategy has been developed, we can discuss how to develop alternative change implementation strategies. Here are some guidelines.

- Provide an example of a change implementation strategy table to strike force members. You can use the example discussed above.
- Begin by having them work together with the change management team to complete the first column and to identify the number of Quick Hit phases. This will get them involved and provide understanding to them of how it works.

- Next, complete the second column upper rows in terms of the current situation. This is a way to generate humor in that people can now openly criticize and summarize the current situation.
- Arrange another meeting where you determine the impacts of the current situation. This shows in a summary form the need for change. It reinforces what has been done to date.
- Go to the last column now for long-term change. Complete the upper and lower parts of the column. This helps in that it solidifies the future vision of the processes or work.

Now pause and have the strike force members think about each row. Take time now to identify alternative change implementation strategy triggers. This will be discussed in detail in the next section. Have a meeting to discuss these triggers for strategies. Try to narrow the field to three or four that are credible.

Now you can hold specific meetings for each trigger and develop an alternative change strategy table. Here are some additional tips.

- Complete the extreme alternative in which there are no Quick Hits first. This is politically useful since it will show members of the strike force teams the benefits of Quick Hits.
- When doing an alternative, cover each row and discuss the sequencing in line with the change implementation strategy trigger. Do not fill out the parts below the line in terms of impacts. This allows team members to think about the logic of the changes and their sequencing. They are not distracted by impacts. It is hard for many people to think of change and the impacts of change at the same time.
- After completion of the alternatives in terms of the changes in the rows about the line, you can now work with the teams to determine the impacts. This may cause some changes in the placement of changes in the phases. It will also coalesce the alternative change implementation strategies since you will likely find that some changes should logically be placed in a specific manner.

DEFINE ALTERNATIVE CHANGE IMPLEMENTATION STRATEGY TRIGGERS

Behind every change implementation strategy is an overriding theme or focus of the change and sequencing. These themes will be called *triggers* for change. If you just sit down and try to think of alternative change implementation strategies, you can very soon become lost and lose focus. Triggers are useful because they provide a theme for arranging the change activities as well as indicating the number and extent of changes. Having triggers can also help you to be more creative at the detailed level.

Let's consider some triggers that have proven useful in past efforts.

- *IT and systems trigger.* Here there would not be much in the way of Quick Hits. Rather, the attention would be on implementation of the network, hardware, and software infrastructure followed by the application system and the changed business process. This has been such a commonly used approach that you must include it to be credible. In a way the IT or systems trigger leads to a radical change approach where there is little or no change until the system is implemented. Then there is radical change.
- *Continuous improvement and avoidance of radical change trigger.* Under this trigger there is an effort to stretch out the change so that there is no possibility of disruption to the work and business. Under this approach there would be many phases of Quick Hits. The elapsed time for implementation would be very long. This trigger is useful since it portrays a conservative approach.
- *Quick Hit phases that have major impacts trigger.* For this trigger, you strive to ensure that there are major, significant changes in the intermediate waves of Quick Hits that lead to long-term change. This is probably one of the most desirable for several reasons. First, it yields significant results with major changes and benefits. Second, the elapsed time for implementation overall is reduced. Third, the change effort receives more credibility due to the results from the Quick Hits.

These three triggers differ in terms of the phases of Quick Hits. There is another way to proceed. That is to consider the rows or areas of change. Here are some examples.

- *Organization trigger.* Here you would consider moving employees who are doing the work to different departments, having different people do the work, and other similar alternatives.
- *Downsizing trigger.* An example here would be to proceed with downsizing prior to changing work or processes. Of course, there are many problems with this approach. First, you don't know what the organization should look like until you carry out the change in the work. Second, downsizing has proven to drive out good employees who can find jobs elsewhere.
- *Customer trigger.* Under this trigger, you would focus change on the customer and what impacts them. This is, in part, the focus of Six Sigma.
- *E-Business trigger.* Here you would implement E-Business with either suppliers, customers, or employees through intranets. Many exceptions and processes would then be changed.
- *Outsourcing trigger.* The approach would be to outsource the work rather than to continue to do it yourself. Change management and process improvement would then become the responsibility of the outsourcing firm.

There is a third set of triggers that represent more general philosophies. These are some examples.

- *Kill the work or starve the work trigger.* Under this trigger you would first cut down the work or process in the early stages of Quick Hits. Then later Quick Hits and the long-term solution would act to build it back up.
- *Automate the work trigger.* Here you would attempt to automate as much of the work and process as possible. Exceptions, workarounds, and shadow systems would be incorporated into the automation or be dropped.
- *Flood the work with resources trigger.* This is almost the opposite of the kill-the-work-trigger in that you would apply many resources to clean things up. This would be in the early Quick Wins. Then you could remove the resources in later phases.

Do you have to use all of these triggers for change implementation strategies? Of course not. However,

The more triggers you consider, the more and deeper you understand the relationship among changes in different dimensions and departments.

Why is this important? Because you can then employ the alternatives for trade-offs in terms of what is possible.

FIT THE SCENARIO AND QUICK HITS INTO THE IMPLEMENTATION STRATEGIES

After you have identified a set of triggers, you can now fit the long-term scenario for change and the Quick Hits into Figure 9.1. Now two examples have been given in Figures 9.3 and 9.4 already.

How do you develop the tables for each trigger? You follow in general the steps discussed earlier along with the following guidelines.

- The first rows in the table should be the major area of focus of change indicated by the trigger. As an example, if you are going to change department functions, then the affected departments would appear in the first rows. If you were going to focus on systems and IT, then the first rows would include specific systems and IT infrastructure.
- Other rows in the upper part of the table would include later factors where there would be change involved.
- Be sure to include each separate area where there will be change as an individual row. Do not group rows or activities as people can become confused when they are considering specific changes.
- Have strike forces first discuss the different triggers and how they impact implementation of change generally.

- Now you are ready to build the tables in a collaborative way. Start with a simple trigger in which there is only one phase of Quick Hits. First, identify the row headings in the first column. Do this all of the way down including performance measures. The second thing to do is to place the long-term change solution or scenario in the last column. This gets people focused on the long-term goal.
- Go to the second column and fill in what the current situation is. This gives the strike force members experience in estimating performance measures. Practice is useful.
- Next, you can move to the individual rows based upon the trigger. You will be fitting individual changes and opportunities into the columns for that row. As you complete the major rows pertaining to the trigger, you can move to the factors in the remaining rows of the top part.
- Having filled in the top part of the change implementation strategy, you can now determine or estimate the performance measures for each column.
- As a result of doing this work, you will have to go back and make changes and updates as people realize that things have to shift, be delayed, or be sped up.

EVALUATE THE CHANGE IMPLEMENTATION STRATEGIES

Now you have several alternative change implementation strategies. You are ready to proceed with the evaluation of the alternatives. The first step is to identify the criteria for the evaluation of the alternatives. Here are several. You will note that these are quite different from each other and relate to political, technical, and business factors.

- *Acceleration of change.* Under the alternative strategy, can you easily speed up the work and implementation of change? Why is this of interest? What if you show results with the first wave of Quick Hits? Alternatively, the financial or political condition of the firm is so desperate that things must be accelerated. Management may want you to speed up the work. If you indicate that it is impossible, things may not look good. How do you analyze an alternative strategy? You start to move the change in the upper part of the table to the left into earlier phases. Then you can add up the changes in the upper rows to modify the performance measures at the bottom of the column. This can be very interesting in that there may be insufficient resources for the work to be done in a single or two phases. The analysis will reveal that.
- *Slowing things down.* Here changes would be deferred. That means that changes are moved into later phases. You proceed as in the above case in that you first move work into later phases and then you estimate and

modify the performance measures. Why would you be interested in slowing things down? There could be political pressure from some departments, for example. Another reason is that there are other projects or work that have higher priority that must be addressed. Of major importance is what happens to the performance measures when change is deferred. Are there still significant benefits, for example?

- *Canceling out some change.* Here you would actually cancel out some of the changes. The issue is what you have left when you do this. Are there sufficient coherent and cohesive changes to make the effort worthwhile. This analysis is very useful in that it helps you identify specific changes that are critical to the overall change effort.

Why is this evaluation useful? First, it reveals the extent of flexibility of the individual change implementation strategy to accommodate alterations in management direction or the situation.

Each alternative change strategy focuses on different activities in different phases of change. Thus, the risks and potential for problems and failure differ by phase and by alternative. Some areas of change are more risky and problematic than others. How do you analyze this? You can employ a radar or spider chart. The dimensions of the chart are the areas of change. Each set of lines represents a phase of change. The lines indicate the degree of importance of each factor to that phase of change. You would construct a separate chart for each alternative. Figure 9.5 applies to the change implementation strategy in Figure 9.3 as an example. In this diagram, the solid set of line segments refer to the initial Quick Hits. The dotted lines refer to the long-term change. Note that the political problems are mostly in the Quick Hits with payroll. In the long-term change, the risk is more with IT being able to deliver the system.

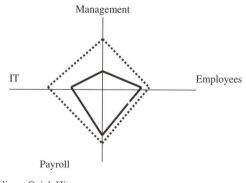

Solid line—Quick Hits
Dotted line—long-term scenario

Figure 9.5   Spider Chart for the Change Implementation Strategy of Figure 9.3

How do you go about doing the evaluation in a collaborative manner? Our approach is to sit down with change management team members first and go through the evaluation. Then you are better prepared to do it with some of the strike force members. We suggest that you use a spreadsheet since you can copy and paste cell entries quickly. First you want to get agreement on what things can move or what can be cancelled. Then you can develop the performance measures.

How many versions of each alternative change implementation strategy do you develop? Time will only permit a few versions.

In doing the evaluation you will find that several different triggers for change implementation strategies may lead to very similar or the same change implementation tables. This is very useful and should be part of your evaluation. This will tend to give more importance to them.

SELECT THE WINNING CHANGE IMPLEMENTATION STRATEGY

How do you select the winning strategy from among 3–5 alternatives? Since there are many factors at play here—political, cultural, business, technical, etc.—you should probably give up on finding an optimal strategy. Selection of the winning change implementation strategy is often by process of elimination.

How can you eliminate specific change implementation strategies? Here are some guidelines.

- Look at the resource requirements levied on individual departments. Can they perform their normal work and participate in the change process at the same time?
- Consider the extent of changes in a specific department. Are these changes too damaging and shattering? Look at our example of Rockwood County and you can see this problem in payroll. Those people are not going to be happy campers if most of the work disappears. They will resist change.
- IT implementations and facilities changes often take longer than you think. What happens if these or other changes lag? Are other changes possible? Can non-systems changes be accelerated? Or, is IT on the critical path and so their delays bog down the entire change effort?
- Are there sufficient changes in the first wave of Quick Hits to raise morale and give management confidence in the change management effort? Getting only minor results at the start could cause management to lose interest.
- Consider drawing a chart of estimated benefits and risk for a change implementation strategy. An example appears in Figure 9.6. In this diagram there are two curves one for each, benefits and risk. You could add more for cost and other factors. As you see, for this change implementation strategy, there are significant benefits in the first wave of

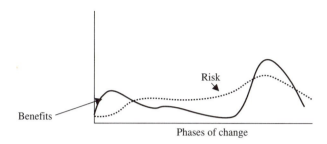

Figure 9.6 Example of Evaluation Graphs for a Change Management Strategy

Quick Hits. Other waves give lesser benefits until the long-term change. This is fine since management and employees see results so that momentum is maintained. The dotted line is that of risk. It behaves as you would expect in that there is more risk in the long-term solution.

- As you and others are selecting winners, people must understand why the others are losers. This is almost more important than figuring out why the remaining one is the best. Don't you see? It may be the best of the worse in some situations. After all, in this chapter you are starting implementation. It is the real world.

EMPLOY THE CHANGE IMPLEMENTATION STRATEGY SCORE CARD

This score card is significant because you are attempting to judge the quality of the selected change implementation strategy as well as the range of alternatives considered and the extent of participation by the change management team, the strike force members, and management. The factors for the score card are listed below. The score card appears in Figure 9.7.

- Elapsed time required to get the change implementation strategy—this is obviously important. However, it should not be short since that may mean little participation or collaboration.
- Extent of participation by change management team—it is critical that the team understands the ramifications of carrying out multiple changes in different areas in the same phase. They must be heavily involved and committed so that when problems arise in implementation, they are comfortable with the setting of the agenda of change.
- Extent of participation by the strike force members—strike force member participation is important since they can point out resource conflicts and other problems that the change management team might not be aware of.

Factor	Score	Comment
Elapsed time required to get the change implementation strategy		
Extent of participation by change management team		
Extent of participation by the strike force members		
Number of different triggers considered		
Number of alternative change implementation strategies generated		
Extent of changes made to the implementation strategy as a result of collaboration		
Participation by management in the evaluation and trade-offs of alternative change implementation strategies		
Feasibility of the change implementation strategy given available resources		

Figure 9.7   Change Implementation Strategy Score Card

- Number of different triggers considered—this shows the extent and range of changes that were considered.
- Number of alternative change implementation strategies generated—remember that some triggers may generate very similar change implementation strategies so that the number of different alternative change implementation strategies is important. It shows the range of what was really considered.
- Extent of changes made to the implementation strategy as a result of collaboration—this indicates the effectiveness of collaborative work.
- Participation by management in the evaluation and trade-offs of alternative change implementation strategies.
- Feasibility of the change implementation strategy given available resources—this is very important since you can have a wonderful strategy that falls flat on its face because it is infeasible.

MARKET THE CHANGE IMPLEMENTATION STRATEGY

You don't market the change implementation strategy by marching around with presentations. That will fail. Managers have to participate and understand the trade-offs that were made in the rejection of some alternatives. They have to understand the passion that people have in being able to do their own work as well as the change work. That is critical.

How do you involve management in the development of change management strategy? Here are some reasonable guidelines.

- Show them the process and the tables. This reveals the method.
- Review the list of trigger elements and get their comments. This shows them that you are considering a broad range of alternatives.
- Now keep the managers informed by showing them some of the alternative change management strategies. Be sure that someone from the strike forces is helping and participating. Management must see that employees are involved since they will be dependent upon them for implementation success.
- Involve management in the final selection by going through some of the trade-offs and the spider chart.

Keep in mind that this is the last time that there will be an overall view of implementation. After this you will plunge into the detail of implementation planning.

EXAMPLES

ROCKWOOD COUNTY

Politics were strong at Rockwood. Many employees were fearful of their jobs. Thus, when changes were identified and placed in tables, there was immediate discussion of the implication on the resources. This became such an issue that Human Resources had to take the step of informing employees what would happen as a result of change. It is too bad that the change implementation strategy work was responsible for this. It should have been done by Human Resources at the start. However, Human Resources did not have any confidence that there would be substantial change. Then later when changes were defined and the discussion turned to implementation, there was some management panic.

LEGEND MANUFACTURING

This phase of the change effort was almost successful beyond expectations. There was a great deal of participation in defining changes and then determining their implications. Resource conflicts between normal work and the change effort were openly discussed. Management even explained to the employees about the rejected alternative strategies. The final implementation change strategy was published for all employees and even included in business reports.

POTENTIAL ISSUES AND RISKS

- Resistance to change may really start to surface here. This is because you are getting into implementation and people are seeing the roadmap for change for the first time in the big picture view. So anticipate that this will happen and start to address it early with the strike force members and those in the change management team.
- There is often a tendency to either think too big or too small. This is a problem and gets in the way of implementing change. People fear doing too little and yet are very fearful of taking on too much. This is a real benefit of the change implementation strategy in that you can do trade-offs with different strategies to determine impacts and performance measures.
- There is sometimes a tendency to avoid this step and plunge into planning. However, the planning will be at the detailed level and people will lose sight of the forest by concentrating on individual trees.

LESSONS LEARNED

- Try to develop several model or "straw-man" strategies to serve as models. Begin with the ones in this chapter. This will give people a better idea of what you are doing.
- If people question whether this work is needed, develop a sequencing problem so that they can see the problems in ignoring multiple changes going on at the same time in related or the same department.
- There is a momentum issue here. People may get bogged down in details. So you might develop several complete change implementation strategy tables with some missing elements to give them an idea and get them started.

SUMMARY

Change implementation strategy is an often neglected area of reengineering, change management, Six Sigma, and other methods. People can come up with absolutely wonderful ideas about changing things. Then they rush into detailed planning and implementation. Later, they are surprised when people resist and resources are not available to work on the change. Why? No one took the time to develop a change implementation strategy. This is a critical success factor to effective change management.

Chapter 10

Plan Ahead for Change

INTRODUCTION

In many methods of process improvement, change management, reengineering, etc., after defining the changes to be made, you would assemble the team and start working on a plan. However, as you saw in Chapter 9, the change implementation strategy was developed. This provided a roadmap and phasing of changes as you saw. But it really does more. Each table entry in the change implementation strategy about the performance line is really a project. That is, it identifies the changes that have to be made in a specific area for a phase of Quick Hits, preparation for long-term change, or the long-term change itself. This makes the definition of the project plan for change implementation more structured and reasonable. Otherwise, you would have to do a lot more work in figuring out the time sequencing and organization of work. With the change implementation strategy, the initial work to divide up the overall work into reasonable subprojects is done.

Traditional project management focuses on single projects. Resources are assumed to be dedicated to the project full-time. People on the team are often assumed to be on the project team until the project work is finished. It is usually assumed that people are enthusiastic about the work. Most projects are treated as either technical, engineering, or standard business projects.

Unfortunately, none of the above apply to our situation. The list below is more typical of what we face:

- Team members are split between their normal work and the change effort.
- Almost all team members cannot be on the change effort for long periods of time—they are needed in their home departments and they can get burned out. So team members will come and go.
- There is resistance, fear, and other emotions that have to be overcome and addressed in the change management.

- There are multiple projects going on at the same time as seen by the change implementation strategy. Coordination among the projects is key to the change effort success.

The above factors are why you need to consider a more modern approach to project management to be successful in change management.

USE A MODERN PROJECT MANAGEMENT APPROACH

In modern projects in information technology (IT), international, and other areas, there are the following major themes for project management.

- Team members must participate in project management so that they become committed to the work and become more supportive of change.
- Resource allocation across multiple projects and regular work is a key issue.
- There is a requirement to perform analysis and do reporting across multiple projects. This requires a standard structure for projects in place of the traditional work breakdown structure. This is the use of project templates—high-level structure for projects and work.
- There is a need to address issues be they problems or opportunities as they arise throughout the project.
- Lessons learned and experience are essential for change management success and for success in many modern projects. These cannot be gathered at the end of the work. Rather they must be gathered, organized, and used throughout the project. This is especially true since change management is a program that lasts a long time.

Modern project management can be characterized by the following themes.

- Collaboration by and among team members and project leaders. Team members help to define their own detailed tasks.
- Templates for all project work. A template is a model for a class of projects that consists of high-level tasks, milestones, general resources, and dependencies. The leaders and the team then take the template and fill in the details to get the project plan.
- Issues management to address problems and focus on their resolution.
- Lessons learned to gather and use experience to prevent repetition of problems.
- Each subproject in the change management implementation effort should have two project leaders with one accountable at all times.
- Most of the tasks in the implementation plan should be assigned to two people.

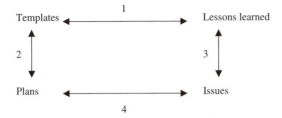

Figure 10.1 Major Components of Modern Project Planning

The templates, the project plans, the issues, and the lessons learned can be related together as is shown in Figure 10.1. Here are some notes on the diagram.

- The templates contain the high-level project plans in which all projects and tasks are numbered. The lessons learned are cross-referenced against these. When you consider a task, then you can easily find the appropriate lesson learned (arrow labeled 1).
- All project plans are created from templates. When the project work is done, experience can be employed to improve the templates (labeled 2).
- As you work on an issue, you look for appropriate experiences in the lessons learned. As you resolve an issue, you can update or create new lessons learned (labeled 3).
- Each relevant issue can be related to specific tasks in the plan. All tasks that have issues should have their issues in the issues database (labeled 4).

Issues can be tracked using databases. We can identify three issues databases: general issues databases for all change management efforts, specific issues database for individual change management projects, and a database of actions that are taken for each issue. The data elements for these three databases appear in Figure 10.2. These allow the issues to be related to projects and tasks.

Three lessons learned databases can be established in a similar vein. One is a general lessons learned database. The second is a cross-reference between lessons learned and the projects and tasks. The third is a database to update the lesson learned based upon experience in applying the lessons learned. The data elements for these are given in Figure 10.3.

Both of the issues and lessons learned databases can be established in a standard database management system such as Access or a spreadsheet such as Excel. If you use Microsoft Project, then you can take advantage of some of its features. Behind Microsoft Project is a database that you can use to customize data elements in tables for issues, lessons learned, risky tasks flag, risky milestone tag, the date the task was created, who created the task, requirement or reason for the task, etc. You can also customize the views, forms, and filters.

General issues database

- Issue identifier
- Title of the issue
- Type of the issue
- General importance of issue
- Date issue was created
- Who created the issue
- Description of the issue
- Situations to which the issue applies
- Who generally handles the issue
- Related issues
- Related lessons learned
- Related projects and tasks
- Impact if the issue is not solved
- Benefit from resolving the issue
- Guidelines for resolving the issue
- Comments

Issues applied to specific projects

- Issue identifier
- Project identifier
- Task identifiers
- Date issue applied to project
- Who created the issue
- Who is assigned to the issue
- Status of issue
- Specific impact of the issue on the project and tasks
- Decision taken, how resolved
- Actions taken
- Date actions taken
- Comments

Actions taken for specific issues

- Issue identifier
- Project identifier
- Task identifier
- Date of action
- Who took the action
- Action taken
- Result achieved
- Comments

Figure 10.2   Issues Database Elements

Microsoft Project also allows you to interrelate tasks between projects. This is using Object Linking Embedding (OLE). You can roll up projects into a general project.

There are many proven benefits to this approach.

- Using templates, the time to develop a schedule is reduced.
- Over time the templates can be improved through experience.

Lessons learned database

- Lesson learned identifier
- Title
- Date created
- Status
- Who created it
- Description
- Situations to which it applies
- Guidelines for application
- Expected results
- Benefits
- Who should use it
- Related issues
- Related lessons learned
- Related projects and tasks
- Comments

Cross-reference for lessons learned and templates

- Lesson learned identifier
- Project identifier
- Task identifier
- Updates to the lessons learned
- Lesson learned identifier
- Project identifier
- Task identifier
- Date of use
- Who created this update
- Situation to which the lesson learned was applied
- Results achieved
- Improvement/correction
- Comment

Figure 10.3   Lessons Learned Database Elements

- Junior project leaders are more effective since they can begin project planning with a template.
- Lessons learned are gathered and applied to the work and related to tasks in the templates and plans.
- Issues can be related to the tasks in the project plan.
- Having two project leaders provides backup if one person leaves.
- You can pair up a junior project leader and a senior project leader together.
- You can draw upon the strengths and different points of view of having two project leaders.
- Assigning tasks to two people means that there is backup and transfer and sharing of knowledge and experience.
- Experience is a key factor in carrying out change and improvement so that you want to capitalize on that.

There is cumulative improvement to your change management work.

- As time goes by, the issues database stabilizes as you see the same issues again and again. So it takes less time to resolve an issue.
- The templates improve as you apply your planning and project experience to updating the templates and making them more detailed.
- The project plans improve in completeness and the time for their development gets shorter.
- The lessons learned expand and become more specific in guidance over time.

CHANGE IMPLEMENTATION PROJECT TEMPLATES

Issues are discussed in each chapter and in the last chapter. Lessons learned are covered in each chapter. A third concept, that of templates, is a critical success factor in organizing your change management effort so that it is complete and logical. In thinking about a template for change management, you begin to realize that change management efforts have similarities and differences. If you create one overall template for change management, each project would have to have its own template given the differences. However, there are also similarities. What to do? The answer is to create smaller templates for parts of the change management effort. Then the overall change management plan is composed of the collection of subprojects of change management.

What are logical parts for change management? Figure 10.4 gives a list of common ones. Note that these include IT, management, organization, facilities, and other subprojects. Space does not permit the display of templates for all of these. However, it is useful to consider two of these as examples. Figure 10.5

- Initial analysis of the business situation through the definition of the long-term process or work
- Development of Quick Hits, change implementation strategy, and the change implementation plan
- Implementation of Quick Hits
- Measurement of work and processes (can appear several times after each round of Quick Hits and long-term change)
- IT work in infrastructure (network, hardware, software, etc.) to prepare for long-term change
- Organization change in preparation for the new process
- Issues management
- Implementation of systems to support the long-term process
- Implementation of facilities changes to support the long-term process
- Training, documentation, and training materials
- Data conversion to the new long-term process
- Testing of the new long-term process
- Implementation of the long-term process

Figure 10.4   Candidate Subprojects for Change Management Templates

1000 Review of previous work
    1100 Review of the long-term process and transactions
    1200 Review of the business objectives and issues
2000 Formation of the strike force teams
    2100 Identification of strike force areas
    2200 Determination of strike force leaders
    2300 Identification of strike force members
    2400 Brief overview training in the change management process
3000 Formulation of opportunities
    3100 Review of previously identified issues
    3200 Identification of new opportunities
    3300 Meetings and documentation of opportunities by strike force members
    3400 Review of opportunities
    3500 Voting on opportunities by strike forces
    3600 Summary and presentation of voting results and opportunities to the operations level change steering committee
    3700 Review by the steering committee
    3800 Report on results to the executive change steering committee
    3900 Feedback to strike force members
4000 Development of business cases for key opportunities
    4100 Review of winning opportunities
    4200 Instruction of strike force team members in doing business cases
    4300 Preparation and review of business cases
    4400 Review of business case financials by audit or finance
    4500 Voting of strike force members on business cases
    4600 Presentation of business cases and voting results to the operations level change steering committee
    4700 Review by the steering committee
    4800 Report on results to the executive change steering committee
    4900 Identification of implementation issues and priorities
    4A00 Feedback to the strike force members
5000 Development of the change management strategy
    5100 Definition of Quick Hit and change activity categories
    5200 Organization and sequencing of Quick Hits by category
    5300 Definition of triggers for alternative change implementation strategies
    5400 Development of alternative groupings of Quick Hits into phases
    5500 Development of alternative change implementation strategies
    5600 Evaluation of alternative change implementation strategies
    5700 Selection of the change implementation strategy
6000 Development of the change implementation plan
    6100 Selection of project management methodology
    6200 Selection of the templates for change implementation
    6300 Set up of databases, project management software, etc., as infrastructure for change implementation
    6400 Identification of initial issues for change implementation
    6500 Identification of the project team
    6600 Development of the project plan for change implementation
    6700 Risk analysis and setting of the baseline schedule
    6800 Resource allocation approach
    6900 Issues management approach
    6A00 Project tracking and reporting approach
    6B00 Project analysis and multiple project approach

Figure 10.5 Template for the Development of Quick Hits through the Change Implementation Plan

1000 Review of Quick Hits to be implemented by the team
2000 Definition of the approach for each Quick Hit implementation
3000 Simulation and modeling of how Quick Hits will be implemented
4000 Identification and definition of the approach for dealing with potential resistance
5000 Preparation of any supporting and preliminary materials for Quick Hit
implementation
6000 Training and orientation for employees regarding Quick Hits
7000 Quick Hit implementation
8000 Monitor implementation of Quick Hits
9000 Address issues raised in implementation of Quick Hits
9A00 Gather lessons learned from implementation

Figure 10.6   Template for Implementation of Quick Hits

gives the high-level template tasks for the development of Quick Hits through the change implementation strategy. Figure 10.6 pertains to the implementation of Quick Hits.

The following guidelines are useful in developing templates and refining them.

- Number all tasks so that you and others can make easy reference and tracking later.
- Use business terminology rather either exotic department or technical jargon.
- Begin with a limited length template and then build on it later.
- To get started, extract the high level, summary tasks from your current efforts and then develop the initial template from this.
- Ensure that no task has complex and multiple verbs as this indicates that the task should be broken up.
- Keep the template size limited to less than 50–75 tasks and milestones to start with.

PROJECT RISK AND ISSUES

Risk in any type of project is a problem. People have different ideas of what risk is and how to deal with it. Change management projects are especially prone to this because of the political and cultural nature of change. You need a tangible and direct method for addressing risk. Here is a definition of risk that is useful.

A task has risk or is risky if it has one or more associated significant issues.

This is simple to use in that it moves the attention to issues. If you want to get at risk, then you resolve issues. It also allows to measure the change management effort in terms of risk and progress. In many change efforts, the cost of the work occurs toward the front end when you modify facilities, procedures, technology infrastructure, and systems.

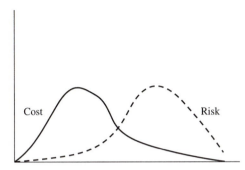

Figure 10.7 The Often Imbalance of Cost and Risk in Change Efforts

However, the risks of change management most often occur at the end when you are striving for employee acceptance of change and trying to prevent reversion back to the old process.

Figure 10.7 points out the situation. Note that this is different from standard construction or other projects where risks and costs are more closely matched. What you are doing in managing the implementation of change is to move the risk to the left, earlier in time. This will help meet your schedule earlier and have less uncertainty. You do this by proactively addressing issues earlier where appropriate.

DETERMINE TEAM MEMBERS AND ROLES FOR CHANGE IMPLEMENTATION

Who should be on the change implementation team? Your first thought probably is to use the same people who were on the strike forces. Of course, given the limited number of people available, some of them will be involved. However, there are six major reasons why you want some new faces and blood.

- The employees on the strike forces may have become too detached from their home departments. Thus, they need to return to reestablish ties.
- The strike force members may have become burned out in the analysis and politics so far.
- Generally, the more people you involve in the department for implementation of change, the more widespread the support will be for change. Therefore, involving new employees is a good idea.
- Some people are more suited to implementation and others are more suited to analysis. You must be sensitive to the differences.
- The more dependent you become on specific people in a department, the more you place the change effort at risk by being overdependent on a few without backup or alternatives.

- The strike force members may have burnt too many bridges politically.
  Their involvement in change might create more resistance.

Overall, it is recommended that you seek out new people to be involved. You can get some ideas from both the department managers and the strike force members. How do you avoid letting the strike force members down? Indicate that you don't want to take too much of their time. Also, point out that there will be a later role in the measurement of results of the Quick Hits. Third, you can point out that there will be other waves of Quick Hits and change so that there will be more opportunities later.

The question generally now is who to involve. Department managers might suggest less effective employees who could actually do harm to the change effort. We have seen several cases in which a department manager deliberately tried to put a less than capable person on the implementation effort, so as to delay the implementation.

Another person you want to avoid is a "queen bee" or "king bee." Remember from earlier that these are people who have been doing the department work for many years and they like things the way they are. They also derive power from their position. They will tend to oppose or delay change. Avoid these people.

A good source for team members is from the strike force members. What attributes are you looking for in the implementation of change? It is interesting that you are seeking different attributes than for analysis in the early work in the strike forces. Here are some ideas.

- Seek out people who have a reputation for getting things done.
- Find individuals who like detailed work, but do not get bogged down in the detail.
- Look for individuals who are even tempered and have a reputation for not being excessively political.

How many people are you looking for? Obviously, it depends upon the number, type, and scope of Quick Hits or long-term change that you are considering. If you involve too many people, then you burn people out for later work. You may also harm the department by taking too many people away from the department. Experience shows that a minimum of two people is necessary. This provides backup, different points of view and perspective, and does not harm the department. Two people also provide flexibility in terms of assignment of specific tasks. You also need people from outside of the department to assist in the implementation. They can provide perspective and encouragement.

What will be the extent of their involvement? More than in the strike forces, but probably over a shorter elapsed time since you are not planning, but implementing.

What are the roles of the change implementation team members? Here is a short list.

- Training employees in new procedures
- Monitoring and guiding employees in the use of the new procedures

- Politically justifying the changes
- Detecting political resistance to change
- Defining on-the-spot ideas and adjustments to deal with exceptions and shadow systems
- Building support and enthusiasm by pointing out the benefits of change

DEVELOP THE DETAILED CHANGE PROJECT PLAN USING COLLABORATION

Let's assume that you have identified a template and that you have the team members selected. What are the next steps? Psychologically you have to create a team atmosphere. You do not achieve this through some social event. You have to provide activities that they perform together, rather than individually. Here are some specific activities.

- *Issue identification.* The team members collectively review the approach for implementing change and point out issues and resistance to change. They might actually role play what some of the resistance might be like. As they identify potential issues, these can be placed in the issues database that was described earlier.
- *Lessons learned.* The employees have had experience in that department. They may also have had experience with past efforts at change in the past. The purpose of sharing and finding lessons learned is that the knowledge is transferred and shared. These things can be placed in the lessons learned database. A side benefit is that the team will more likely avoid repeating problems that occurred in the past in the department.

The third activity is that of developing the detailed change project plan. Now you have the template. What you do now is to carry out the following steps. These will ensure that the people understand, support, and commit to the plan. Because if you do not have that, then you are likely to have problems and even failure. Notice that these steps are collaborative in that team members are participating in project management. The project leader is not defining the detailed tasks—the team members are.

- Project leaders assign areas of the template to pairs of team members. Team members define detailed tasks down to a period of one to two weeks.
- Team members match up the issues and lessons learned with the detailed tasks. This will uncover additional missing tasks and/or issues.
- Project leaders review the work and assess how complete the work is and the extent to which the team understands the work.
- Team members now define resource requirements and relationships among tasks. These are reviewed by the team leaders.
- Team members define the duration and dates for the detailed tasks. These are reviewed by the team leaders.

There are some useful observations to make here.

- By making the detailed tasks one to two weeks long, the plan will be reasonable to update later during the work.
- The team members link the issues and lessons learned to the tasks— important for understanding the impact of issues and where the experience of the past will likely pay off.
- The team members first define tasks and discuss them so that any problems or lack of knowledge surfaces. It is important that there is no pressure to define the schedule until later in the process.
- Validation of both the issues and the tasks comes when the team and leaders match up the tasks and issues with each other.

What if someone cannot estimate how long a task will take? Have them break up the tasks into parts. This will isolate the part that cannot be estimated. Now, perhaps, because it is smaller, it can be estimated. If this does not work, then ask why it cannot be estimated. Presto! You have a new issue. Better to find out about this now before work begins than later when the impact can be more severe.

How do you deal with contingencies and people's natural tendency to over-estimate to be safe? Emphasize that all estimates will be reviewed. Also, have them identify contingency tasks and work that may (the word is may not will) occur if there is a problem. These can be added to the bottom of the plan.

Now at this point the team leaders can put together a plan. They can also relate the work that they are overseeing with that of other teams working on change. However, in the real world when you put together the schedule from the team members you find that the elapsed time for the work is too long. Then what do you do? Avoid the temptation to go to the critical path in the project. Instead, follow these steps. First, try to break up tasks so that more work can be performed in parallel. This will shorten the time to some extent. Second, consider the tasks that have issues. If you are able to resolve some of the issues, the duration of the corresponding tasks can be shortened. Third, you can consider the critical path.

DEFINE AN APPROACH FOR RESOURCE ALLOCATION

Early in the implementation effort it is important to identify what other work team members will have to perform outside of the change effort. This will help show potential resource conflicts before they become a problem. You need a proactive approach for allocating and tracking resource use as well as dealing with resource conflicts in which demands for your team members' time come from many sources.

A basic and direct approach is to institute a weekly allocation meeting in which the change management team and line managers and supervisors meet to discuss what change implementation team members will be working on during the next week. This can be a short meeting and only has to deal with the individuals who are critical at that time.

There are several advantages to this approach.

- By doing this weekly there are fewer chances for miscommunications.
- The employee will receive the same allocation story from both the change implementation managers as well as their own line managers.
- Politically, this shows that the project leaders for the change effort respect and are trying to involve the line managers.
- The meetings also provide a forum to address any problems or issues.

What happens if there is a resource conflict? There are several options. If the line manager and change leaders cannot agree, the issue can be escalated. However, you want to avoid this if you can. There are several politically acceptable solutions that do not require either side to lose face. First, the person's time can be allocated down to smaller periods of time. Second, the change management tasks may be shifted. Third, the department might be able to change the work assignments. Fourth, it might be possible to find another person in the department to do some of the work.

TRACK THE CHANGE IMPLEMENTATION WORK

There is both informal and formal tracking. We will consider both. For informal tracking of work you should visit the team members and ask them how it is going. Their tone and mood will indicate if there are problems in many cases. Another method is to go out into the department where there is change going on and observe the work. Talk to the employees. In that regard, change management is easier to gauge than projects that are more subtle such as IT efforts. A third method is to have team members make presentations at team meetings.

Team meetings represent a borderline between the formal and informal. It is sad and a waste that many people waste team meetings in gathering status about the change effort. In such meetings individual team members do not want to discuss sensitive political issues or problems. When one person talks, no one else is participating. It is not a true team meeting.

A better, more positive and productive approach is to gather status prior to a team meeting and then summarize it at the start. Then you can spend the time in the meeting on either discussing issues or lessons learned. We recommend having two meetings on issues and one on lessons learned. There are a number of good topic areas for the lessons learned meetings. These include the following:

- Presentation of experience by a new team member. This gets them psychologically involved in the team.
- Presentation by a vendor. This helps transfer knowledge from the vendor or consultant to the employees.

- Name of the project
- Date
- Purpose of the work
- Scope of the work
- Expected benefits
- Summary GANTT chart of the work
- Cumulative budget versus actual graph
- Milestones achieved
- Upcoming milestones
- Major outstanding issues

Figure 10.8   Regular Reporting Information for a Change Effort

- Presentation by a key employee. This aids in transferring knowledge and becoming less dependent upon this person.
- Presentation of a milestone document or result by the team members who did the work. This helps you find out where potential problems may lie in the work.

Now let's turn to the formal side. Teams involved in change efforts need to report in on a regular basis with a minimum of overhead and a maximum of information. We have had success in change management efforts with a form (either paper or electronic) that contains the information given in Figure 10.8. Note that not all of these elements are needed if the scope of the Quick Hits is limited. The reporting approach is scalable. Also, note that there is a focus on issues.

There are the standard methods of determining status. One is percent complete and the other is budget versus actual. However, as was noted earlier in this chapter, risk and issues often occur later in the project. Therefore, these indicators are not as useful as in traditional projects because they do not reflect either issues or risk.

An alternative measure can be created by returning to the project plan. Here you have developed the tasks, identified the issues, and associated the issues with the tasks. Therefore, you can now calculate the following measures.

- Percentage of the tasks that have issues that have been completed (a very rough measure since this is not duration sensitive).
- Percentage of the work that lies ahead that is associated with risk and issues (a very good measure that is future, not past oriented).
- Age of the oldest major outstanding issue (this is a good indicator of how the change effort is addressing issues).
- Average time that it takes to resolve a significant issue (good for tracking management involvement).

ESTABLISH THE PROJECT MANAGEMENT FRAMEWORK

What do we mean by a project management framework? Well, it is taking the elements that have been discussed and creating a framework or infrastructure to support multiple projects of Quick Hits and change. Here are the critical ingredients.

- Guardian and keeper of the issues database, the lessons learned database, and templates.
- Instructor in the change management methods, project management approach, and general counseling to the change implementation teams.
- Coordinator of measuring status across multiple change efforts.
- Guidance counselor in kicking off the change implementation effort.
- Coordinator of measuring costs and benefits of the change effort.

You can have these duties performed by one or more people. The work should be rotated among different people so that it does not get institutionalized and overly formal.

Note that this is different from the concept of the Project Office. The Project Office deals with the bureaucracy of projects and project management. This applies to projects in general. Here you are concentrating on change efforts, not general projects.

As you look down the list, you might think that these duties can be performed by the people involved in the change. Not a good idea. They are too close to the action. It should be done by others.

EMPLOY THE CHANGE PROJECT MANAGEMENT SCORE CARD

How did you do? Use Figure 10.9 as a guide. Here are some comments on the factors in the score card.

- Elapsed time to organize the implementation effort. This is important since you do not want to spend too much time in planning. You want to start implementing change.
- Extent of participation of employees in planning. Collaboration is a critical success factor in change management. While this is subjective, it is a useful measure here just prior to implementation.
- Percentage of tasks that are joint between two team members. This is a second indicator of collaboration.
- Number of issues identified. The more issues you can identify in general, the fewer surprises you will have later.
- Mixture of issues by type identified. If the issues are skewed toward one or two areas, it is likely that a number of issues have been missed.
- Support by line managers in the resource allocation process. This will be crucial during any extended change effort.
- Establishment of the implementation coordination roles. This is important to provide the structure for the change implementation work.

Factor	Score	Comments
Elapsed time to organize the implementation effort		
Extent of participation of employees in planning		
Percentage of tasks that are joint between two team members		
Number of issues identified		
Mixture of issues by type identified		
Support by line managers in the resource allocation process		
Establishment of the implementation coordination roles		
Percentage of employees in affected departments that have been involved in the change effort so far		
Establishment of the databases and templates for the change implementation		

Figure 10.9   The Change Project Management Score Card

- Percentage of employees in affected departments that have been involved in the change effort so far. This is a cumulative measure of participation.
- Establishment of the databases and templates for the change implementation. This is a simple measure of the setup of the infrastructure for the change work.

MARKET THE CHANGE IMPLEMENTATION PLAN

There are a number of things that have to be marketed. First, you are going to market the project management approach that you select. That is why so much space and time has been spent in this chapter on the benefits and approach. A successful marketing method is to appeal to people's self-interest. The approach here will take up minimal time and have as little bureaucracy as possible. People are participating so that there will be more support.

A second marketing job is required to get people to join the implementation team. In a way this is easier than getting people on the strike forces. Why? For one reason there is momentum and enthusiasm for change. This diminishes reluctance to participate. For another, more people like to do things than to study and analyze things.

The third marketing area is that of the plan itself. Here you should start with a high level summary plan that contains the milestones. Then you can move to the resource allocation and conflict approach. Next, you can identify and discuss key issues that will have to be addressed.

EXAMPLES

ROCKWOOD COUNTY

While it became easier to get participation from employees during the work through the change implementation strategy, things slowed down and resistance started to increase.

Managers now began to resist assigning good employees to the change effort. This caused an alternation in the change implementation strategy so that certain departments started on change earlier. These were the departments who support the change effort more. It was thought and later proven that showing success by example would be useful. It worked out that way.

This also proved that having the change implementation strategy was a good idea. It was much easier to analyze the effects of changes.

LEGEND MANUFACTURING

There were many fewer problems at Legend. More people wanted to participate than were needed. So the planning for the implementation had to cross several phases of Quick Hits to figure out where to place people. This proved useful in that additional issues surfaced earlier that would not have been anticipated otherwise.

POTENTIAL ISSUES AND RISKS

- There is sometimes a tendency to plunge in and just develop the plan with the project leaders. While that will give you a plan faster, it will not have the quality, completeness, or support of the people. The approach that has been presented here is based upon joint work and collaboration. This requires some elapsed time for people to get involved. It pays off during the work.
- Resource allocation is often ignored since people often assume that the change effort will receive high priority and attention. However, this cannot be assumed in any change effort that consumes substantial elapsed time. Therefore, you must proactively nail this down with line managers.

- Even though issues are negative, they must be tracked if not addressed. Many view issues as negative and so they put off solving them. They then can fester and negatively impact the change effort.

LESSONS LEARNED

- Lessons learned are a key ingredient to keeping a team effort going. People share experiences and gain knowledge. This is just the same as it was thousands of years ago.
- There is a need for the coordination role being established early. Otherwise, there can be much information lost. Moreover, the methods of project management and the change effort may not be consistent.

SUMMARY

Change implementation requires a different approach than standard project management. Because change management is a program and not one project, there is a need to accumulate lessons learned, improve templates, and track issues over time. This is different than a single project. In addition, change management is more political than standard projects so that any project management effort must be sensitive to the issues that were discussed.

Part III

Implement Change

Chapter 11

Get Quick Hit Results

INTRODUCTION

When you read many books on change management and related areas such as process improvement or reengineering, you find that the materials end with implementation still ahead. Based on all of the problems and things that can go wrong in implementing change, experience shows that implementation is critical if you are going to actually perform change and get lasting change.

This part of the book is divided into four parts:

- Implement Quick Hits
- Install and carry out major change
- Measure results
- Prevent deterioration and reversion

It looks all so nice in this sequential form. A book is a sequential document so we have no choice. However, it must be emphasized that all four activities go on in parallel. When you implement Quick Hits, you want to measure the results. When you have carried out some major change in one area, you will probably be carrying out Quick Hits in another area. Then after you have implemented any change, you have to ensure that there is no deterioration or reversion. Keep these remarks in mind as you read the chapters.

Let's checkpoint where you are now. You have the long-term change and Quick Hits identified. You have organized these through the change implementation strategy and roadmap. Using the strategy, you have developed implementation plans for the work. All along you have involved employees and managers through the strike forces, steering committees, and participation in planning. Now it is time to implement change.

REVIEW THE CHANGE IMPLEMENTATION STRATEGY

There are some things to review at the start. You want to review the writeups of business cases, opportunities, and the change implementation strategy. The strategy is important since you must have the sequencing of the different change activities foremost in your mind. You don't want to get out of sequence. If you deviate from the change implementation strategy, management and employees may raise concerns and question what is going on.

ORGANIZE FOR THE FIRST ROUND OF QUICK HITS

Taking the project plans you have developed for the first round of Quick Hits, you want to get the employees involved in implementation together. You want to discuss and simulate how changes will be undertaken. Here are some specific tasks that you should perform:

- Review the current situation and determine if there is anything new since the analysis was performed. Consider the following:
  — Have there been any manager or supervisor changes?
  — Is the staffing doing the work the same?
  — Have there been any changes in the systems used, including the shadow systems?
  — Are the facilities the same?
  — Has other work that will not be changed been altered?
  — Have interfaces between the employees or work and those of other areas changed?

  Why is it important to do this review? There could have been changes if there has been substantial elapsed time since the original analysis was performed. Notice that you are reviewing more than the work itself. You are reviewing interfaces, other work that will not be changed, and the systems, infrastructure, and organization as well.

- Review the issues and problems that surfaced in the initial analysis. Answer the following questions:
  — Are the issues still present?
  — Have the impacts of the issues gotten worse, stayed the same, or improved?
  — Are there new issues that are present?

  Why is this important? This is vital because you want the employees to again recognize that the problems exist and that the impacts are substantial. You always must keep pushing to keep people motivated for change. Another reason is that you want to acknowledge to the employees that they are correct and that their ideas counted. This helps give them a sense of ownership.

- Now review the proposed changes that were developed earlier. Here are some additional questions to pose.
  — Are the changes still valid? Do they address the issues?
  — If there are new issues that have arisen or changes, do the changes deal with these?
  — Do the changes deliver the intended benefits?
  — How would these benefits be validated?

  Notice here that you are concerned with whether the changes are valid, complete, and deliver the estimated benefits. Politically, this will help the change effort since employees will now be focused on the changes and their impacts. However, do not, we repeat, do not consider implementation. That is separate. After you have covered these questions, you can move onto implementation.

- Encourage employees to discuss implementation and any problems that might occur.

  This is a good time to bring up concerns about jobs, tasks, and related items. You can even volunteer some of the points of resistance from Chapter 3.

PLAN THE IMPLEMENTATION OF CHANGE

Now turn to the implementation of change. How will the changes be undertaken? This, of course, depends in detail upon the exact situation and the nature of the change. Here are some general guidelines for planning the changes. Note that resistance has already been defined so that the emphasis is on how to deal with the concerns. This planning session must be carried out soon after the meetings in the last section.

- Involve employees in the planning from the beginning.
- Indicate to the employees that they must be involved for this to work.
- Cover the scope of what has to change and get inputs from them on sequencing of the individual changes. This is important because it is difficult for most people to cope with many changes at the same time— especially when it involves their jobs.
- Now turn to each individual change. Discuss how to implement each one. Define what people would expect to see different in their work after each step.
- Determine a kick-off time and method for starting the change implementation.

- Simulate how the new, changed process will work through some sample transactions. This can be useful later for training.
- Indicate that there will be a small celebration after the Quick Hits are implemented and measured.
- Indicate that the employees will participate in evaluating the implementation process for the Quick Hits as well as the results themselves. This will be accomplished through score cards.

Now having provided some general guidelines, we can turn to individual situations and instances of change for more detailed comments. A logical approach is to consider a variety of different types of change. Remember that these are Quick Hits and not major change. That comes in the next chapter.

CHANGE IN PROCEDURES

While seemingly simple, changing procedures means that people have to do their work differently. How they will make this transition and stick with the new method or procedure is covered. There is typically a need for supervisory reinforcement.

CHANGE IN POLICIES AND PROCEDURES

Policy changes result in more complex change. When you change a policy, you have to consider how the policy will be interpreted in terms of the work. This is the same as in the law where legislation is enacted and then interpreted by the court system. Many people make the mistake that people assume how the policy is to be interpreted. However, most of the time it is not automatic. Figure 11.1 can help here. In the first column (labeled A) you enter the areas that the new policy will address. In column B you place the current policy in terms of interpretation. In column C the new policy is placed for that area. Column D contains the interpretation of the new policy. The last column (E) is for the new procedures.

You cannot rely on what managers say about the use of current policies. You need to talk to different supervisors. After all, different supervisors may interpret the same policy differently. You also want to talk to employees without the

Areas covered by policy	Existing policy	New policy	Interpretation of new policy	New procedures
A.	B.	C.	D.	E.

Figure 11.1   Analysis of Policy Changes

supervisors around to see how they do their work. This might be a different result than what you heard from the supervisors.

On implementing new policies you define both the interpretation of how the policy is to be employed and used as well as the procedures. Here are some questions to answer with regard to new policies:

- Are there any new exceptions generated by the new policy?
- Are exceptions to the old policy covered by the new policy?
- Are there fuzzy or unclear areas of the policy in terms of what the policy applies to?
- Can people get around the policy? An example might be a policy to use a specific method or tool if the work is more than a certain cost. Some people might then state that the cost was lower, thereby avoiding the policy.
- Is the new policy consistent with the systems and automation in place? If not, then there must be systems changes before the policy is changed.

MINOR SYSTEMS CHANGES

For Quick Hits these changes must not take more than a few weeks. Any extensive change would fall into the major change and not Quick Hits. The scope of any systems change must be very limited. Testing must be allowed.

What types of changes could be made to systems in such a short time? Here are some examples.

- New or modified reports
- Modified screens in terms of data element placement or text on the screen
- Automation of simple exceptions
- Modifications of business rules to eliminate workarounds
- Changing of permissions and security levels
- Simple modifications to interfaces

FACILITIES OR LAYOUT CHANGES

Changing someone's workplace when it has been the same for many years is difficult. You have to think about where and how people will work during the changes. It is important that they see some benefit from the change. In one case, a facility layout change resulted in people being more cramped and working in poorer lighting. It then had to be redone. Employees should be involved in terms of selecting furnishings and colors. You can imagine the feeling of powerlessness when someone comes in and tears up and reorders the place.

SHIFT OF WORK ASSIGNMENTS

Let's first consider some examples that can be considered as Quick Hits. Suppose you had a customer service group in which everyone was allowed to answer any call. You found in the analysis that a number of employees could not handle the difficult or complex calls. As a Quick Hit it was decided to create a position of specialist so that other employees could refer the calls to these people. In order to implement this and similar shifts, the following steps are required:

- Develop and get approval for new position
- Develop procedures and standards for the new position
- Screen current employees to determine those who qualify for the new position
- Train the employees who will be specialists
- Train other employees on call referrals

As you can see, there are multiple steps, but each is reasonable.

IMPLEMENTATION OF MEASUREMENTS

In many cases we have found that the existing work is not measured. After doing the measurements to determine where the best opportunities are for change, you often find that it is useful to implement a measurement process. This paves the way for a more formal measurement process when the long-term change is put into place.

ADDITIONAL TRAINING

All of the changes require additional training. Rather than address it in each area, it is covered here. Training begins with defining the new procedures for the work. You want to have those for the current work on hand along with the issues that were identified earlier. The next step is to develop a short training outline in preparation for the training materials. Here is a successful outline:

- Overview of current work—this is familiar to people and it shows that you respect what they do.
- Issues involved in the current work—this gets the employees to acknowledge again the need for change and improvement.
- Change management approach—here the Quick Hits are described along with the long-term change.
- New policies and procedures—these are presented in a summary form.
- Detailed procedures and workflow.
- Benefits and measurement from the change—this shows that change management is to be taken seriously. It also helps to set expectations.

You can probably reuse the work on the new process and changes that was done earlier.

CHANGES IN INTERFACES BETWEEN OR AMONG GROUPS

This can be tricky. You are implementing change in one area that impacts another group. Alternatively, you are implementing changes in work that spans multiple groups. The approach is basically the same as that for a single group. However, you should employ these guidelines.

* Focus on the issues in the current interface and the problems generated for both groups.
* Even if the two groups are of unequal power or prestige, you should treat both groups as equals.
* When doing training, focus on the problems with the interfaces and their impacts.
* Train both groups at the same time so that the training and message are consistent.
* Involve employees and supervisors from both groups in planning work and meetings.

ELIMINATION OF EXCEPTIONS

There may be opportunities in Quick Hits to eliminate one or more exceptions. This is carried out in the simplest cases by changes in procedures. However, in some cases there may need to be a policy change. Some guidelines here are:

* Focus on the problems and extra work that the exception generates.
* Show how the new approach that eliminates the exception will work.
* Indicate how any questions or issues that remain with that exception will be handled.

ADDRESSING A SHADOW SYSTEM

Recall that a shadow system is a system created within a department. It can be automated through database management software or spreadsheets. There are several approaches to take with a shadow system.

* You can eliminate it. Here it is treated as an exception so that the above guidelines apply.
* You can formalize it. This means that it will become part of the standard business practices until the long-term changes are put into place.

If you formalize it, then typically this means some systems work, development of procedures, and training. Then you have to explain how it will be used in conjunction with the regular work.

COPING WITH A WORKAROUND

A workaround is a set of procedures that are followed because the existing system does not handle or address a specific collection of transactions or work. People have gotten in the habit of using the workaround. It is ingrained by habit. What are alternatives here?

- You can eliminate the workaround by changing the system to handle the work. This is a good idea, but it may go beyond what is possible in a Quick Hit.
- You can formalize and streamline the workaround so that the workaround is performed more consistently and efficiently.

IMPLEMENTING ADDITIONAL OR NEW WORK

It may be the case that you have to add some additional work steps to prepare for the long-term change. Examples of this are:

- Measurements of the work
- Additional editing or quality control work
- Improved customer service

Employees are often naturally resistant to new work. They feel that they are already working at full steam. Thus, it is important to stress the following points:

- The additional work is temporary and will disappear when the long-term change is implemented. This can help get the employees to support long-term change faster to get rid of the work.
- The additional work is necessary and should have been performed all along.
- Demonstrations of how people can do this additional work and their regular work must be done so that the people feel comfortable with the feasibility of the total workload.

COMBINATIONS OF CHANGES

Now these are individual changes. You also may plan to implement a combination of changes. Then you are concerned with the sequencing of the changes.

Remember that you are working at a detailed level with a very limited scope. That is good. Here are questions to address regarding dependencies of changes and parallelism.

- You want to get the changes implemented as soon as possible. One reason is to start getting the benefits. A second reason is to give credibility to the change management effort. A third reason is that you do not want to disrupt employees for too long a time.
- You want to first determine the maximum number of changes that can be accomplished in parallel. This will give you the shortest time period. However, it has not yet been shown to be practical.
- Next, you identify the dependencies that have to exist due to the non-employee factors such as IT, facilities, work, policies, etc. If you put this step and the previous one together, you have the most optimistic schedule for completing the Quick Hits.
- Now you must consider the loading of people onto the schedule and changes. Here you should prepare a table like the one in Figure 11.2. This table shows who has to be involved in each change.
- Using Figure 11.2 you can now prepare alternative sequencing of tasks. For this you can work with Figure 11.3. This table has as columns the stages of the changes. There are two sets of rows. One is for changes. The other group of rows is to indicate the degree of involvement of each employee. You would enter all of the tasks and employees. Then for the tasks or changes you would place an "X" where they are performed. Once

	Tasks			
Employee				

Figure 11.2   Employee Involvement Table for Quick Hits

	Stages			
Tasks				
Employees				

Figure 11.3   Phasing Table of Changes for Quick Hits

you have completed this, then you can enter the degree of involvement required by each person in the stage.

- You can generate alternative sequencings by moving the changes or tasks between the stages. Then you can recompute the loading of resources. This amounts to manual resource leveling.

The above approach is useful since it highlights how dependent the changes are upon a small number of people, if that is the case.

PLANNING WITH SUPERVISORS AND MANAGERS

Now that you have covered the employee part of planning, it is time to consider the supervisors and managers. Of course, the supervisors are going to be involved during the planning as are some of the middle level managers. However, you also want to do planning with supervisors without the employees. There should be an initial meeting to go over the following items:

- Potential problems with employees in terms of resistance
- Identification of individuals in the department or group who should be trained in the changes first, second, etc. (sequencing of employees)
- Timing of the implementation in terms of peak or trough workload periods

As the planning progresses, you want to have follow up meetings with the supervisors to determine how things are going, what their reactions are, and also address these specific points.

- Can specific individuals be freed up from their regular work to participate in the change effort?
- How can the supervisor review work after changes to ensure that reversion or fallback does not occur?
- How will resistance be addressed—either covert or overt?

Managers need to be assured that the work will not be disrupted. Therefore, you should have some employees and supervisors in the meetings with managers when you provide updates. This will also show the managers that the employees and supervisors are committed to the changes.

Do you have to do all of this planning if you are just implementing Quick Hits? We think so for a number of reasons. First, it shows that the change management team and management are sensitive to their concerns and feelings. Second, it gives the employees a greater sense of ownership in the change process. Third, you may uncover hidden issues that were not noticed before. Some issues may be more substantial or less important than previously thought.

CONFLICTS BETWEEN QUICK HITS AND LONG-TERM CHANGE

It is sometimes necessary to address specific problems and issues in the Quick Hits. The actions taken for the Quick Hits may be contradictory or extraneous to the long-term change. Why does this happen? One reason is that there is urgency to address the problem. Another political reason is that you want to shake things up so that people move from the status quo.

Here are some guidelines to deal with this.

- Point out that the change is necessary because of the problem and its impact.
- Delineate how not making the change will make things even worse.
- Explain how things will improve with the long-term changes.

IMPLEMENT THE FIRST QUICK HITS

After all of this planning, the installation of the first Quick Hits should be easier. It will be. However, there can still be issues that arise.

- People get pulled off of the change effort due to pressing regular work. This is addressed in the next section.
- Pockets of resistance still surface even if the supervisors, managers, and many employees support the change.

To kick off the change, an upper level manager should introduce the Quick Hits. The manager should not only explain that change is needed, but give fairly detailed management expectations and a timetable for change.

You can now follow the training outline given in the planning section to implement the change. Wherever possible you should convert everything that you identified in your strategy for implementation at the same time so as to reduce disruption. You should create a quiet and calm atmosphere and then kick-off the training for the change.

In the training for the change, have the supervisors and employees perform the training. They know the language and their fellow workers. They can answer questions more quickly and easily than the change management team. However, several members of the team should be present.

After you have carried out the changes, monitor the work. Get opinions of employees. In this initial change, this is crucial to build confidence for further change. Here are some guidelines.

- Encourage employees to pose questions as they do their work.
- Have a supervisor on hand to address any concerns.
- Ask employees after a few days what they think.
- Gather positive opinions and write these down.

What if you find that you have to make some changes to the new procedures. Be careful here. What may be happening is that people are attempting to revert back to the old process. They may be testing you to see how far they can go. Think through any changes with the change management team and supervisors outside of the ears of the employees. Do not improvise on the spot. There is no need. If you do, you may be sending a message that you are desperate to have the employees carry out the change.

A useful thing to do is to hold a group focus meeting. This can be done several times. The first one can be after 3–4 days of operation. Another can be held a week later. The supervisor and a member of the change management team can co-chair the meetings. Here are some things to cover in the meetings.

- How is the work going now?
- What are any problems that have arisen? Do not attempt to address these in the meeting. Write them down for later analysis with the supervisors and members of the change management team.
- What are some lessons learned and guidelines that they have identified in how to do the work? Answers here can be helpful for both further Quick Hits and long-term change.
- What are the benefits of the changes? Here you want people to identify the benefits along with how they impact the group. What do the benefits result in?

ADDRESS RESISTANCE TO QUICK HIT CHANGE

Employees may continue to raise issues and potential problems from planning through initial operation after the change. This can occur in the middle of training, for example. Typically, an employee will ask "How will we do xxxx?" You should take this initially as a positive step in that they are trying to visualize how something will now be done. It starts to become resistance if the same individuals raise similar questions repeatedly. Here are some guidelines to handle this.

- Do not respond with a hair trigger idea.
- Gather more details using the supervisor and other employees to delve into the situation.
- For each question go into impacts, need for action now, and other related problems.

EXECUTE SUCCESSIVE QUICK HITS

You have just carried out one round of Quick Hits. Maybe it went well. Typically, however, the road was bumpy at first. The change management team and management have gone through a learning experience. This is a good time to gather more lessons learned. Here are some additional steps to prepare for more Quick Hits.

- Revisit the schedule and sequencing of Quick Hits to see if there have to be any changes.
- Involve employees who were successful in the change effort in later waves of Quick Hits. This is very useful to generate more grassroots support for change.
- Gather and use comments from employees as testimonials.

In general, the successive waves of Quick Hits will carry out more and greater changes. However, you are better prepared with the experience.

PREPARE THE ROAD FOR LONG-TERM CHANGE

As you carry out the Quick Hits you are conducting measurements of the work and results. You are also collecting guidelines that will be valuable when you come to the long-term change.

Another step to take in preparation is to keep the employees who were involved in change informed as to the status of the long-term changes. This shows that you are interested in their feelings.

EMPLOY QUICK HIT PLANNING AND IMPLEMENTATION SCORE CARDS

There are several Quick Hit implementation score cards to use. These are divided into two groups—planning and implementation as well as employees and management. Think of it as a 2 × 2 table with four score cards. You should develop the score cards during each wave of Quick Hits. As before, you should do this in a collaborative way involving managers, supervisors, and employees where appropriate. The completed score cards should be shared with the people involved in future waves of Quick Hits. Let's discuss each of the score cards in more detail now.

QUICK HIT IMPLEMENTATION PLANNING SCORE CARD FOR EMPLOYEES

The purpose of this score card is to assess how the employees performed in the implementation planning. It is used to help in future implementations of Quick

Factor	Score	Comments
Number of employees involved in planning		
Percentage of total employees involved in planning		
Quality of participation in planning		
Number of meetings held		
Number of surprises encountered in implementation that should have surfaced during planning		
Lessons learned gathered during planning		
Elapsed time for the planning		
Performance of the change management team		
Planned versus actual schedule		
Planned versus actual cost		

Figure 11.4   Quick Hit Implementation Planning Score Card for Employees

Hits. It also helps to evaluate the change management team's effectiveness. This score card is shown in Figure 11.4.

Some comments on the factors in the score card are:

- Number of employees involved in planning.
- Percentage of total employees involved in planning.
- Quality of participation in planning—this is subjective but important. The score can be arrived at through discussions in meetings.
- Number of meetings held with employees—you may want to add the total time here as well.
- Number of surprises encountered in implementation that should have surfaced during planning—you may also want to include the types and impacts of the surprises. This will help to improve your future efforts.
- Lessons learned gathered during planning—always important.
- Elapsed time for the planning—this should get shorter as you implement more Quick Hits.
- Performance of the change management team—also subjective.
- Planned versus actual schedule.
- Planned versus actual cost.

QUICK HIT IMPLEMENTATION PLANNING SCORE CARD FOR MANAGEMENT

The intent of the planning score card for management is to evaluate the role of management and supervisors as well as the change management team. Figure 11.5 contains the score card. Remarks on the specific factors are as follows:

- Number of supervisors involved—almost all should be involved.
- Percentage of supervisors involved.
- Number of meetings with supervisors—there should be many formal and informal meetings or gatherings.
- Number of surprises encountered—surprises are also a reflection of the supervisors and management.
- Extent and impact of surprises—you definitely want to include impacts here.
- Extent and degree of participation.
- Performance of the change management team.
- Support of supervisors with employees—this is subjective and should be addressed.

Factor	Score	Comments
Number of supervisors involved		
Percentage of supervisors involved		
Number of meetings with supervisors		
Number of surprises encountered		
Extent and impact of surprises		
Extent and degree of participation		
Performance of the change management team		
Support of supervisors with employees		
Performance of management involvement		
Resolution of issues by supervisors		
Resolution of issues by managers		

Figure 11.5   Quick Hit Implementation Planning Score Card for Management

- Performance of management involvement—this is subjective and can be estimated by the change management team and the supervisors first.
- Resolution of issues by supervisors—this includes outcomes as well as elapsed time to resolve issues.
- Resolution of issues by managers—same as above.

QUICK HIT IMPLEMENTATION RESULTS SCORE CARD FOR EMPLOYEES

The goal of the employee implementation score card is to assess how effectively the employees embraced, participated, and supported the changes. The score card is given in Figure 11.6. Remarks on the specific factors are as follows:

- Number of employees trained.
- Percentage of employees trained.
- Employee turnover during and after change—this indicates both positive and negative factors (e.g., you lose a queen bee).
- Number of surprises in training—surprises can surface during both implementation and training. You might include the types as well.
- Number of surprises in implementation—same as above.

Factor	Score	Comments
Number of employees trained		
Percentage of employees trained		
Employee turnover during and after change		
Number of surprises in training		
Number of surprises in implementation		
Impact of surprises		
Extent of surprises		
Elapsed time to install		
Planned versus schedule		
Planned versus actual cost		
Cost and effort of surprises		
Performance of the change management team		
Willingness of employees to embrace change		

Figure 11.6   Quick Hit Implementation Results Score Card for Employees

- Impact of surprises—this can be financial, morale, structural, etc.
- Extent of surprises— this is the scope or range of surprises.
- Elapsed time to install.
- Planned versus actual schedule.
- Planned versus actual cost.
- Cost and effort of surprises.
- Performance of the change management team.
- Willingness of employees to embrace change—this is subjective and can be estimated by the change management team and supervisors.

QUICK HIT IMPLEMENTATION RESULTS SCORE CARD FOR MANAGERS

The manager implementation score card addresses management and supervisory participation in the Quick Hit implementation work. It is shown in Figure 11.7. Comments are:

- Extent of supervisor involvement—this is critical and should include quality of involvement.
- Degree of support of supervisors for change—this is an overall measure in terms of actions taken by supervisors that indicate support.

Factor	Score	Comments
Extent of supervisor involvement		
Degree of support of supervisors for change		
Extent of management involvement		
Degree of support of managers for change		
Elapsed time for supervisors to resolve issues		
Elapsed time for managers to resolve issues		
Number of issues surfaced		
Number of issues resolved		
Extent of revisions needed		
Enthusiasm of supervisors		
Enthusiasm of managers		
Performance of change management team		

Figure 11.7 Quick Hit Implementation Results Score Card for Managers

- Extent of management involvement—this is a balance between micromanaging and aloofness.
- Degree of support of managers for change—this is an overall measure in terms of actions taken by managers that indicate support.
- Elapsed time for supervisors to resolve issues—this can be an average.
- Elapsed time for managers to resolve issues—same as above.
- Number of issues surfaced—this can also include the type of issues.
- Number of issues resolved—this is a measure of completion.
- Extent of revisions needed—surprises may require revisions.
- Enthusiasm of supervisors—this is subjective and can be estimated by employees and managers.
- Enthusiasm of managers—this can be estimated by supervisors.
- Performance of change management team.

MARKET SUCCESSIVE WAVES OF CHANGE

Once the Quick Hits, it is tempting to think that marketing of the change effort can stop. It can't. Employees who resist change may start rumors that things are not going well. Managers who oppose change and see a power shift may lobby to slow down the pace of change. Trust us these things happen frequently.

It is imperative that you keep key managers informed about status, issues, and progress. You should get them involved in some of the issues. As changes occur, invite managers to visit with employees after the changes have been made and the work has settled down. You want hands-on involvement in addition to formal presentations and informal meetings.

In terms of formal presentations on Quick Hits, here is an outline that we have used many times.

- Summary of the overall change implementation table—gives an overall perspective.
- Quick Hits that are active now—zooms in for detail.
- Results of the implementation planning for the Quick Hits.
- Summary of the issues and problems in the current work—reinforces the need for change.
- Example of a transaction—before and after change—proves the change.
- Benefits from the change—relate to the transaction.
- Surprises and lessons learned—this is often of great interest to the managers who get more insight into the work.

Using these steps management becomes more hands-on without getting in the way of change or micromanaging change.

EXAMPLES

ROCKWOOD COUNTY

The tendency of management was to bypass the planning and implement the changes. However, the problems with this were substantial due to the cross-impacts of changes on each other.

How was this attitude overcome? Examples of impacts and issues in implementation were given to show the effects of lack of planning. A king bee was selected to do. He did this in a monotone, deadpan way so that management was suitably panicked and impacted.

LEGEND MANUFACTURING

Legend management was behind the planning and phasing. They insisted on the lessons learned. As progress was made, there was increasing pressure to speed up the schedule. This was given support by the substantial benefits. However, the employees could only take so much change at once.

POTENTIAL ISSUES AND RISKS

One of the major areas of risk is the resistance by the king and queen bees. When you get to implementation, resistance that was once in the background may now surface. It may not surface openly as a challenge, but as repeated questions. Many change implementation methods stress the importance of getting these people on board. However, this may not always be possible. If you push too hard for their support, you may compromise the changes. Then the successive waves of change may be in jeopardy. Moreover, word will spread that the change effort can be manipulated.

How do you address these people? First, you have them identified through the planning work. Second, you can involve lower level employees in planning first. Then you can bring in the king and queen bees. Both supervisors and employees should be encouraged to support the change and answer any questions that the "bees" raise.

Another situation is that an individual may not openly resist during the planning and implementation. They may just continue to do the work as if there was no change. Supervisors need to oversee these people to detect this. Then the supervisors can step in and take corrective action.

Another area of risk surfaced in the Legend Manufacturing situation. Once it is seen that the Quick Hits work and that there are real benefits, there is often a tendency to speed up the change. As has been pointed out, this can be very disruptive. What is the best way to deal with this? Assume that it will happen and address it in planning with the managers and supervisors. Point out the problems of changing too quickly.

LESSONS LEARNED

- Throughout this chapter there has been a stress on gathering lessons learned. This is important for many reasons. First, it helps further change by making it easier. Second, you show employees that you can learn and adapt to a degree. Third, you can show management what has been learned. Fourth, you ease the way later for long-term change.
- Be willing to modify the schedule for specific changes to a degree. Be more flexible on this if there is a legitimate business reason. However, resist modifying the change itself.
- The change management team should meet amongst themselves to share experience and issues. During implementation it is easy to be drawn into specific detail and for the team to be split up.
- If you have a three shift operation, don't ignore the third shift. You might want to rotate supervisors. You might want to implement the changes one shift at a time. Think of these as options in your planning.

SUMMARY

Implementation of Quick Hits is a proven approach to implement both near and long-term change. If you are successful with Quick Hit planning and implementation, then the installation of longer-term change will be easier and more predictable. A critical success factor is the gathering of lessons learned during this work.

Chapter 12

Carry Out Major Change

INTRODUCTION

You might think that after doing the Quick Hits, you could just plunge in and implement the long-term change. The reality in most cases is different. There is a natural urge to pause. Implementing the Quick Hits took a lot of work. People are tired. The Quick Hits yielded good benefits so management pressure is reduced. Moreover, the employees may have gotten comfortable with the situation and really do not desire more change. For these reasons it is recommended that the following steps be undertaken.

- Determine how far you have to go to get to the long-term change.
- Encourage management to make a direct decision as to whether to go on with the long-term change or stop.
- Update the change implementation plan.

Once you have completed these steps, then you can move ahead with implementation.

MEASURE THE GAP BETWEEN THE LAST QUICK HITS AND THE LONG-TERM CHANGE

The Quick Hits brought you a considerable distance on the road to long-term change. However, you are not there yet. There were surprises along the way. You may have made fewer or more extensive changes than you had originally planned. For these reasons you should sit back and consider the gap between where you are at the end of the Quick Hits and the long-term change.

How do you go about measuring and determining the gap? It is useful to revisit the change implementation strategy or roadmap. As you recall, the rows of the table were divided into two groups. The first group consisted of the areas of change. The second group consisted of impacts such as cost, risk, schedule, benefit, and other factors. Keep the first group of rows as the first column. Create a second column that gives the status of the situation after the Quick Hits. The third column consists of what is needed for long-term change. The fourth column indicates the distance or gap for each row. Figure 12.1 provides an example of this for Rockwood County. The application is to handle calls from the public with questions about county government. An old system was in place that required many manual procedures. The procedures had deteriorated over time.

The Quick Hits focused on cleaning up the procedures, instituting new policies, periodically measuring the performance of the group, installing the network for the new system, installing the hardware and system software. Here are some comments for each area of change.

- Network—in place. It needs to be tuned and adjusted for the new software.
- Hardware—in place. Nothing more is needed.
- Application software for handling calls—acquired, but not yet installed or customized.
- Procedures—manual procedures have been streamlined. However, there will still be substantial change.
- Policies—new policies have been implemented and will have to be modified to fit with the system.
- Performance reporting and tracking—this is done now and then manually. The labor required prohibits any regular performance reporting.
- Staffing changes—none have been implemented. This will wait for the software.

Area of change	After Quick Hits	Long-term change	Gap/distance
Network	In place	Same	Needs to be optimized
Hardware	In place	Same	Nothing
Application software	Acquired	Installed	Need to install software
Procedures for calling	Manual with old system	Automated synchronized with software	Substantial change
Policies for handling calls	In place	Modified somewhat	Slight change for system
Performance reporting and tracking	Manual; occasional	Automated with system	Needs to be implemented
Staffing changes	None	Needs to be done	After installation of system

Figure 12.1 Measuring the Quick Hits Long-Term Gap for Rockwood County

There were some benefits from the Quick Hits. A greater volume of calls could be handled. There was additional training in new policies and procedures that improved the consistency of the application of the policies. However, major benefits await the new system. Using a similar approach you can measure the gap for each change area as well as the overall change.

STOP OR GO ON?

Why even bring this up? Raising this question gives management an out to stop the change. That is precisely what should be done. You want to ensure that management has the will to implement the long-term change. After all, long-term change is disruptive to the employees and customers.

How do you approach this question? Make it a part of the overall change management approach. Formalize it in the method. This will ensure that there is no surprise when it is brought up.

There are a variety of decisions that can be made by management.

- Stop the change effort. Live with the Quick Hits. Declare victory and move on.
- Follow the long-term approach as it was envisioned.
- Modify the long-term approach based upon the experience and lessons learned from the Quick Hits.

What are some of the factors that could influence and affect the decision? Here is a list.

- The elapsed time for the Quick Hits could have been long. Things could have changed in terms of the business situation and management attention. Technology may have changed as well.
- The need for the long-term change may have been affected by external factors such as the business, competition, regulation, etc. Internal factors may also be present. There may be another area that deserves more attention for change management.
- The Quick Hits may have produced over 80–90% of the benefits of those that the long-term solution may yield. There is little point in going on unless the costs are low, the risks are limited, and the schedule is short.
- During the Quick Hits most of the funds required for the long-term solution may have been spent. There is little incremental cost to finish the job.
- The need for the long-term solution may have changed due to the experience with the Quick Hits.

The analysis of the alternatives begins with whether the long-term solution has now changed based upon the additional, new experience and information. You can revisit earlier chapters that developed the long-term scenario for the work. If you determine that there is change that is substantial, then some of the past work must be redone and updated. Benefits, risks, and costs will be updated. A new change implementation strategy will have to be prepared.

The change management team must make the utmost effort to be unbiased in preparing the analysis. The pros and cons for each alternative should be presented. The approach for presenting the analysis results might follow this sequence.

- Summarize the results and lessons learned from the Quick Hits.
- Present the gap analysis in the previous section so that management understands where they are now versus the long-term solution.
- Indicate whether the long-term solution has changed based upon the experience.
- If there is change, then the modified and updated change implementation strategy is presented.
- Present the advantages and disadvantages of going ahead or stopping.

Figure 12.2 gives lists of factors that affect the decision. If the decision is made to stop, then a political story must be prepared for the employees and managers. The change management team needs to be either disbanded or redirected. The most common story is that since most of the benefits have been achieved, there is little point in incurring the additional cost and effort and pain to go on. Management would also indicate that the decision would be revisited in 6 months to a year.

Advantages in going ahead

- Morale will drop if the effort is stopped.
- There are substantial benefits to the long-term solution.
- The long-term solution is still valid. Stick with the plan and go ahead.
- The job should be finished.
- Change management will fall into disrepute if the effort is halted.
- There are no more pressing areas that require attention or the resources.
- The incremental cost of completion is small.
- The time to complete the work is limited.
- The risk in completion is manageable.
- There are adequate resources to finish the job.

Disadvantages in going ahead

- People are tired of change. They need a rest.
- There is substantial risk still ahead in implementing the long-term solution.
- There is substantial cost still ahead in implementing the long-term solution.
- There are more pressing areas that require change.
- The gap between the Quick Hit results and long-term solution is very small.
- The gap between the Quick Hit results and long-term solution is too large.
- The Quick Hit implementation did not go well.
- There was high turnover in the change management team. There is a lack of experience.
- The technology or other factors have changed significantly so it pays to wait.

Figure 12.2   Advantages and Disadvantages in Going Ahead with the Long-Term Change

For Rockwood County you can see from the table in Figure 12.1 that most of the expense has already been incurred. The software, hardware, and network have all been acquired. The remaining costs are labor hours. Moreover, the long-term solution offers many substantial benefits over the situation at the end of the Quick Hits. Thus, there is a substantial gap. These factors clearly indicate that Rockwood County should finish the implementation. They did.

REVIEW AND UPDATE THE CHANGE IMPLEMENTATION PLAN

With the decision to go ahead, you next move to update the change implementation plan for the long-term change. Here is where there will probably be substantial change based upon the experiences and lessons learned of the Quick Hit implementation. Each situation is unique. However, there are some guidelines that can prove to be useful.

- Review the tasks of the implementation plan. Look for missing tasks given the experience. Typically, there will be missing tasks in dealing with exceptions, etc.
- Revisit the change implementation team. Some employees may not have panned out and may need to be replaced. Make any necessary changes.
- Analyze the list of implementation issues and see if there have been changes or additions. This will probably then impact the tasks for the work.
- Evaluate the dependencies between tasks in the implementation plan based upon the lessons learned from the Quick Hits. There may be more opportunities to implement change in parallel.
- Have the team members now review the tasks, dependencies, and issues. They may want to add more detailed tasks. The project leaders then review the results.
- Work in a collaborative way to estimate the duration of the tasks. A tip here is not to start with a copy of the old plan. Start from the beginning and re-estimate the duration of the tasks. This approach will prevent people from just copying over the old durations.

The overall schedule will likely have changed. It could be longer or shorter. Figure 12.3 lists potential influences on the schedule. This is not a complete list. You can probably add even more.

When you made the changes and updates to the plan, you are ready to present it to the management. Here is an outline for the change implementation plan presentation.

- Experience shows that the employees are supportive of change or more resistant to change.
- There is additional, unplanned work in doing facility modification.
- There is more work to modify and implement the system.
- New technology has appeared that will be part of the long-term solution.
- There are additional or fewer changes needed in terms of policies and procedures.
- Based upon experience, there will have to be more or less training required.

Figure 12.3   Potential Influences on the Updated Change Implementation Plan

- Summarize the items that have changed since the original plan was developed.
- Indicate how the new plan was developed. This will give management confidence in the results if there was substantial collaboration and participation.
- Present the high level tasks and milestones of the new plan along with the schedule.
- Identify the potential areas of risk and uncertainty to the schedule along with the assumptions used.
- Go into an assessment of costs.
- Review the roles and responsibilities.

Why do the last step? The review is necessary to review what the management's role will be. Some managers may assume that their main responsibilities ended with the Quick Hits. You want to politically show that the role continues and that more issues lie ahead. This approach will provide sufficient opportunity for management to review and comment on the detailed plan.

CREATE TEAMWORK AND A TEAM SPIRIT

One issue regarding the team is to assess the team members involved in the Quick Hits and see if changes are needed. Some employees may be burned out from the effort. Others must return to their normal work. If the Quick Hit implementation went on for a substantial time, the core change management team may need to be changed as well. Some team members may not have performed adequately. Remember too that the implementation of the long-term solution is different and more demanding than that of Quick Hits. Another factor in replacement is that a team member could have acquired too many political enemies.

How do you undertake team member replacement? First, have the core change management team meet to review the employees who participated. See if you can get consensus about each of them. For each person that the team wants to replace, answer the following questions:

- What are political issues in returning the employee to the department full-time?
- Is there a suitable replacement person with similar knowledge and experience?
- What is the political fall-out if the person is returned to the department?
- What would be the estimated learning curve to get the new person up to speed?

There need not be a one for one replacement. You could replace someone with two or more employees on a part-time basis.

Next, someone must go to the department manager and get approval for a change. In doing this you want to begin by laying out the requirements of what is needed for the long-term change. Indicate that the person currently assigned has been spending a great deal of time on the Quick Hits and that you are sensitive to this. Also, point out that the department work probably has been affected by this person's absence. Then move on to suggest one or more people who might be suitable. Hopefully, this should work. If the manager resists, then you may have to go into the problems with the person continuing on the team.

Now that you have identified and gotten the team members for the long-term solution in place, the next action is to get them involved in activities together. In that way will you create a team spirit. The first opportunity is to get the team members involved in defining the detailed tasks. Use the guidelines in Chapter 10. Each new team member should be paired with a remaining team member.

Another activity is to have project leaders give short presentations on where their parts stand in relation to the long-term change. This gives them a more complete and detailed picture of what is ahead.

With these tasks completed, you can move to implementation issues. Have the team review the existing list of implementation issues. New members can indicate how these issues might be addressed.

IMPLEMENT THE CHANGES

As was stated several times, the exact implementation depends upon the situation. A typical situation is that the long-term change involves automation. The Quick Hits are the steps leading up to the installation of the application software system. Specific comments on implementation of systems as well as E-Business appear in Chapters 15 and 16, respectively.

Another case involves outsourcing. Then the Quick Hits were the efforts to clean up the process and work in preparation for outsourcing. For this situation, there must be a clear understanding of what will happen to the employees. This must be effectively communicated to them.

There are several approaches for implementation. There are three basic ones: pilot approach, parallel approach, and total change-over approach. There are advantages and disadvantages to each that are discussed below.

PILOT APPROACH TO IMPLEMENTATION

Here you would implement the changes in one unit first. This is a pilot approach. By testing out the new system and process in one group, you can shake it down and then roll it to other areas. If you were to pursue this course of action, you would gather lessons learned after this initial implementation and then use these with the next group. You can also use some of the employees from the first group to assist in implementation with other groups.

The pilot approach has several advantages, including:

- If there are problems, they are of limited impact and scope.
- There is limited risk since only a small area is affected.
- The overall implementation can be accomplished sequentially or in parallel after the pilot.
- There is greater time and flexibility to deal with issues.

However, there are also disadvantages to the pilot approach. Some of the major ones are the following:

- The elapsed time to implement the new process is long since you must not only undertake the pilot, but also learn from that, make modifications, and then continue the roll-out.
- The pilot approach is not suited to operations in which there is a great deal of integration between activities and processes. Making a change in one group means that the interfaces to other groups must be changed. However, the other groups are still working with the Quick Hits version of the process.
- There may be substantial differences between different groups so that what is learned in one group from the pilot may not be applicable to others.

The pilot approach is best suited to situations in which there are multiple locations that are performing the same or very similar work. It is least suited to firms in which processes are tightly interrelated.

IMPLEMENT THE CHANGES IN PARALLEL

Alternatively, you can implement the changes in parallel to the existing process. This is done in accounting systems most frequently. It is very expensive. In information systems it was widely used over 20–30 years ago when systems were more limited. It is used rarely today. Some of the problems that arise are:

- There is much more effort required.
- The same people may be needed in both efforts.
- There is a shortage of people who have knowledge and can go the work.
- Just thinking that you can do duplicate work raises issues about costs and organization.

However, there are some advantages, including:

- There is immediate fall-back if there is a problem. You just revert to the old process.
- There is an opportunity to speed up or slow down the transition to the new process.

Overall, the parallel approach is not practical for most business processes. Even in cases where the parallel approach is taken, the time for the parallel effort is very short—a day to a week—no more. It is most suited to situations in which there are very complex and intricate business rules.

USE THE "BIG BANG" APPROACH FOR CHANGE IMPLEMENTATION

Here you implement the changes all at once. This is the "big bang" approach. It can be successful or it can result in true disaster. A leading retailer implemented a major system that way. It did not work. There were many dissatisfied customers. Sales dropped substantially. The company had to take a big loss in one quarter. It took several years to recover.

With that said, it is still a common approach. Here are some reasons for using the "big bang" approach.

- It may be the only feasible method for accomplishing change. It is the best of unattractive options.
- It completes the change-over to the new process in the least time.
- Disruption generally is limited to the change-over and a "settling down" period.

Disadvantages include the following:

- Much greater coordination is required.
- Continuous monitoring of work is needed to detect any problems.
- Management must be on hand to make decisions about any issues that arise.
- It may be necessary to create workarounds, exceptions, and shadow systems to fix problems temporarily. However, temporary things have a habit of becoming permanent.

In order to carry out this approach, you need a slow period of business so that you can recover from problems quickly. You also must have managers, IT staff, and others in addition to the change implementation team on standby in case of problems.

PERFORM TRADE-OFFS IN SELECTING THE IMPLEMENTATION APPROACH

The choice among these is not simple. Some firms have employed a combination approach. That is, they carry out a pilot. In the pilot, they do a very limited parallel implementation to ensure that everything works. Then they drop the parallel and complete the pilot. At the end of the pilot, they do the "big bang" approach.

Some of the things to consider in making the decision are:

- Existence of a cyclical down time of business for cut-over
- Staff availability to support the implementation
- Interdependence among processes and work
- Extent to which you can fallback to the old process in the event of major problems
- Availability and willingness of management to deal with issues and problems and to make decisions quickly during implementation

STEPS IN THE IMPLEMENTATION OF MAJOR CHANGE

Having discussed approaches, we can turn our attention to the specific activities. Of course, there are all of the ones involved in Quick Hits. After all, major change is a superset of Quick Hits. Without repeating these here are some of the major activities along with some observations and comments.

- Data conversion. Information has to be converted from the old process and system to the new. This is normally not part of Quick Hits. There are many problems in data conversion that are discussed in Chapter 15.
- Testing of the new process. This is necessary to ensure that the system works in conjunction with the new process, that the business rules are implemented properly and correctly, that the system is reasonable to use, and that the system performs satisfactorily.
- Completion and testing of networks, communications, and facilities.
- Training of the employees in the new process and system.

- System and process interfaces and integration.
- Preparation of documentation—operating procedures for the system, procedures for the process and users, training materials, and troubleshooting guidelines.

DETERMINE CUT-OVER

It is almost unbelievable, but sometimes people do not consider the exact turnover to the new process and the cut-off of the old. Another related factor is the archival or destruction of the old. Isn't the timing automatic? You really do not know when this should be accomplished until you are deep in the implementation. Only then will you have sufficient knowledge to deal with this decision.

What happens when you cut-over? You stop using the old process and system. You only work with the new one. There is little opportunity or inclination to go back.

Here are some things to consider in cut-over timing.

- Training has to be completed.
- The data that will be used has been validated that it is sufficient, accurate, and complete.
- All interfaces work properly.
- The system is tested.
- There has been advance given to employees, customers, and/or suppliers that change is coming.

Most often, the cut-over comes as soon after training as possible. Otherwise, employees tend to forget the new process as they continue to work with the old. Normally, you select a very slow time or weekend to do the cut-over.

After the cut-over, you will monitor the work, measure the results, and deal with lingering problems and issues. These are discussed below. However, it is important to root out and slay the old process. Notice the words used. We could have used "put away" or "store." Those don't work politically. You have to symbolically destroy the old process so that people know there is no going back. In one case, we destroyed the old documentation in a shredder in front of employees. In other, where fire was permitted, the documentation was burned.

Here are some steps in killing off the old work and process.

- Remove and destroy all manuals and training materials.
- Remove any computer or office equipment that was used by the old process and not necessary for the new.
- Visit all work locations and collect "cheat sheets," yellow sticky notes, etc. that people have around for the old system and process.
- Have people clean out their desks and offices.
- Put up new posters, guidelines, etc. for the new process.
- Put up a poster indicating the date of birth and death of the old process.

COPE WITH RESISTANCE TO MAJOR CHANGE

Ah, here we are—back at resistance. This has been present in every chapter. You might think that most of the resistance was dealt with and overcome in the last chapter with the implementation of Quick Hits. But that is seldom the case. If there were problems during the Quick Hits, then there may be more resistance to further change. In addition, some people can deal with small change, but have much more problems with major change.

By now you have identified employees who are likely to resist change. Don't make the mistake and assume that this is the end of it. Assume that there will be more. That way you will be safe and not be taken by surprise.

Let's turn to preparation for the change in anticipation of resistance. You will want to hold meetings with employees and their supervisors to go over the plan for the long-term change. You will want to generate desire for the long-term change beyond the benefits to the overall organization. Here you should focus on the remaining problems and issues in the work even after the Quick Hits that will be addressed by the long-term change. Encourage the employees to discuss these issues and problems. Show that doing more Quick Hits will not resolve the problems.

Quick Hits do not tend to eliminate jobs. Long-term change, on the other hand, enables management in some cases to downsize. This is another reason that there may be more resistance now. It is very important to meet with Human Resources management to discuss the situation. You should first get from them an understanding of what they think will happen with staffing in the new process and work. If they believe that there are substantial savings, then you must emphasize that there is a need for a policy and position that will help in the implementation of long-term change. From experience it is suggested that there be no layoffs during or immediately after implementation. Here are some reasons that you can provide to Human Resources.

- No one really knows about the staffing requirements or job duties exactly until the new process is in place. This is true since there are still unpredictable things in implementation.
- Making changes to staffing during implementation could easily and most likely disturb the implementation—having a potentially devastating effect.
- No one knows which employees should be retained or let go. If you make some general announcement, then it is possible that the best employees will leave—remaining will be a collection of gnomes and trolls.

However, you must suggest an approach. Here is a useful one. When it is evident that someone is redundant, then have additional work assignments ready for them. Get them out of the department so that the implementation can continue. They will not disrupt the operation of the department. Another idea is to rely in part on attrition. Some people may not like the new system or process and want to transfer. Human Resources should be ready for this.

All of this is to prevent what occurs too often. People make major changes to processes without thinking through the exact staffing implications. Then when the impact occurs, a mess of a situation arises. Why don't people plan better? We think that a major reason is that people have been told about major impacts and changes and then they never occurred. This is the flip side to the promised labor savings of new systems that never materialized.

DEAL WITH LINGERING ISSUES

There are always lingering issues and problems that exist when there is major change. Here are some of the most common.

- There are workarounds and exceptions that are still present or were created during implementation.
- Some additional enhancements and additions to software are needed.
- There may be shadow systems that have to be addressed.
- There could still be remnants of the old process present.

It is important that both management and the change management team stay around to deal with this. The change implementation teams can be disbanded after lessons learned are gathered. The problem here is that:

If lingering issues are not addressed, there can be
midinstallation paralysis.

This is not an infrequent curse in change management. People think that the work is done and success is declared. In reality a mess is created of the old and new. Productivity declines and the benefits of the new process and work are not realized.

How do you deal with lingering issues? Create a list of these along with a schedule and assignment of responsibility. Identify for each what is necessary for cleanup. Create a project plan, if necessary, to get these done if there are a substantial number.

MEASURE CHANGE RESULTS

The next chapter is concerned with overall measurement of change in mostly quantitative. Here we discuss some of the major steps involved in measurement in qualitative terms.

You could go around and ask what people think about the new process and work. Often, they will be too intimidated to say much except for general positive comments. There are better approaches. Go back to Chapter 7 where there were guidelines for data collection. Use these here.

Here are some measurements that you should make.

- Extent, range, number, and impact of lingering issues
- Existence of shadow systems and exceptions

- Degree of acceptance by employees of the new process
- Number and type of new problems that surface

USE THE CHANGE IMPLEMENTATION SCORE CARDS

There are four of these in Figures 12.4–12.7. They deal with four perspectives of change: employee, management, process, and change management. Let's address each of these in succession.

EMPLOYEE SCORE CARD

The employee score is intended to measure the performance of the employees during implementation of the long-term changes. Figure 12.4 presents the score card. Specific comments are as follows:

- Percentage of total employees involved in implementation—this should be very high.
- Employee involvement in procedures—there should be intensive involvement since the procedures are so important.

Factor	Score	Comments
Percentage of total employees involved in implementation		
Employee involvement in procedures		
Employee involvement in training materials		
Employee involvement in training		
Number of surprises during implementation		
Degree of help in resolving issues		
Elapsed time of implementation		
Involvement of employees in resolving issues		
Involvement of employees in dealing with problems		
Participation with other employees		
Degree of support for change		

Figure 12.4 Employee Score Card for Implementation

Factor	Score	Comments
Average time for management to resolve an issue		
Number of management issues		
Involvement of management in change		
Commitment of management to change		
Support by management of change effort		
Effort in resolving resource allocation problems		
Percentage of managers involved in change		
Budget versus actual cost		
Schedule versus actual time		
Number of surprises		
Impact of surprises		

Figure 12.5   Management Score Card for Implementation

- Employee involvement in training materials—same as above.
- Employee involvement in training—the employees should participate in both initial and ongoing training.
- Number of surprises during implementation—by now this should be low. If it is substantial, then there are probably problems in the change process.
- Degree of help in resolving issues—employees should participate and own issues.
- Elapsed time of implementation—employee participation affects elapsed time of implementation.
- Involvement of employees in resolving issues—degree of help refers to depth of help; involvement indicates the range of participation.
- Involvement of employees in dealing with problems—this is the extent to which employees provide solutions to problems.
- Participation with other employees—this is a measure of interaction among employees.
- Degree of support for change—this measures the support for change.

MANAGEMENT SCORE CARD

The management score card is designed to assess management performance (see Figure 12.5). Remarks on the elements of the score card are as follows:

- Average time for management to resolve an issue—from before.
- Number of management issues—this indicates how many issues surfaced during implementation that required management involvement.

Factor	Score	Comments
Benefits from process change		
Incremental benefits from long-term change		
Issues that arose during implementation		
Number of shadow systems handled		
Number of shadow systems remaining		
Number of exceptions handled		
Number of exceptions remaining		
Number of workarounds handled		
Number of workarounds remaining		
Average time to handle a transaction		
Volume of work addressed		
Customer/supplier satisfaction		
Availability of measurements of process		
Number and type of lingering issues		
Flexibility of the change management process		
Adequacy of the change management process		
Completeness of the change management process		

Figure 12.6   Process Score Card for Implementation

- Involvement of management in change—this is a measure of involvement.
- Commitment of management to change—this is indicated by the degree and involvement of management in change.
- Support by management of change effort—this is measured not by involvement, but by actions taken.
- Effort in resolving resource allocation problems—this specifically relates to dealing with personnel issues.
- Percentage of managers involved in change—this measures the degree of commitment of management overall.
- Budget versus actual cost.
- Schedule versus actual time.

Factor	Score	Comments
Overall quality of team effort		
Extent and quality of lessons learned		
Organization of lessons learned		
Use of lessons learned		
Extent of cooperation and collaboration among team		
Average time to resolve issues		
Number of surprises addressed		
Average time to address a surprise		
Problem resolution ability		
Teamwork		
Cost performance		
Schedule performance		
Turnover of team members		
Lessons learned for future efforts		

Figure 12.7 Change Management Score Card for Implementation

- Number of surprises—this is partially due to management.
- Impact of surprise—management should work to mitigate the impact of surprises.

PROCESS SCORE CARD

The process score card is probably the most important in that it relates to results of the change.

- Benefits from process change—this can be measured in a number of dimensions as indicated in the next chapter.
- Incremental benefits from long-term change—this is the difference measure from the Quick Hits.
- Issues that arose during implementation—this is an indication of the condition of the process.
- Number of shadow systems handled—hopefully, this number will be large.
- Number of shadow systems remaining—this number should be small.
- Number of exceptions handled—similar to above.
- Number of exceptions remaining—similar to above.
- Number of workarounds handled—similar to above.

- Number of workarounds remaining—similar to above.
- Average time to handle a transaction—this should improve.
- Volume of work addressed—increases should occur here as well.
- Customer/supplier satisfaction—this can be measured by volume and type of complaints.
- Availability of measurements of process.
- Number and type of lingering issues.
- Flexibility of the change management process.
- Adequacy of the change management process.
- Completeness of the change management process.

CHANGE MANAGEMENT SCORE CARD

The change management score card measures both the performance of the change management team and the change management process. Comments on the elements of the score card are as follows:

- Overall quality of team effort
- Extent and quality of lessons learned
- Organization of lessons learned
- Use of lessons learned
- Extent of cooperation and collaboration among team
- Average time to resolve issues
- Number of surprises addressed
- Average time to address a surprise
- Problem resolution ability
- Teamwork
- Cost performance
- Schedule performance
- Turnover of team members
- Lessons learned for future efforts

MARKET THE CHANGE RESULTS

Aren't the benefits obvious? Yes, but people tend to take them for granted after a short time. Hence, you must market the benefits of the new process. You also have to market the change management process. It worked successfully.

There are some specific tips for marketing. One is to give credit to the employees. Involve them in management presentations. Another is to focus on the lessons that were learned. This will show details. Document several specific transactions before and after change and publicize these. This will back up the benefits.

EXAMPLES

ROCKWOOD COUNTY

The pilot approach was used to implement a new dispatching process and system at the operations bases of the county. Rockwood County has four major bases. Each operates semi-autonomously at the detailed level. This made it possible to implement in one location while leaving the other ones alone. Moreover, the detailed operations performed at each county base were the same. Thus, what was learned and done at one location could be applied to the other three. The approach described above was employed successfully. What was even more successful was that the staff of the first base who were involved in the roll-out to the second base could provide information on the system and its benefits. They could also calm fears and give detailed guidelines to the next group of employees.

Due to resource limitations it was not possible to roll-out the new process to the remaining three bases at the same time. Therefore, the approach was to do a sequential roll-out. That is, each base was installed in order. The experiences learned in the installation at later bases was also rolled back to the first base. The training approach was to use the people from the first base to train the second, to use the people at the second base to train the third, and so on. This provides an opportunity for much more widespread involvement and commitment of employees.

LEGEND MANUFACTURING

Legend considered all three methods of implementation. The pilot one was not suitable since the operations and processes of Legend were highly integrated. Doing a parallel approach was totally infeasible due to cost and limited resources. Thus, the "big bang" approach was selected.

In preparation for the change-over, there was extensive training and communications among implementation teams. A slow period and long weekend were chosen for the change-over to minimize any impact on sales and service. There were intensive simulations of the processes and what would happen. The new software system was extensively tested and retested. Training materials were tested. It was decided to train a core of employees in each department. Then, using the train-the-trainer method, these employees with assistance from the change implementation team and change management team trained the remaining staff in each department.

The implementation was successful, but it was also gut-wrenching. There were several times when implementation was held up by an issue. Management devoted themselves 100% to addressing these issues right away. In two cases, the decisions had to be changed after implementation.

POTENTIAL ISSUES AND RISKS

- A major issue may arise if the software system that is to be installed does not meet the needs required by the new work. It may be several months before those issues are addressed. What do you do in the meantime? One option is to fall back to the situation that existed at the end of the Quick Hits. However, this may not be possible since there have been additional changes that cannot be easily undone.

  Another option is to implement modified procedures or policies to deal with the shortcomings of the system. The system may still go live, but there will be restrictions or limitations on use.

  A third option is to implement workarounds and shadow systems that get around the shortcomings of the new system. This is often the best course since at least the problems are being addressed consistently.
- The information that the employees work with was converted, but it turns out to be faulty, in error, or incomplete. This is not a rare occurrence. Then you have to make a decision on what action to take.

LESSONS LEARNED

A basic point here is to gather extensive lessons learned and experience as you go. You can use the methods described in the preceding chapter. Here though you go beyond just identifying them and organizing them for current work. You want to gather lessons learned to do the following:

- Improve your approach for change management.
- Establish measurement methods for ongoing use.
- Create a lessons learned database for use in subsequent change efforts.
- Create an atmosphere that encourages sharing of information and knowledge about processes.

You see, a major benefit of undertaking change is that you can change and impact the culture of the organization through a change effort. What you hope to accomplish is that employees and managers will be more open in discussing process problems and opportunities. They will be more willing to invent Quick Hits to improve the situation. They will be less reluctant to just sit there and do the work and assume that no change is possible. That is what change management is all about.

Through participating in a change effort, employees will become supporters of change and improvement.

SUMMARY

Even with the Quick Hits, the implementation of long-term change can be very stressful and demanding. It is here that employees often have the greatest sense of anxiety and fear. Moreover, there can be additional problems in the implementation of systems that cause the implementation to falter or be delayed—jeopardizing the overall change effort. With that said, the Quick Hits provided experience to the change implementation team as well as the change management team so that they are more prepared to deal with issues and problems.

Chapter 13

Measure Results and Generate Enthusiasm and Support

INTRODUCTION

Measurements are necessary at multiple points in change management for the processes, including:

- At the start when selecting what work to change
- In detailed analysis of the process selected
- For the new process or work that will replace the long-term existing one
- For each stage or phase of Quick Hits
- After all Quick Hits have been implemented
- At the onset of the long-term change
- After the long-term changes have been made
- On an ongoing basis

It is essential that a consistent approach be adopted for measurement. However, there are also differences due to the individual situation and timing.

Going beyond the process, you want to measure other aspects of change management as was done in some of the previous chapters. These include:

- IT involvement
- Business employee involvement
- Management and supervisor involvement
- Vendor and consultant support and involvement
- The change management team

- Project management of change
- The change management process

All of these are covered in this chapter.

However, measurement does not end here. All through the change management effort there was an effort to gather, organize, and use lessons learned. Measurement links to lessons learned as both can be employed to improve the change management process as well as the results. Issues and lessons learned are intertwined. Prevention of process deterioration and reversion are discussed in the next chapter where issues are addressed.

All of this represents substantial initial and ongoing effort. There must be a hub or center for coordination. This is similar to having a project office for project management or having a strategic planning group for business planning. That is why we identify and cover the role of measurement and process coordinator. It is much more than a casual activity.

GOALS AND APPROACH TO MEASUREMENT

You measure something to find out what is going on. Then you may have to take actions to correct a situation. You may do nothing. You may take further measurements. Most of the time you want to either leave something alone or collect more information. The problem is that sometimes measurement triggers people to take actions. Then the actions are not thought through and the situation worsens as a result. Consider a simple example. Many parents in some countries rush children with colds to a doctor for antibiotics. This is done at the first sign of a cold—a measurement. The child then becomes overtreated with antibiotics. When the child really gets sick, the antibiotics have limited benefit.

The lesson learned here is that you have to define more than just what to measure and how to measure as part of measurement. Here are some specific components of a measurement process.

- *Goals of measurement.* There should be technical, business, and political objectives.
- *Definition of a measurement process.* This begins with data collection and proceeds through analysis of the data, presentations of results, and taking actions.
- *Structure of measurements to be taken.* Here you determine what, when, why, who, and how of measurement.

GOALS AND CONSTRAINTS OF MEASUREMENT

There are three types of goals: technical, business, and political. In change management, the technical goal is to collect the information that satisfies the

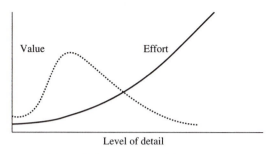

Figure 13.1 Trade-offs in Measurement

business and political goals, is of high quality, but has the least cost and impact on the work. There are trade-offs here as revealed in Figure 13.1. In this figure the horizontal axis reveals the level of detail of measurement. There are two lines. The solid one shows the rapidly escalating effort required to do the measurement; the dotted one shows the value of the measurement. There is little value in collecting only a small amount of information. After some level of detail, the value diminishes due to the amount of information and potential negative impact on the process. There is also the Heisenberg uncertainty principle that applies here in that when you observe a process or work too closely (shine a light into space), you disturb the process and affect productivity (you disturb the particles).

The business objectives for change management measurement are: (1) ensure that the work or process has not deteriorated or reverted back; (2) identify potential additional activities for change; (3) give management sufficient understanding of what is going on in the work to determine if resources or other actions are needed.

There are political goals to measurement that are often neglected. However, these are critical for change management. A primary goal to provide evidence that change management works in that the changes are effective. Another goal is to support the management, supervisors, and employees who provided sustenance for the change effort. A third objective is to support standardized measurements for key processes for control and planning purposes.

However, there are also constraints that limit the goals and measurements themselves. Examples are:

- *Systems.* Measurements are limited by the existing systems that can capture measurement data in an automated form.
- *Information.* The type, level of detail, validity, and amount of data available is a constricting factor in measurement.
- *Resources.* Measurements are restricted by the resources made available.
- *Schedule.* There is a limited amount of time to collect and analyze the information.
- *Management expectations.* Management typically sets goals for any measurements in terms of their expectations.

- *Process*. The actual work constrains the measurement in terms of what is possible.
- *Facilities and geography*. The location and facilities for the work may restrict what can be done by measurement.

DEFINITION OF A MEASUREMENT PROCESS FOR CHANGE MANAGEMENT

In organizing a formal measuring process, you can proceed by steps.

- *Step 1*. Define the goals of measurement. This was discussed above.
- *Step 2*. Determine how measurements will be employed.

With defined goals you can now move to the end of the measurement process and ask how measurements will be used. For change management, the applications include the following groups. For the process itself you have:

— Assess the effectiveness of employees in doing the work
— Review the performance of managers and supervisors in overseeing the work
— Determine the effectiveness of systems and technology
— Identify any additional steps within the work that is needed

For multiple processes there are additional applications of measurements.

— Perform comparative analysis among processes
— Assess the effectiveness of organizations through their processes
— Make decisions overall on the direction of the change management effort
— Be able to perform benchmarking with other firms and industry statistics

- *Step 3*. Identify what measurements are necessary to achieve the goals along with the details of measurement. This is discussed in the next section.
- *Step 4*. Conduct a simulation or modeling of the measurement process to ascertain if the approach is practical.

Once you have identified the details in the previous steps, there is often a tendency to implement the measurements. However, you must see how the entire measurement mosaic will work in practice. This is best performed through simulation in meetings with employees, supervisors, information technology (IT), and managers.

- *Step 5*. Implement the measurement process.

Implementation goes beyond manual data collection. You really want the systems to collect and even perform initial analysis on as much of the information as possible. Thus, there may have to be changes to the systems to collect, aggregate, organize, analyze, and report on the measurements.

Employees and managers should be provided with some overview training on the measurement process. This has the political advantage of removing the fear factor. It will also result in less disruption to the work.

After implementation, there may have to be tuning or refinement of the measurement process. Additional information may be needed. Some information might be dropped. The analysis methods may be changed.

STRUCTURE OF MEASUREMENTS

In planning and conducting any sort of measurement, there are some basic questions that have to be addressed to support the goals.

- What information is required for measurement? This can be wide ranging and consist of both subjective and objective information.
- What is the best source of the information in terms of accuracy, quality, and completeness? There may be multiple systems or sources of data. In general, you want to employ systems as much as possible to reduce manual effort and error.
- When should the data be collected? You can collect data on either a periodic or on a demand basis, or both. Frequency of collection impacts the cost.
- What is the least expensive method for collecting and analyzing the information? Every measurement costs something for collection, retention, and analysis.
- How should information be collected? You can employ systems. You can use questionnaires. You can contact a sample of individuals or use meetings or focus groups.
- Where will information be collected? If you are dealing with multiple locations such as factories, branches, or stores, then you must define which are to be measured.
- How will the information be organized and retained for use over time? You will undoubtedly want to perform longitudinal analysis over time as your database of measurements builds up.
- Who should collect and analyze the information? This is important since it relates directly to the cost of the effort and available resources. This also supports the establishment of an ongoing coordination role.
- How will measurements be sustained over time? You can make a big one time push to collect information, but you also have to consider the ongoing effort.

Again, these are all trade-offs. You should identify several alternative measurements that can be compared. Here you can prepare a table for the alternatives that you have identified. Use the table in Figure 13.2. In this figure the columns are the alternatives. The rows are divided into two parts. The first collection of

Alternatives

Areas of measurement		
Process/work		
IT and systems		
Employees		
Management		
Vendors/consultants		
Facilities and layout		
Performance measures of alternative		
Cost of measurement		
Extent of data provided		
Human resource demands		
Ability to address ad hoc management requests		
Effort to implement		
Elapsed time and schedule to implement		
Elapsed time and schedule to use		

Figure 13.2   Table of Alternative Measurement Approaches

rows characterizes the measurements. The second collection defines what can be done, benefits, costs, and risks.

GENERAL MEASUREMENT OF BUSINESS PROCESSES

Let's examine three areas for measuring processes and work.

INFORMATION REQUIRED FOR MEASUREMENT

You can divide up the information into these categories.

- Performance—this relates to how the work is performed. This represents the output side of the measurement. Elements can include:
  — Cost of the process. This is more meaningful than just IT or systems costs.
  — Sales generated by the process. This may not be applicable to a process.
  — Throughput or volume of work handled in a specific time period.
  — Response time. This is the average time to do the work.
  — Shadow systems. Here you can measure the number, the dependence of the work on them, the condition of the shadow systems (documentation, stability, etc.).
  — Exceptions. This can include the number, percent of volume in exceptions, percent of work in exception handling.

— Workarounds. Similar to exceptions and shadow systems.
— Stability in handling peak and trough workloads.
— Number of complaints and/or errors noted in a specific time period.
— Responsiveness and flexibility in handling new types of work.
- Resources—these are ingredients that support the work. These are the input for the process and include:
  — Employees
  — Policies and procedures
  — IT and systems
  — Facilities and layout
  — External factors, systems, and processes. This measures the interfaces between this work and other processes and systems in the same groups and other organizations within and external to the firm.
  — Vendors and consultant involvement.
- Management—this is the oversight, direction, and supervision of the work. Elements are the following:
  — Ability to handle and address issues and problems
  — Results in dealing with lessons learned and opportunities
  — Involvement in the change effort
  — Ongoing involvement in the processes and work

SOURCES OF INFORMATION

Where to get the data depends upon the specific situation. However, with systems support, the basic performance information should be available through the system. The system should be designed to capture transaction information on what happened and when and record it in a database. An example for the customer information process for Rockwood County appears in Figure 13.3. This is not a complete list, but it gives you some idea of what is needed. The customer information process handles calls from the public about the county services.

It is not possible for the supporting system to provide all of the data. Therefore, you must expand your search. You can go to the finance and accounting group and obtain cost information. Marketing can provide sales information, if applicable.

Now you can turn to manual data collection. You can collect information in several ways, including:

- Individual interviews using questionnaires with employees. This can be done but it diverts them from their work and may slant the answer due to the formal nature of the method.
- Focus groups or meetings of employees. Here you can provide a checklist of areas and get their observations, concerns, ideas, and opinions. This is

Data	Source
Number of calls from public	Telephone system
Number of completed calls	Telephone system
Number of dropped calls	Telephone system
Number of abandoned calls	Telephone system
Origination of calls by zip code	Telephone system
Number of calls in a specific language	System
Number of calls handled	System
Number of calls handled per employee	System
Average time per call	System
Average time per call per employee	System
Average number of screens accessed	System
Number of calls by type of request	System
Volume of materials mailed by type	System
Most difficult or complex requests	Focus group
Problems and issues	Focus group
Ideas for improvement	Focus group
Total cost of systems	IT and accounting
Total cost of process	Accounting/finance
Facilities and layout	Accounting/finance
Issue tracking	Change and process coordination

Figure 13.3   Example of Data for Customer Information at Rockwood County. (Listed below are data elements and comments on the source for selected data elements.)

extremely valuable since it provides insight into what is behind the measurements.

- Direct observation of the work. Here you visit the work location and gather information informally.

The best approach often is to do the focus groups and meetings augmented by limited direct observation. The direct observation can validate what is said in the focus group and also allows you to investigate what is behind some of the measurements.

TIMING OF INFORMATION COLLECTION

When should you collect process information? From previous chapters, here is a list.

- Limited measurement when a process is being considered as a change candidate
- Detailed measurement for the selected work prior to change when you are in the planning stage

- Detailed measurement at the onset of Quick Hit implementation
- Detailed measurement several times after stages of Quick Hit implementation
- Detailed measurement after the new, changed work is in place
- Periodic detailed measurement on an annual or semiannual basis
- Reactive measurement to address a specific issue or directive

MEASURING IT INVOLVEMENT AND PARTICIPATION

A process or work is supported by one or more systems. The systems are in turn sustained by:

- IT staff for operations and network support
- IT programmers for maintenance, enhancement, and operations support
- IT support for systems analysis
- IT management for handling issues and directing the support

Specific measurements along with comments on sources are given in Figure 13.4. Some people give too much importance to these statistics over the others. This is often due to IT management using the information that they have. There is a basic point here that is:

IT is only a part of the process unless the work is completely automated.

After all, you can have a process which is falling apart and where the systems are working flawlessly.

Information	Source
Number of outstanding problems	IT management
Average time to handle a problem	IT management
Number of problems by type	IT management
Overall cost of IT support	IT management
Availability of system	Network and Operations
Average response time	Network and Operations
Total volume of transactions	Operations
Total transactions by type	Operations
Worse response time	Operations
IT resource usage by type (programming, etc.)	IT management
Number of problems handled	IT management

Figure 13.4 Measurements for IT Involvement in Process Support

MEASURING BUSINESS EMPLOYEE INVOLVEMENT

Here you are measuring the participation of employees in the process as well as in the change. Figure 13.5 presents some commonly used measures for employees. Again, this is a partial list. Notice that you want to get Human Resources involved in terms of measurement for several reasons. First, they have the information. Second, they are outside the department and so are more unbiased. Third, you do not place the burden on the department. A basic lesson learned is:

Where possible, you should avoid excessive dependence on data collection in a department to minimize the impact on operations and production as well as to ensure that the information is not slanted.

MEASURING MANAGEMENT AND SUPERVISOR INVOLVEMENT

Score cards have been presented in previous chapters about management and supervisor involvement. The key here is that you are measuring management by what they do and their degree of participation. Here is a list of things that you can collect:

- Total number of issues presented to management
- Number of issues by type presented to management
- Total number of issues handled by management
- Number of issues by type handled
- Age of the oldest outstanding unresolved issue
- Mix of unresolved issues by type
- Average time that it takes for management to resolve an issue
- Extent of involvement of managers in the process
- Extent of involvement of managers in the change effort

Information	Source
Turnover of employees	Human Resources
Number of employees trained	Human Resources, training, department
Number of errors made by employees	Department
Absenteeism of employees	Human Resources
Number and type of personnel problems	Human Resources
Participation of employees in change effort	Discussed before
Extent and type of ideas supplied by employees ongoing	Discussed before

Figure 13.5 Measurements for Business Employee Involvement

- Turnover of supervisors and managers
- Communications between management and employees in terms of meetings, etc.

MEASURING VENDOR AND CONSULTANT SUPPORT

Often, there will be one or more consultants or vendors involved in providing either or both of change support or ongoing support. There are a number of measurements possible here. These are listed in Figure 13.6. Note that in most cases, vendors work according to project plans and projects so that many of the items listed are project management related.

MEASURING INTERFACES WITH OTHER SYSTEMS AND PROCESSES

Very few processes function in a vacuum. There are additional processes in the departments where the work is performed. Multiple departments may be involved in the work. There can be external interfaces to outside organizations. The same

- Number of vendor staff assigned to the project
- Turnover of vendor staff
- Percentage of team members that are vendors
- Number of vendor-related issues
- Number of vendor-related open issues
- Percentage of open issues that are vendor related
- Percentage of issues that are vendor related
- Average time for vendor to resolve an issue
- Age of the oldest outstanding vendor issue
- Number of future tasks assigned to vendor
- Percentage of future tasks assigned to vendor
- Percentage of future effort assigned to vendor
- Vendor task schedule performance
- Number of requirement changes from vendor
- Quality of vendor work
- Relationship of vendor staff in team to other vendors
- Percentage of vendor tasks that are joint with IT
- Percentage of vendor tasks that are joint with users
- Percentage of vendor tasks involving more than one person
- Knowledge level of vendor staff in project
- Number of surprises from data supplied by vendors
- Costs—actual versus planned
- Schedule performance
- Milestone quality

Figure 13.6 Measurement of Vendor/Consultant Involvement

comments apply to systems. Figure 13.7 contains a list of measurements that are possible for interfaces. Note that the most of the list pertains to a specific interface so that the list would have to be replicated for the other interfaces.

MEASURING THE EFFECTIVENESS OF THE CHANGE MANAGEMENT TEAM

In this and the next three sections we turn our attention from the process and its support to the change management effort. Let's begin with the change management effort. Some measures to use are given in Figure 13.8.

- Number of system interfaces
- Number of manual interfaces
- Type of system interfaces—interfaces can be batch or on-line
- Extent of dependence of the work on interfaces—this measures how tightly the work is interrelated with other work
- Staff time consumed in supporting the interface
- Cost of the interface
- Documentation quality and validity of the interface
- Dependence for the interface on specific people—this indicates a potential weakness and bottleneck
- Existing problems and shortcomings of the interface
- Number of times an interface has broken or had problems
- Average elapsed time required to solve problems with an interface
- Changes made to interfaces
- Reasons for changes to interfaces
- Frequency and timing of an interface
- Total number of problems and issues reported for the interface

Figure 13.7   Measurement of Interfaces

- Total number of people who participated in the team—this should be a moderate number
- Turnover of team members—you don't want this to be too low or high
- Dependence of the team upon consultants and vendors
- Number of surprises that the team encountered
- Number of issues that the team was given
- Number of outstanding and remaining issues
- Number of outstanding issues by type
- Age of the oldest outstanding issue
- Communication and collaboration performance of the team

Figure 13.8   Measurements of Change Management Team Performance

MEASURING CHANGE PROJECT MANAGEMENT

Here you are measuring the leadership of change management. Figure 13.9 contains some sample measures for these project leaders. In this area and others you will note that many factors are subjective. How do you deal with this? Here is an approach. First, discuss the areas of measurement with a group (this depends on the specific area). Second, have each person develop their own score. Then hold a meeting to see if the group can arrive at a consensus on the score. This will also point out additional things that you might not have noticed because each person has his/her own perspective. The logical audience for measuring change project management are the project leaders, managers, business unit managers, and team members.

MEASURING THE CHANGE MANAGEMENT PROCESS

Going beyond the people, you want to measure any change management process that you employ. Figure 13.10 gives some factors to consider in measuring the process. The participants for this measurement can be wide ranging across

- Budget versus actual cost performance
- Schedule performance—planned versus actual
- Total number of issues
- Total number of open issues
- Open issues by type
- Age of the oldest outstanding issue
- Communications and collaboration abilities
- Number of surprises
- Impact of surprises
- Overall handling of issues and surprises
- Average time to handle an issue
- Allocation of team resources in the change management work
- Dealing with team member problems
- Dealing with resource allocation problems between change management and regular work
- Turnover of leaders
- Quality of handoff of information among leaders
- Communications with management
- Adherence to the change management methodology
- Gathering of lessons learned
- Use and organization of lessons learned
- Quality of communications with management
- Quality of communications with team members
- Quality of communications with business staff
- Quality of communications with vendors and consultants

Figure 13.9 Measurements of the Change Management Project Leaders

the change management team, management, IT, vendors and consultants, and business unit staff.

ORGANIZING LESSONS LEARNED

Chapter 5 provided you with a database of lessons learned. In order to use lessons learned, you have to analyze the raw experience, extract the lesson learned, analyze the lesson learned, organize it for use, and then use. Then you have to be able to update the lessons learned. Figure 13.11 gives a schematic view of this approach. Notice that there is a feedback loop so that you can refine and improve on the lessons learned.

- Ability of the process to be flexible during the change effort
- Understandability of the change management process
- Training required in the change management process
- Problems encountered in using the change management process
- Average time to resolve issues
- Severity and impact of problems and issues encountered
- Stability of the change management process
- Fit of the change management process with the vision, charter, and mission of the organization
- Fit of the change management process with the organization culture

Figure 13.10   Measurements of the Change Management Process

Gathering of raw experience from change management or process work

Analysis of the experience to determine the lesson learned guidelines, when and where to use it, expected results, benefits, and players in using the lesson learned

Organization of the lesson learned into the lessons learned database; establishment of cross-referencing so that the lessons learned are accessible

Discipline to use the lessons learned

Gathering additional experience after the lesson learned is applied

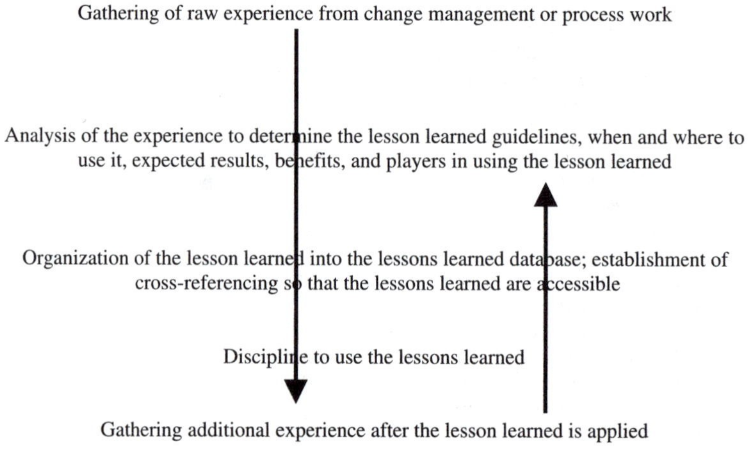

Figure 13.11   Structure of Dealing with Lessons Learned

CREATE THE ONGOING PROCESS MEASUREMENT

As was stated earlier, you want to create an ongoing measurement method and process. A key ingredient is the role of the process coordinator. This is discussed in detail in the next section.

Other key components of ongoing process measurement are:

* Lessons learned database
* Issues database
* Coordination of measurement efforts
* Support of management requests for analysis, and information
* Development of measurements, analysis and reporting
* Longitudinal analysis of measurement information

THE ROLE OF THE PROCESS COORDINATOR

The process coordinator is a full-time role. Many organizations bridle at this. They don't want to spend the time, resources, and energy as they view it as overhead. However, without this role being defined, there is no home for the measurements. Experience shows then that the measurement process will fall flat on its face.

Even though the process coordinator is full-time, it should be handled on a rotational basis by different people. A good approach is to have two people assigned on a part-time to cover the role. This provides backup in case someone leaves. It also provides you with multiple perspectives. Another benefit is that you could stagger the assignment to effect an easier hand-off. For example, you could have one person start in January and one in July for overlapping terms. Figure 13.12 gives the duties of the process coordinator.

* Maintain and support the lessons learned database
* Maintain and support the issues database
* Monitor and keep track of activities and research in change management
* Coordinate ongoing measurement of processes
* Coordinate measurements within change management efforts
* Coordinate, analyze, and report to management on processes
* Support management ad hoc requests for information
* Provide specific process guidance when requested
* Interface with IT and other organizations on process changes
* Provide training in the change management process
* Support documentation and training materials of the change management process

Figure 13.12   Duties of a Process Coordinator

USING MEASUREMENTS TO EFFECT CHANGE

Not many want to go through the effort to measure and then not do anything with the results found. Here are some examples of how the measurements and lessons learned can be employed.

- Use the measurements as part of the basis of promotions and advancement.
- Employ the measurements to support incentive programs for employees in teams.
- Measurements can detect deterioration and process problems. This can help you prioritize where you should direct change energy.
- Use measurements as the basis for benchmarking with other firms and with industry statistics.
- When selecting systems projects to work on, management can apply the measurements to determine the best candidates.
- Apply the lessons learned in training of new and current employees.

MARKETING MEASUREMENT AND LESSONS LEARNED COORDINATION

Why go through all of this? Doing it all is a great deal of overhead. You have to be selective. Here are points in justification that can be employed in management presentations and communications.

- If no measurements are taken, then how do you know where you have been and where you are going?
- If there are measurements taken one time only, then there is nothing to compare this information with later?
- If measurements are taken on an individual, ad hoc basis, there will be no consistent information—limiting comparative analysis.
- Measurements can lead to identification of problems and issues early— before they become crises.
- Measurements can provide tangible support for the change effort beyond management support of change.
- Capturing information on processes through measurements and lessons learned are major methods for long-term and sustained process improvement.
- Measurements can provide early detection of reversion and deterioration.

EXAMPLES

ROCKWOOD COUNTY

Management at Rockwood did not want to take the time for measurements. They felt that it was too much overhead. A crisis arose when a senior member of the overseeing board of supervisors asked what the differences were between a new process and the old version. Managers scrambled for answers. However, there were no measurements available so the response was very weak. Management was then forced to implement regular measurement. The lesson learned here is that:

It is better to be proactive in implementing measurement and lessons learned than be reactive.

LEGEND MANUFACTURING

Because of their long manufacturing experience, Legend management knew the value of measurements and lessons learned. However, these had not been carried out in a consistent, complete, and organized approach. Each division did its own measurements. As a result of the change management effort, a more formal, organized approach was installed. A major benefit was that the ongoing measurement had less overhead than the disorganized previous effort. Moreover, lessons learned were structured and organized so that they were used more often and to greater positive effect.

POTENTIAL ISSUES AND RISKS

- People can go overboard on measurement. In applying Six Sigma some firms tried to measure too many items. They measured at too low a level of detail. There was too much data. In addition, measurements interfered with the performance of the work and skewed the work toward the measurements.
- It is not wise to establish the formal measurement process at the start. You want to start with a change management effort so that measurements can become more natural and represent a normal outgrowth of change management. This will also yield more political support for measurement.

LESSONS LEARNED

- There must be care taken when you have found analysis results from measurements. There is sometimes a tendency to jump to one conclusion. It may be faulty. You should validate the measurements in the process first hand. This will not only back up the analysis, but meet the recommendations with accurate knowledge.
- Measurements are sometimes placed in the internal audit or IT group. This can be a problem since these groups may have their axes to grind. It is better to have a separate function established for this.

SUMMARY

Measurements and lessons learned are the reasons for carrying out change in the first place. Unless you have good measurements that are credible, much of the change management work may be attached. That is why we have given so much attention to these areas and to widespread participation in measurement and developing score cards.

Chapter 14

Prevent Deterioration and Expand the Change Effort

INTRODUCTION

What do our bodies, homes, cars, appliances, and processes all have in common? They deteriorate over time. We will say that deterioration occurs if the performance of the process or work fails to meet set standards or expectations. Work may appear to be going on very smoothly, but underneath and unnoticed, there are changes afoot. Many people who do research and work in change management like to think that after change has been made and measured, the story ends and the people and the work live happily ever after. Unfortunately, processes are subject to a large number of internal and external pressures. Keeping a process from major deterioration requires will, guts, and stamina.

Because you want to have lasting improvement, considering deterioration is important. Deterioration can be unintentional. Or it can happen because employees institute changes. They may attempt to bring a process back to the old state. We call this reversion. There is a body of literature on software maintenance that shows how systems deteriorate over time. The situation with business processes is worse because there are even more factors that can cause problems. Factors contributing to deterioration can interact as well. In this chapter, you will learn how to detect and deal with deterioration and reversion. The focus will be on detection, prevention, and solution if it occurs.

WHY DETERIORATION OCCURS

Consider any significant business activity and you can see that there can be a number of factors that impact the performance of the process. These include:

- Systems—these are the systems that support the process
- IT infrastructure—this includes the network, hardware, and system software
- IT staff—these are programmers and analysts that support the process
- Facilities—this includes the buildings, location
- Environment—this includes the climate, the economic conditions, and culture
- Competition—activities of competitors can affect your processes
- Employees—these are the people who perform the work
- Supervisors
- Managers
- Other processes—these are processes that interact or share resources with the process
- Other systems—these interact with the supporting system

In all of these areas there is change. Each factor is dynamic. Consider the table in Figure 14.1. There you see some examples of changes that occur and their potential impacts.

Why does deterioration occur? Here are some common reasons.

- People make changes and do not think of the process.
- Employees and supervisors focus on short-term actions to fix something.
- There is no sponsor or monitor of the process to help protect it from damage.
- Attention focuses on employees and systems and not on the process.
- The process is not sufficiently flexible to accommodate new requirements.

Example	Impact
Loss of key IT programmer	Changes to the system are not possible easily
Government regulations change	This requires system and process change
Management turnover	New directions are set
Replacement of supervisors by less capable people	Process oversight is weakened
New employees in the department are not trained in the process	Improvisation occurs creating exceptions
Competition causes marketing to define new promotions	The system cannot handle them so exceptions are generated
Network response time worsens	Productivity of employees plummets
Employee turnover	Key people who supported change are gone
New managers	Lose interest in change management
Related system has a change	Impacts the system for the process

Figure 14.1   Examples of Deteriorating Factors and their Impacts on Processes

- King and queen bees interfere with the process and change the rules.
- Supervisors are not trained in detecting and dealing with deterioration.

What are some impacts of deterioration?

- More exceptions are created, impacting productivity.
- King and queen bees move the process backward in time.
- It takes longer to perform the same amount of work.
- Errors increase along with rework due to inconsistent application of policies and procedures.
- Employees lose faith in the systems and technology and revert to using shadow systems more.

DETECTION OF DETERIORATION

There are always signs of deterioration. For a car, it can be a puddle of oil under the crankcase. It can be worn tires. For a house it can be signs of termites. What is the equivalent for processes and work? Here are some telltale signs of deterioration of processes.

- It is taking longer or more resources to do the same amount of work.
- Employees are complaining about the workload—more than they have before.
- There are signs of increased use of the shadow systems.
- More pieces of paper are appearing on people's desks as they keep manual records, given that there are problems in the system.
- There is no updating of the operations manual or training materials for the business process.
- There are more complaints from customers or suppliers about the work or responding to problems or questions.
- Information Technology (IT) has not carried out any systems changes.
- There is a lack of measurement for the process.
- Absenteeism is increasing.
- Turnover of employees is increasing.

SCORE CARD TO DETECT DETERIORATION

These things and others are visible if you look. To help you get going, Figure 14.2 gives a score card to detect process deterioration. Here are some comments on each of the scoring elements.

- Turnover of employees—very low turnover or very high turnover may not be good signs. High turnover may indicate morale problems. Very low turnover may mean that there is too much complacency.

Element	Score	Comment
Turnover of employees		
Absenteeism		
Updating of operations procedures		
Updating of training materials		
Training of new employees		
Extent of requests for changes to system		
Activity in using the system		
Involvement by supervisors		
Involvement of king and queen bees		
Evidence of manual work		
Evidence of exceptions		
Evidence of workarounds		
Evidence of change of attitude		
Evidence of use of shadow systems		
Lack of process measurement		

Figure 14.2   Score Card for Process Deterioration

- Absenteeism—excessive time away from work by many employees is a sign of problems.
- Updating of operations procedures—if there is little activity here, then there is not much going on with the process support.
- Updating of training materials—same as above.
- Training of new employees—if the training drops off or is viewed as not important, then there are probably problems.
- Extent of requests for changes to system—processes change and so generate the need for changes to systems. If there are no requests, then this indicates that the systems are not being used as much.
- Activity in using the system—if the activity level drops, then this could be a sign of problems.
- Involvement by supervisors—supervisors should be hands-on and on top of what is going on. If they lack details, then they are not sufficiently involved.
- Involvement of king and queen bees—if their involvement is increasing, then this could be a problem.
- Evidence of manual work—the changed work was supposed to reduce this.
- Evidence of exceptions.
- Evidence of workarounds.

- Evidence of change of attitude.
- Evidence of use of shadow systems.
- Lack of process measurement.

CHARACTERISTICS AND DETECTION OF REVERSION

Reversion is different. It is more insidious in that some people are directly or indirectly trying to warp the work back to the way it was done before. This happened many times in the past with industrial engineering. After the engineers left, the employees reverted back to their old ways. Why does this happen? One reason is that some people such as the queen and king bees have a vested self-interest in restoring their power in the organization. Another reason is it is hard for people to break old habits. A third reason is that the change management approach did not give enough stress to the need for employees to denounce the old process and recognize the problems. So the employees never faced up to the problems with the old ways.

Here are some characteristics of reversion.

- The king and queen bees are more in evidence in the department.
- Employees are seeking the help of the king and queen bees rather than the supervisors.
- The supervisors indicate that they are not involved directly in the work—in other words, they may have given up power to the king and queen bees.
- There appears to be more manual activity in the department. This is a sign of increased exceptions.
- Old shadow systems have not been addressed and are still being used.
- Some of the issues and problems in the old process are reemerging.

OUTSIDE FACTORS AND IMPACTS ON BUSINESS ACTIVITIES

There can be many outside factors that impact a process or activity. These have been listed above. What you want to understand are the ways in which these factors can impact the work. Here are some examples.

- *Government regulation.* Regulations are first defined and accepted and then promulgated to organizations. The organizations then have to interpret these. Proactive interpretation is essential here to minimize the impact on the work. The organization must then determine how the work will be impacted. This cannot just be handed off to supervisors in a memo. An organized approach is needed using the change or process coordinator. Then the additional or changed work has to be designed into the process so as to have minimal impact on productivity.

There are several types of impacts. One is additional reporting. This is, perhaps, the simplest, since it is backend, overhead work. It is not integral to the work itself. Another change is the business rules for performing the work change. This can result in a major impact. Then there may have to be systems changes as well as procedure and policy alterations.

- *Other processes in the department.* The department employees typically work on several processes during the day. If there are changes to one process, the others are affected. After all, there are only a limited amount of hours in the workday. It is a "zero sum" game. Thus, changes to other processes have to be considered in terms of their overall impact. For example, what if you increase the workload for another process by 20% and that process consumes 40% of the work of the department. The net impact is that the department workload has increased by 8%. But there are the same number of people. If there are 25 people in the department, then the additional work just consumed two people. There is a lesson learned here.

> *Pay attention to all of the processes in the department,*
> *not just the ones that have been changed.*

- *Other departments.* The process may depend upon inputs from surrounding departments. Alternatively, the department may send work to another department. If there are changes of staffing or a different emphasis on the work, this can impact the process and work.
- *Management.* Management may have been very supportive of change. However, there may have been some management turnover. New managers may have different priorities. The supervisors and employees want to satisfy the managers' needs so they in turn change priorities. This can affect the quality of the work, the dedication, and the work itself.
- *Competition.* Competitors may institute changes to processes such as new marketing campaigns, new systems, new products or services, etc. As a competitor, you have to respond if their changes are successful. This often translates into changes in policies and procedures. For example, if a bank changes its lending strategy, then you may have to change your credit policy. This impacts all processes and work dealing with application processing for credit.

- *External economic conditions.* If the economy improves, the workload may increase. If the economy worsens, then there can be other changes beyond workload level. There may be increased pressure to cut back on staffing. This then has a major impact on the process if people disappear.
- *Other systems.* The system supporting your process may be unchanged. However, if interfacing systems are altered, then the interfaces are modified. This can impact system performance as well as system availability.

ESTABLISH A METHOD TO DEAL WITH DETERIORATION AND REVERSION

Based upon the above discussion, you have to think about a more formal approach to detect, prevent, and deal with deterioration and reversion. Here is a proven method that consists of the following steps.

- *Step 1.* Take measures to detect deterioration. Some of these include:
  — Initiate the measurement of deterioration through the score card.
  — Conduct measurements of the processes—not only the ones that have changed.
  — Informally visit departments and supervisors to find out what is going on.
  — Encourage employees to come forward when something new has surfaced in the work. Here you can use the form in Figure 14.3.
  — Conduct periodic focus groups among employees to comment on what is going on.
  — Seek feedback from IT as to what they are working on and the performance statistics of the system.

- *Step 2.* Make management aware of the dangers of process deterioration. Specific actions include:
  — Gather examples of process deterioration in the literature and on web sites.
  — Create presentations for management using measurements of processes.
  — Raise awareness of deterioration.
  — Develop levels of actions to take: level 0—continue to monitor; level 1—gather more information; level 2—take action.

- *Step 3.* Take action on deterioration. Some of these include:
  — Form a mini change management team to investigate and recommend changes.
  — Move into the process and work to collect much more information.
  — Cut off the outside influences that are impacting the process.

Date: _____

Process or work: _____

What happened that was new: _____

_____

Was there any forewarning of this? _____

How many transactions fit into this new work? _____

What is the problem that was raised by the new work? _____

_____

What was the impact on your work? _____

_____

What did you do? _____

What do you suggest in terms of handling this work? _____

_____

Figure 14.3   Form for Detecting Changes to Work

Notice that many times you will observe deterioration, but that it will be too early to take actions. Why? Because you lack information about the situation. The problem may not be severe. Taking action too soon could disrupt the work of the process.

DEPLOY THE METHOD FOR DEALING WITH DETERIORATION AND REVERSION

Now that you have formulated a method for addressing the problem, you have to consider how to implement the method. Here are some basic guidelines.

- Gather managers and supervisors in meetings to discuss process deterioration and reversion. Indicate the impact on productivity and morale of staff. This should get them to take this seriously. Point out the early signs of deterioration that have been discussed. Give examples. Distribute the form in Figure 14.3.
- Follow up on the meeting with visits to the departments where the work is being performed. Conduct focus groups among employees to discuss what has changed or occurred since the changes were put into place. Go over the form.

- Take an example where there has been deterioration and show the employees how to deal with it. This will make process and work deterioration sink in with them.

PREVENT DETERIORATION AND REVERSION

There are some additional guidelines to help prevent deterioration and reversion. Here are some proven ones.

- Work with the king and queen bees to try to get them to participate and have ownership. This should be easier after the changes have been implemented.
- Work with management to show them that they should insist on measurement of processes.
- Try to implement a more formal method for dealing with external changes such as the ones listed above.
- Implement awareness workshops on maintaining the integrity of processes.
- Ensure that new employees are trained in the processes and work in the new mode.
- Periodically, go through the department to detect exceptions, workarounds, and shadow systems.

CREATE A POSITIVE ATMOSPHERE TO REINFORCE THE CHANGES

All through this effort, you are trying to create a positive environment to support change. The best way to do this is to appeal to their self-interest. It is in each group's self-interest to see that the processes do not deteriorate. Here are some ways that each perspective of a process can be harmed.

- *Employees.* The work can become more difficult and complex. There may not be equivalent rewards.
- *Supervisors.* The more that work deteriorates, the more likely it is that the supervisors will have to become involved in the detailed work of the process.
- *Managers.* If processes deteriorate, the productivity, service, and other factors get worse. Costs may increase.
- *IT.* IT may get blamed for process deterioration since it is easy to blame systems for problems.
- *Vendors and consultants.* Same as IT.

Remember to appeal to self-interest. It is a proven method of success.

APPLY THE DETERIORATION PERFORMANCE SCORE CARD

Figure 14.4 gives a score card for deterioration. Here are some comments on the elements of the score card.

- Management awareness of the importance of deterioration—this can be seen by their attitude and participation in things related to deterioration.
- Implementation of methods for detecting deterioration—this indicates that the methods have been deployed.
- Continued use of measurements—this is critical if you are going to detect deterioration and determine the effectiveness of your countermeasures.
- Existence of process coordinator role—this is center post for the effort.
- Number of instances of deterioration detected—there should be some here. Too many indicates there is too much control. Not enough may mean a lack of measurement.
- Impact of deterioration—this can be measured by meeting with employees and supervisors.
- Average time to respond to deterioration—this is the time between when deterioration is detected and when the countermeasures have been implemented.
- Effectiveness of actions to respond to deterioration—this can be based upon measurements later.

Factor	Score	Comments
Management awareness of the importance of deterioration		
Implementation of methods for detecting deterioration		
Continued use of measurements		
Existence of process coordinator role		
Number of instances of deterioration detected		
Impact of deterioration		
Average time to respond to deterioration		
Effectiveness of actions to respond to deterioration		
Support of supervisors in dealing with deterioration		
Support of employees in dealing with deterioration		

Figure 14.4   Score Card to Assess Response to Deterioration

- Support of supervisors in dealing with deterioration—this can be measured by supervisor attitudes.
- Support of employees in dealing with deterioration—same as above.

EXAMPLES

ROCKWOOD COUNTY

Rockwood did not take deterioration seriously. Management assumed that once change had been made, it would remain in place. With several employee bases operating semiautonomously, deterioration in this instance was unavoidable. This came to light when the labor union for a large group of employees pointed out the inconsistencies of policy implementation at the bases. All hell broke loose. Standardization was implemented. Measurements were formalized. Today, there is an active effort to identify deterioration.

LEGEND MANUFACTURING

Legend had had experience with deterioration and reversion when they had spent a large amount of money on a system. Then, after implementation, they found that the employees had reverted back to their old procedures. There were no benefits to the system. This triggered an increasing awareness of deterioration. When the change management work began, there was an emphasis on lasting change.

POTENTIAL ISSUES AND RISKS

- Some people may not take this seriously. They make think that it is normal business and a part of the work. It should be left to the individual employees. This is a recipe for disaster. You can help prevent this attitude through examples.
- Deterioration management may be associated with change management. The impact is that only the changed processes and work get this attention. This is a big mistake. The best way to implement addressing deterioration is to work with existing processes that are not changed.

LESSONS LEARNED

Where do you begin with deterioration measurement? Do you wait until you have changed work. No. Start with any major existing process. Go out and determine the history of the process, staffing, and systems. Assess what changes have occurred since the system was implemented. Use this as a base date. Then work forward first to analyze what changes have been made to the system. Look at what changes have been requested and what actions were taken. This will be tangible and should be easily available from the IT organization.

Now move out into the department. Look at the current state of training materials, procedures, and training. Have these been kept up-to-date with the systems changes? Go to Human Resources to see what staffing changes and turnover have occurred.

With this preparation you are ready to go into the department and see the work. Direct observation is best. Talk with supervisors informally about the work. Then talk with employees as they perform the work.

Now you can create a case example of deterioration and what the organization did to deal with it. You can likely show the benefits of an organized approach to deterioration. This can be easily applied to all processes—not just the ones that changed.

SUMMARY

Deterioration and reversion are natural parts of life and work. You can never be totally successful in preventing these, but you can take measures to minimize these and their impact. Remember too that preventing deterioration to processes is as important as the method for changing work. Dealing with deterioration and reversion are key ingredients to change management.

Part IV

Address Specific Situations and Issues

Chapter 15

Implement New Technology and Systems

INTRODUCTION

A common way to achieve change is through implementation of new systems and technology. Yet, many systems implementations have met with failure to deliver the estimated benefits. In many cases the systems have been installed, the people trained in the use of the system, and success in implementation proclaimed. Then this is followed by resistance and lack of use of the new system. In this chapter we explore how change management can be employed as a tool alongside and mutually supporting systems implementation. When you stop and think about it, IT and change management are often closely linked.

> *Persistent and lasting change is often best supported through*
> *automation; getting results from investment in IT often*
> *requires change in the work and processes.*

Automation tends to standardize the work and makes it more difficult to change by the employees. Hence, it is more stable. On the other hand, if people do not use the system properly or fail to use the system, then there really is no change. In fact, things can get worse and result in lower productivity. Benefits of automation only come through change.

If you carry out change that does not involve systems and automation, then the stability and persistence of the new process and methods depends upon the people consistently and constantly supporting it. This requires more training and supervision. Change is reinforced by automation.

SYSTEMS AND TECHNOLOGY ISSUES

There are a number of systems and technology issues that are relevant to change management. These include the following:

- Many existing systems are old and fail to meet changing needs of the business. This results in the employees in business units having to invent workarounds and shadow systems as well as to generate exceptions.
- Systems, like processes, deteriorate over time. The program code becomes more complex to maintain and enhance due to multiple programmers working on the system as well as increased size and number of modules.
- Software packages (off-the-shelf software) has great appeal since managers envision that it can be used with little change. However, many packages are relatively inflexible and cannot be substantially customized. Moreover, a number of software packages are old and so have even greater inflexibility.
- IT looks at systems for a department or process and sees the existing system so that replacement in their eyes focuses on a one-for-one replacement. However, it is not that simple. From the business employee view, the situation is quite different. They see the system, shadow systems that they built, workarounds, and manual exceptions. They have become comfortable with this mélange of systems.

FOUR MYTHS ABOUT SYSTEMS IMPLEMENTATION

There are so many myths that you can identify given what we have covered in change management.

- *Myth 1*: Requirements for a new system can be defined one time and are stable.
  This is fundamentally flawed in most cases. As you have seen, requirements change as the business needs change. If you implement a system that takes a long elapsed time, then the system is not likely to meet all of the requirements of the new situation.
- *Myth 2*: It is necessary to understand all of the requirements for a new system.
  This has been shown to be false. First, you cannot identify all requirements since there are too many exceptions. You cannot possibly automate everything. You have to draw the line somewhere.
- *Myth 3*: User acceptance occurs after the training and installation of the system are completed.

This is often much too late. There may be a major buildup of resentment and resistance. Moreover, users often resist accepting a new system since it means that they have to make changes in their processes and become more accountable for the benefits. User acceptance must be gained even before the system is installed through user dissatisfaction and unhappiness with the current system and situation.

- *Myth 4*: User participation in systems implementation can be limited. This is a sure recipe for failure. If employees do not have to be involved, they do not participate. They are remote from the new system and the effort. They will not become committed to change. They assume no ownership.

WHY SYSTEMS IMPLEMENTATIONS OFTEN FAIL

Here are some key reasons why so many system implementations fail.

- The project to implement the new system ends when the system is installed. However, there are additional steps. The business process must be changed. Also, the benefits must be measured. Without these additional steps, the project ends and the business employees are under less pressure to change their processes.
- The scope of the systems effort is limited to the existing system. Shadow systems and exceptions may often be ignored. Then the system will not meet all of the requirements of the business. Furthermore, employees in the business departments may have to invent new shadow systems to match up to the new system.
- The system project relies too much on "king bees" and "queen bees." As was pointed out earlier, these people like the status quo and resist change.
- IT selects new technology to implement with the new process. However, there is long learning and expertise curve and time to be endured. This can doom the system implementation.
- IT staff often want to please the employees so they collect requirements from interviews as to what is desired. This is often different from what is needed. The result may not only be extra effort, but a more complex system than is really needed.
- IT staff pay too much attention to exceptions so that enormous programming effort can be expended on automating relatively rare and infrequent transactions.
- Many business staff want the new system to do the work the same way the old system did the work. Hence, they will make requests and issue requirements that tend to warp the new system back to the old. This is natural since they have worked with the old process and system for years and are loath to give it up.

A MODERN APPROACH FOR IMPLEMENTING
NEW SYSTEMS

Change management and systems implementation need to be more tightly integrated. We have seen above that each often depends upon the other. The linking of these two has ramifications for how the systems implementation is planned, organized, and undertaken. From experience here are some guidelines.

- Ensure that the major scope of the system implementation is to change the business process. Within this policy and procedure change, staffing, and systems fall as components.
- Early in the systems project, aim to kill off or eliminate exceptions. This will reduce the elapsed time for development. It will also reduce any customization of the software if a package is selected.
- In the early analysis work to define requirements, identify the shadow systems. You need to understand why these systems were created and what situations they are intended to address. After all, these were created after the old system was implemented so that the shadow systems meet new requirements.
- When you are collecting requirements, it is important to define the new process through transactions as well as to identify problems with the current process and system. Requirements and benefits can then be defined. Business employees must be heavily involved in these activities for several reasons. First, they see the problems with the current process and so will be more supportive of change. Second, business employees can define detailed benefits in more detail than IT employees.
- Since the systems work will take a substantial amount of time to carry out, implement the Quick Hits described earlier in parallel. Why is this a good idea? First, you pave the way for the new system. Second, you can address political resistance separate from the system being installed. Third, you raise morale and support for the new system and change.
- Traditionally, much of the documentation of the system including procedures and training materials were prepared by IT staff. This often runs into trouble since the language of procedures does not match that of the users. Moreover, the user procedures do not encompass the entire business process. There are often significant gaps and holes. Therefore, a better approach is to embed the user procedures into the operations procedures for the business process. Training materials and operations procedures should be written by the employees in the business with the help of IT staff. This will help them assume ownership.
- Training in a new system is most frequently performed by IT. The training scope is restricted to the system. This is also flawed. Consider a new employee who comes into the department 6 months after the new system

is in place. The person needs to be trained in the process that includes the system. This is best done by the business department not IT. IT, in fact, may not even know that the new employee is there. The guideline here is that recurring training should be done by the business users. The scope of training should include the process as well as the system. Thus, training in the new system initially should be carried out by the users with IT support.

There are a number of impacts when you combine change management and system implementation using the approach above. First, the business employees have a wider role and more responsibilities than is the case traditionally. Second, the employees are more likely to be supportive of change and will work harder to ensure that the process is changed.

ALTERNATIVE IMPLEMENTATIONS OF NEW SYSTEMS

After you define the new process, you are in a position to consider a wide range of automation alternatives.

- Live with the current system and change the process around the existing system. You can do this through changing policies and procedures. This greatly lowers the cost of change and vastly reduces the scope of the effort.
- Change or enhance the current system to handle some of the exceptions or shadow systems. This also is less effort than development or software package purchase. An example might be to add a web based front end to an existing system.
- Undertake new development while trying to salvage the useful part of the current system.
- Undertake massive new development.
- Acquire a software package for the new process.
- Adopt a combination of development and a software package.

Often, these alternatives are not all considered. Only new development and software packages are considered. This is a big mistake and often results in extra work.

You should also note that the fundamental purpose changes from getting a new system through development or purchase to trying to find the best solution that will be most affordable and consume the least amount of time. In general,

To minimize risk, you seek to avoid wholesale replacement of the current system unless absolutely necessary.

There are also additional guidelines for both development and software package acquisition. Figure 15.1 provides guidance for software development. Figure 15.2

Guideline	Comment
Avoid undertaking projects with technology you are not familiar	This raises the risk and unpredictability of the work. It also will more likely alarm users.
In developing a prototype focus on carrying out specific transactions rather than on entire user interfaces	This is in line with the approach of dealing with where the risk is
Pay much more attention to system interfaces early	This helps to reduce the risk
Select programming tools that minimize new written code	This is in line with the goal to minimize work
Try to implement the new system for some transactions as soon as possible rather than waiting for completion	This will tend to get more political support for the new system

Figure 15.1   Guidelines for Software Development

Guideline	Comment
Select software that covers the most functions not features	Functions are necessary capabilities. Features are often things that are nice to have.
Try to avoid any substantial customization of the system	Customization often ends up warping the new system to be the old. Customization increases time, risk, and cost.
Select any consultant who will help in the package implementation at the same time that you are selecting the package	The consultant will turn out to be as important as the system in many cases
Aim at a minimal implementation of a software package	Avoid implementing all parts of a package at the same time to reduce risk

Figure 15.2   Guidelines for Software Packages

provides guidance for software packages. For packages, it is important to distinguish between features and functions. Functions are basic capabilities. If a function is missing, then you have to invent, customize, or develop software for this missing capability. Features are things that are nice to have. A number of these are not critical. An example on a new car is cruise control—nice to have but not essential. Figure 15.3 shows the features of two packages A and B. Traditional evaluations would have you select A because it has many more features. Yet, consider Figure 15.4. Here package B has more functions than A. The outer box is the total required functions. The lesson learned is:

> *Select the package that covers the functions best so as to minimize extra work and time.*

Now for whatever method you select, you are faced with the situation that one selected, or in fact all of them, will not lead to a perfect fit with the new process and work as defined. There is almost always some gap between the real and ideal.

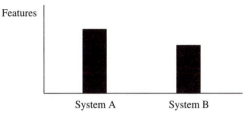

Figure 15.3 Comparison of Two Systems in Terms of Features

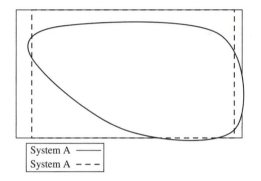

Figure 15.4 Comparison of Two Systems in Terms of Functions

Therefore, the business department and IT have to become engaged in trade-offs as to what effort to expend to approach the ideal closer.

RISK IN SYSTEMS AND TECHNOLOGY IMPLEMENTATION

Experience has indicated that the following areas of system implementation have high risk.

AREA OF RISK: END USER INVOLVEMENT

You should have continuous business staff involvement. What can the users be expected to do? A list for the business staff appears in Figure 15.5. Note that IT staff will have to participate in these tasks too.

This is a powerful and lengthy list of things to do. What if the business managers balk at having some of these things performed by their staff. They can use many excuses. Here are some common ones.

- Analyze the current business process and work
- Uncover issues and problems in the current work
- Define the new business process
- Help to define Quick Hits from this analysis
- Help in defining requirements
- Define the benefits and how they will be measured
- Participate in design and development
- Be involved in software package evaluation and selection
- Participate in data conversion work
- Be involved and support policy and procedure changes and other Quick Hit activities
- Support measurement of Quick Hits
- Participate in testing
- Develop the training materials
- Develop the procedures for the new process and system
- Train the business staff in the new process and system
- Support the cut-over to the new process and system
- Eliminate the old process and its vestiges including shadow systems and exceptions and workarounds
- Change the process to fit the new system and work
- Measure the benefits after change and implementation
- Provide on-going training for new employees in the process and system
- Support on-going measurement of the process and work
- Help to prevent process deterioration

Figure 15.5   Activities in System Implementation Suitable for Business Staff

- There are no employees available. Then the new process is not a priority. Why are we doing the work then?
- We do not know how to do this as we have not done it before. IT can help and the users can participate.
- It is mostly IT work. Wrong! It is almost entirely business work that needs some limited IT involvement.

None of these are really valid. After all, if the business wants the system and new process, they have to be willing to put "skin in the game" or be part of the effort. They cannot just be spectators. They have to be participants. One reason for this is that these tasks are not appropriate for IT to do. They don't have the knowledge or experience of the business staff. They do not know their terminology. They may produce work that is not complete or acceptable.

AREA OF RISK: REQUIREMENTS DEFINITION AND PROJECT SCOPE

Scope creep and unstable requirements are big problems in almost all major systems efforts. Prevention of these things requires that there be constant user involvement. The user activities defined in Figure 15.5 provide for this.

Another method for reducing these risks is to revisit the business process and work to see if there have been changes after the requirements have been gathered. This will help keep the people involved in implementing the new process and system in touch with the people doing the work.

A third method is to ask the following questions when someone wants to make a change to requirements or add to the scope. Answering these questions will dissuade people from changes. Here is a tip. Point out that these questions will be asked every time that there is a change early in the implementation effort.

- What is the change needed?
- What are the benefits of the change?
- Why did this change surface now? Why was it not detected earlier?
- How would the benefits be measured?
- What is the requestor willing to do to support the implementation of the change?
- If there are multiple requests, maybe the entire effort should be stopped and the requirements revisited since the entire situation has changed substantially?
- What if the change is not done? What will the business unit do?
- What if the change is deferred? What will the business unit do?

As you can see, these are very pragmatic questions that deserve answers.

AREA OF RISK: GETTING THE BUSINESS RULES

Business rules are the detailed directions for how specific pieces of work or transactions are handled. As such, their understanding is key to whether the new system and process meet the requirements of the business and deliver the benefits.

Where are the business rules? In the process. However, many are in the program code of the existing, old system. Here is a tip. Begin to gather business rules from the IT programmers and staff who support the old system. They tend to be more familiar with them than most of the business staff since they have to know their programs. Once business rules are programmed, many users then just assume they are there and do their other work. After you have exhausted the IT staff, then go to the "king bees" and "queen bees." These people are now useful here in that they can provide the business rules as well as how and why they were created. This is your best use of these people.

Area of Risk: Process Documentation and Training Materials

It has already been pointed out that these are properly the domain of the business staff. IT employees can work with the business staff to get these documents started. Here are some additional guidelines.

- Assemble and organize documents from past IT projects and implementations that can be used as models. There is nothing wrong copying or following what has worked before if it is relevant.
- Have people develop procedures using the method of successive refinement. That is, the employees develop successively more detailed outlines. This will lead to reduced risk since you know the status of the documentation at any one time.
- Have other business staff review end products for language, tone, politics, and content. These are the best people to do reviews.

Area of Risk: System Interfaces and Integration

This is an area of major concern. Most new systems do not operate in a vacuum. They have to interface to surviving parts of the old system or to other systems. Some of the problems with interfaces are:

- Systems change over time so that interfaces have to be monitored and maintained.
- Systems were written at different times by different people so that there are likely to be differences in meaning, format, creation, and other attributes of data elements.

System interfaces have to be designed in terms of content, timing, frequency, validation of interface, backup if there is a problem, recovery if there is a problem, and format. Thus, you want to gather interface information early in requirements.

Similar comments apply to system integration. Design of integration of systems and how to test the integration are key ingredients to systems success. This is so important that system integration should be pulled out as a separate subproject.

Area of Risk: Data Conversion

Converting data from the old system to the new has been a real curse and problem for us over the years. Some of the problems are:

- There is missing data
- The data elements of the new system are more comprehensive than that of the old

- The data elements of the new system have meanings different from that of the old
- The data in the old system is of questionable validity and accuracy
- Data quality is bad in the old system

As with interfaces, you want to start analyzing the current data early. Then you want to map in to the data elements of the new system. You also have to make provision for data cleanup. In more than one systems effort, this was ignored and the result was that the entire system implementation was held up while the data was cleaned up for conversion.

There are some critical activities and areas to address in data conversion, including:

- What is the quality and nature of the current data?
- How does the data in the old system map into or relate to that in the new system?
- What data is missing?
- What will be done about the missing data? There are several options: live without it, add it to the old system and then convert it, or add it to the new system.
- What will be the conversion approach?
- What is the timing of the conversion? If you convert too early, then the data in the old system that is still in production has changed.

AREA OF RISK: USER ACCEPTANCE OF CHANGE

In traditional system implementation user acceptance of change is a milestone left to the end. The dream is that people who had resisted change will see the new system. The light will then come on. Then the users will wholeheartedly endorse the new process and system. In your dreams!

A more realistic approach is to get as many different users involved in the system implementation. Also, you want the users to acknowledge the problems in the current process and system. Then they can be involved in the implementation of Quick Hits. With these steps you achieve user acceptance. User acceptance does not come overnight.

Moreover, just because a business manager accepts the system does not mean that the lower level business staff do. They may just continue to do things the old way even after implementation and acceptance. This brings up the major questions of "what is acceptance?" and "what does acceptance mean if the lower level users do not accept it?"

AREA OF RISK: BENEFITS ATTAINMENT

Attaining benefits is a major concern that has been pointed out in this and previous chapters. The ingredients of achieving benefits are the following:

- Initial definition of benefits
- Definition of how benefits will be measured
- Determination of what will happen when the benefits are achieved
- Implementation of the new process as well as the new system
- Measurement of the actual benefit
- Decision on what to do with the benefits

These are important. Just because you get benefits, if you do nothing with them, then there are really no benefits.

Another guideline is that all benefits must be translated into tangible benefits. That is, you should not allow fuzzy benefits. Systems projects are often cursed with fuzzy benefits. Let's take an example of how to do the conversion from fuzzy to tangible. Suppose that the new system is much easier to use and is more "user friendly." What does this mean in the real world? Training time should be less. Documentation should be simpler and faster to develop. There should be greater throughput of work. The time to do the work may be less. These are all tangible.

Now remember our discussion of benefits for the new process. You measured not just the new process, but also what would happen if the old process were to continue to live. There would be more deterioration. Keep this in mind when measuring benefits.

AREA RISK: PROCESS MEASUREMENT

Many organizations implement new systems and then perform a post-implementation review. If this is successful and the business unit is not unhappy, measurement often stops. There is no provision of on-going measurement in IT systems implementation. Big mistake! Remember that the system and process can deteriorate individually and collectively. Thus, there must be the on-going process measurement that was discussed in Chapters 13 and 14.

QUICK HITS FOR TECHNOLOGY IMPLEMENTATION

There are some Quick Hits that apply to systems and technology implementation over and above the process oriented ones that were mentioned earlier. Here are some common ones.

- Enhance or fix some of the problems in the current system if this does not consume too much effort. This can buy time for the long-term system solution.
- Improve or upgrade PC's or servers so that the response time using the old system is better. This is not wasted since the new system may require these upgrades anyhow.
- Improve the network so that there is greater capacity and improved performance.
- Retrain users in how to use the old system properly.
- Make a shadow system more standardized and provide support for it.

These things may seem like wasted effort since you are implementing a new system. Also, you may not want to divert resources from the new system implementation to these tasks. However, these negatives can be offset by the benefits that are provided as well as the time bought for new system implementation.

UTILIZE THE SYSTEMS AND TECHNOLOGY SCORE CARD

Figure 15.6 displays the systems and technology score card for implementing new systems and technology. The following comments apply to the score card components:

- Involvement of business staff in analyzing existing system and process— the more and greater the involvement, the more likely will be the support for change.
- Involvement of business staff in benefits estimation—this is critical since the business staff will be analyzing the benefits later.
- Number of exceptions to be included in new system—the more exceptions that are included in implementation normally means trouble since the elapsed time will be longer for implementation.
- Extent of replacement of shadow systems by the new system—the more functions of shadow systems that are replaced by the new system the better.
- Availability of performance data for the process through the new system— having the new system provide automated performance information helps in on-going measurement of the process and deterioration.
- Elapsed time of system implementation—this is critical; the longer the implementation the more the requirements change, the less confidence the users have in the new system, and the more chance of erosion of management support.
- Amount and extent of new technology employed—from before the more new technology that is used, the greater the risk due to the learning curve.

Factor	Score	Comments
Involvement of business staff in analyzing existing system and process		
Involvement of business staff in benefits estimation		
Number of exceptions to be included in new system		
Extent of replacement of shadow systems by the new system		
Availability of performance data for the process through the new system		
Elapsed time of system implementation		
Amount and extent of new technology employed		
Involvement of business staff in documentation and training		
Number of business staff involved in implementation; percentage of total staff involved		
Stability of scope and extent of surprises during implementation		

Figure 15.6   Score Card for Systems and Technology Implementation

- Involvement of business staff in documentation and training.
- Number of business staff involved in implementation; percentage of total staff involved.
- Stability of scope and extent of surprises during implementation.

EXAMPLES

ROCKWOOD COUNTY

Rockwood employed the traditional approach for system implementation. As a result many systems efforts resulted in little or no benefits. It got worse. Process improvement and change management efforts were addressed outside of IT systems. This meant that many changes that were implemented were neither persistent nor long lasting. In some cases, the process improvement effort resulted in new shadow systems making the overall situation worse.

The situation was only improved when a new management policy was put forth. It required that all significant IT efforts had to be linked to process improvement and change management. After this things greatly improved. However, there were still efforts to minimize systems efforts so that some could avoid the process and work change.

LEGEND MANUFACTURING

Legend had experienced two major systems failures where the systems were completed at great cost and yet the benefits were not achieved. They implemented the same rule as Rockwood County. When the change effort started, this was reinforced. All shadow systems were tabulated and analyzed. More useful requirements were found here than in some parts of the old systems. Legend implemented different solutions depending upon the conditions: enhance the current system, buy a package, develop modules for the current system, and develop a new system.

LESSONS LEARNED

- Long-term change often depends upon systems being improved or implemented. The pace of implementing long-term change often lags due to the time required for software change or installation.
- The details of a business process and the transactions must be linked closely to the automation. If the automation effort leaves significant manual work and steps, then there is higher likelihood of reversion and process deterioration.
- In terms of user involvement, you must have as many different users involved as possible. This will increase support for change and for the new process and system.

SUMMARY

System implementations often fail or run into trouble because there is a lack of change in management elements in the implementation planning, organization, and execution. Specific steps that you can take to reduce risk and problems in system implementation come directly from the concepts of change management. To be successful in change management, automation provides stability over time. To be successful in system implementation, you have to implement changes to processes and work. Change management and system implementation are intertwined.

Chapter 16

Achieve Success in E-Business

INTRODUCTION

E-Business (electronic business) is the automation of transactions and work within a company through intranets or with customers (business to consumer) or suppliers (business to business). Another term used is e-commerce or electronic commerce.

E-Business while treated as new is really just the next step in automation of work.

In the early days of computers, systems worked alongside the work. That is, you would typically perform the transaction and then record the results into the computer system afterward. This was often done with batch processing systems in which the day's work was processed at one time. Automation here was an extra step—double entry of information. In retail sales, the individual sale was recorded after the event.

The second stage of evolution was the recording of the information as the transaction was being done. Employees enter the information as the work or transaction is done. Actual updating of master databases and files could be done immediately or later in a batch mode. This stage eliminated the extra step, but did not necessarily improve the work. This was the stage of on-line systems. In retail sales electronic point-of-sale (POS) systems along with bar coding became the common approach.

E-Business can be seen as the next stage because it automates the entire transaction. In the retail sale example, the consumer could either shop from home or check themselves out at the store. Total automation brings many more benefits than the previous two stages, including:

- There is greater tracking of detail so that a wider variety of performance and management statistics are more readily available in more depth.
- Customers, businesses, and employees are doing the transactions themselves so that the support structure for the transaction and work is reduced to the systems and technology.

- Work is standardized to a much higher and greater degree. This is because the work must be programmed and structured. There is no room for exceptions unless these are put into computer code.
- Since humans adapt to new situations faster than systems can be changed and programmed, E-Business requires much more planning and strategy to be successful.

E-Business has itself evolved. In Berlin Airlift planes landed seconds apart and had to be unloaded quickly and goods organized and distributed. It became clear that with different countries and companies involved, there were many different forms with the same information. To make the system work, a standardized format was instituted for the operation. This made the effort possible.

With this success, the potential for standardization in logistics and transportation became evident. Previously, if you shipped goods on a route that involved several railroads, you would have to complete what amounted to duplicate paperwork for the same goods. This was the next area of standardization.

Computerization of interfaces and information between organizations started up with Electronic Data Interchange (EDI). In EDI, companies work in standard organizations to agree on standardized formats for each type of transaction. Using this standard, software is modified or constructed to translate information to and from the EDI format. The data is then transmitted to an intermediary organization in a batch mode. The receiving organization checks their "mailbox" and downloads the work.

EDI has been successful, but probably not as much as people projected. This can be traced to several factors. First, the technology was more complicated then. Second, there were substantial barriers to entry for smaller firms and for some industries.

E-Business has changed that and also represents a step in evolution from EDI. E-Business is on-line oriented for one thing. Next, E-Business has taken advantage of newer and modern technology such as the Internet, the web, and Extensible Markup Language (XML). Programming languages such as Active Server Pages (ASP) and Java have emerged that make implementing E-Business simpler and faster.

WHY E-BUSINESS FAILURES OCCURRED

Yet, there has been much hype around E-Business. We have all witnessed the dot com startups and disasters. There were many faulty and flaky business models. Concepts were implemented that made no common sense. In some cases, the technology was not sufficiently mature. Another major reason for perceived failure was that the expectations for what E-Business could do were set too high. People thought of E-Business in terms of technology when it was really much more business than information technology (IT).

With all of the attention on the failures, E-Business still continues to rapidly expand. One reason is that it is the next stage in evolution of automation of business work and processes. Another reason is that the benefits of E-Business are so compelling. Examples of the military organizations, retail chains such as Wal-Mart and Home Depot, banking, and others point to this success. When a leading firm in a specific industry segment embraces E-Business and makes it work, then the other competing firms are forced either to retreat or to follow very quickly to stay alive. The example here that is cited often is that of Wal-Mart and K-Mart.

Nevertheless, there have been failures in E-Business. These should be considered so that lessons can be learned and applied in the future in E-Business implementations. Here are some factors in E-Business failures.

- There was no clear strategy for what E-Business was to do and how E-Business and regular business were to relate. This resulted in confusion for customers and employees.
- There was an effort to automate too many or all exception transactions and work. This leads to a situation in which E-Business capabilities are delivered too late.
- The strategy for E-Business was to automate one area such as sales while not addressing other areas such as customer service or distribution.
- Automation was directed at the work as it was. There was not much thought given to changing the process.
- There was a lack of attention to performance measurement.
- There was no thought given to potential change generated by changing requirements after E-Business was in operation.

E-BUSINESS AND CHANGE MANAGEMENT

Looking at the bullet list above, there are some useful lessons learned here.

- Changing and simplifying the work are all part of the overall E-Business implementation effort.
- When implementing E-Business, you have to clearly define how the regular business will work alongside or with E-Business.
- Due to the level of effort required for E-Business, thought must be given as to what few exceptions can be retained.
- E-Business is not just a project; rather, it is an ongoing program.

Now you can see that success in E-Business is dependent upon success in change management. E-Business implementation is much more linked to the business than it is to systems and technology. Here are some basic factors that describe the relationship between change management and systems for E-Business.

- You must have an overall strategy for E-Business and the regular business. This is really how you will manage change to establish E-Business and change the regular basis.
- Just like change management, E-Business is a program so that there will be waves of change and additional E-Business implementation and expansion.
- Just like effective change management, E-Business is best accomplished with multiple steps that lead up to E-Business being operational. Thus, early steps or Quick Hits might eliminate exception transactions paving the way for automation of regular, common transactions.
- Change management in the future will link to customers, suppliers, and employees since the scope of work is increasingly seen to be cross-organizational. Hence, change management will increasingly depend upon E-Business systems and technology.

The bottom line is that:

> *Change management and E-Business will become increasingly interrelated and interdependent to ensure success in either one.*

Now consider the title of this book. Two words that appear are breakthrough and enduring. E-Business supports change management by providing scalability and reliability if properly implemented in addition to standardization. This is dynamic. Lasting and enduring change means that the work and business process will not revert back to what was there before. One of the best ways to accomplish this is through E-Business.

APPLY THE CHANGE MANAGEMENT APPROACH TO E-BUSINESS

Given the interdependence between change management and E-Business, it is useful to apply the change management approach that has been developed to E-Business.

- Change management starts with understanding the business and identifying work and processes as well as specific transactions for change. *Selected transactions will be targets for E-Business implementation.*
- Change management requires that you develop a strategy for dealing with all of the process and related processes while you go ahead with change. *E-Business success requires that you have a strategy for defining the relationship between regular business and E-Business.*
- Change management is best carried out in phases or stages of Quick Hits that lead to long-term change. *E-Business implementation is best carried*

out in the same phases of Quick Hits that lead to E-Business being operational.

- Change management succeeds and persists when employees see the problems in the current work and support the implementation and sustenance of the change. *E-Business succeeds when there is widespread grassroots support and participation among employees.*

Figure 16.1 presents an overall approach to E-Business implementation that takes advantage of what has been learned and proven successful in change management. Note the similarity with the change management approach outlined in the first chapter. Here are additional comments regarding the steps in the figure.

- *Understand the business and select the group of processes that are most suited to E-Business.* Here people make the mistake of selecting one process. You have to select multiple processes that are relevant to a customer, supplier, or employee. For retailing you would select cataloging, ordering, credit card processing, order fulfillment, shipping, and accounting.
- *Select the specific common transactions that make sense for E-Business implementation.* In general, you select fewer transactions across multiple processes as opposed to all transactions across one process.

1. Understand the business and select the group of processes that are most suited to E-Business.

2. Select the specific common transactions that make sense for E-Business implementation.

3. Get employee participation and recognition of the problems in the work and the need for change and automation.

4. Develop an overall E-Business strategy that links business and E-Business.

5. Define Quick Hit opportunities that can lead to E-Business implementation and simplify the technical work required as well as the schedule.

6. Determine the change/E-Business implementation strategy for phasing in Quick Hits.

7. Employ a collaborative approach along with balanced score cards in implementation.

8. Establish ongoing coordination of change and E-Business expansion.

Figure 16.1 Approach to E-Business

- *Get employee participation and recognition of the problems in the work and the need for change and automation.* This is directly from change management.
- *Develop an overall E-Business strategy that links business and E-Business.* This step is important since it determines how E-Business and regular business relate.
- *Define Quick Hit opportunities that can lead to E-Business implementation and simplify the technical work required as well as the schedule.* This is from change management and focuses on elimination and simplification to get ready for E-Business.
- *Determine the change/E-Business implementation strategy for phasing in Quick Hits.* This has been shown to be critical to organize change, deliver results with Quick Hits, and prepare for E-Business.
- *Employ a collaborative approach along with balanced score cards in implementation.* Collaboration is important for getting support for change.
- *Establish ongoing coordination of change and E-Business expansion.* In most E-Business books and methods, this step is ignored. The problem is that processes can deteriorate. New requirements surface for E-Business as well.

DETERMINE YOUR OVERALL E-BUSINESS STRATEGY

You have to think about business and E-Business. Let's make this simple. Think of business as a circle and E-Business as a square. Figure 16.2 shows the four possible arrangements of the two shapes. Each of these results in an alternative E-Business strategy as follows.

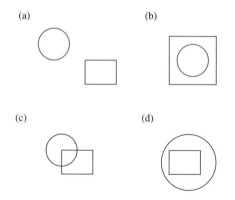

Figure 16.2   Alternative Strategies for E-Business. (a) Separation, (b) Replacement, (c) Overlay, and (d) Integration

- *Separation.* Here E-Business is separated from business as a separate enterprise. This is Figure 16.2(a).
- *Replacement.* E-Business contains business (the circle is within the rectangle). This is Figure 16.2(b).
- *Overlay.* E-Business and business overlap (the circle and rectangle overlap). This is Figure 16.2(c).
- *Integration.* This is incorporation of E-Business into the business (the rectangle is within the circle). This is Figure 16.2(d).

Now let's consider each of these. Separation appears to be a simple solution. You just create E-Business on its own. However, there are many issues with this strategy. Most companies that have attempted it have either failed or have had limited success. In separation much more work is required because there are no established processes. The elapsed time to implement E-Business is too long. Moreover, there are problems because customers or suppliers become confused between E-Business and regular business as they grow apart.

In the replacement strategy, E-Business replaces the business. The company moves to the web. A number of businesses have done this—again with limited success. On the other hand, this is the model for E-Business startups that are exclusively web based. Examples are travel and other retail sites.

Overlay has been the most common approach for implementing E-Business. This is, perhaps, the fastest way to get into E-Business. However, there are many problems in synchronizing E-Business and regular business.

The most successful strategy for E-Business is integration where the change and automation are carefully linked and planned. Here E-Business expands within the business. Moreover, the business and E-Business are mutually supportive.

Each organization must decide upon its own strategy for E-Business. The problem often is that a company just plunges in and pursues an approach without consideration of the alternatives.

DEFINE THE SCOPE OF YOUR E-BUSINESS EFFORT

The scope of your E-Business effort includes the range of processes, policies, systems, and transactions. This must be carried out much more carefully than in IT projects. What is difficult is that you are "cherry picking" the most common transactions and work. What happens to the rest of the work? How about the exceptions? Well, if you address the most common work, then what is left over are the exceptions. Now if E-Business does not need these, then the issue will be what the regular business will do. In one case, after the standard transactions are removed, attention can be directed at the exceptions since the high cost of operations for these transactions is visible in the manual effort.

How do you deal with a shadow system for E-Business? If the shadow system is employed in common transactions, then it must be addressed. If it only supports exceptions, then you pass it up. You cannot afford to spend too much time. What if people ask what will happen to these? The honest answer is that it is not within the scope of E-Business. E-Business pushes standardization.

In analyzing transactions you normally define how the work is done. It is different in E-Business. In E-Business you have to give attention to what flexibility is required. An example is sales promotions related to business-to-consumer E-Business. If you do not pay attention to the variety of potential promotions, then you will be driven crazy when marketing and sales propose new promotions that require substantial new development and testing.

DEVELOP THE E-BUSINESS IMPLEMENTATION STRATEGY

The E-Business implementation strategy involves Quick Hits similar to those in the earlier chapters. However, it also involves setup effort in getting web content established, defining marketing, conducting marketing and sales promotions, and other similar activities. Experience has shown that the scope of the E-Business implementation strategy tends to be more broad and to cover more areas than the change management implementation strategy.

DEFINE THE E-BUSINESS IMPLEMENTATION PLAN

As you recall from the guidelines in change management, you want to employ a template of standard high-level tasks in order to create the detailed implementation plan. An example of the template tasks is given in Figure 16.3. In reality you would split this up into smaller subprojects. The team members would then be involved in defining the detailed tasks within the template as well as the dependencies, duration, dates, and resources.

EMPLOY THE E-BUSINESS SCORE CARD

There are several E-Business score cards that are useful. One pertains to planning and organization of E-Business. This one is shown in Figure 16.4. Comments on these elements are:

- Alternatives considered for the E-Business strategy—it has been pointed that if you pick a strategy too soon without analysis, you are likely to run into more problems.
- Alternatives considered for the processes—the most common problem here is that too few processes are selected.

1000 Overall E-Business vision, objectives, and plan
    1100 Develop E-Business vision
    1200 Define the E-Business objectives
    1300 E-Business management
        1310 Identify issues management approach
        1320 Identify management approach
        1330 Establish project steering committee
        1340 Establish the E-Business executive committee
        1350 Identify project leaders
    1400 Identify organization roles
2000 E-Business strategy
    2100 Define overall E-Business goals
    2200 Determine mission of organization with E-Business
    2300 Identify alternative strategies
    2400 Perform strategy evaluation
    2500 Document/present strategy
    2600 Strategy review
3000 Implementation approach
    3100 Evaluate the vision of the organization
    3200 Assess supplier alliances and relations
    3300 Assess current marketing initiatives
    3400 Approach to technology
    3500 Perform comparative analysis
    3600 Define approach
    3700 Review approach
4000 Identify E-Business processes
    4100 Define core processes to support E-Business
    4200 Group processes to include related processes
    4300 Create comparison tables for processes
    4400 Identify finalists
    4500 Evaluate finalist processes
    4600 Make final selection
5000 Competitive and marketplace assessment
    5100 Define ongoing competitive assessment approach
    5200 Identify internal resources to participate
    5300 Investigate benchmarking
    5400 Identify specific sources of information
    5500 Define evaluation methods
    5600 Collect information
    5700 Organize information for long-term use
    5800 Perform analysis
    5900 Present results of analysis
6000 Technology assessment
    6100 Evaluate hardware in terms of E-Business
        6110 Suitability and support of E-Business
        6120 Identify missing hardware components
    6200 Network assessment for E-Business
        6210 Internal network capacity and performance
        6220 Security available and required
        6230 Extranet/intranet requirements

Figure 16.3 *Continued*

6300 System software assessment
    6310 Core operating systems
    6320 Database management systems
    6330 Desktop systems
    6340 Utility software
6400 Test environment
    6410 Test hardware
    6420 Test network
    6430 Test software tools
6500 Development environment
    6510 Development hardware
    6520 Development network
    6530 Development software tools, languages, libraries, environment
6600 Identification of alternatives for E-Business support
    6610 Hardware
    6620 Operating systems
    6630 Network software/management/security
    6640 Development environment
    6650 Test environment
6700 Define technology direction for E-Business
    6710 Hardware
    6720 Operating systems
    6730 Network software/management/security
    6740 Development environment
    6750 Test environment
    6760 Interfaces with legacy and existing systems
    6770 New software
6800 IT staffing
6900 Develop comparative tables
6A00 Documentation of technology assessment
7000 Gather information on current processes
    7100 Direct observation of processes
    7200 Identification of issues in processes
    7300 Interdepartmental interfaces
    7400 Review of process documentation
    7500 Assess current web activities
    7600 Perform analysis and develop comparative tables
    7700 Determine fit with E-Business
    7800 Documentation
    7900 Review current processes
8000 Define the new E-Business processes
    8100 Generate alternatives for new processes
    8200 Assess alternatives in terms of regular/E-Business
    8300 Develop comparative tables
    8400 Technology requirements for new processes
    8500 Staffing requirements for new processes
    8600 Compare new with current processes
    8700 Documentation

Figure 16.3 *Continued*

8800 Review new processes
    8810 Current business
    8820 E-Business
9000 Measurement
    9100 Identify areas of risk
    9200 Define E-Business measurement approach
    9300 Infrastructure/technology/support
    9400 Measurement of current business
    9500 Measurement of web business
    9600 Measurement of web visitors
10000 Develop the implementation strategy
    10100 Define alternative strategies for processes
    10200 Define alternative strategies for technology
    10300 Define alternative strategies for organization/policies
    10400 Define alternatives for marketing
    10500 Conduct assessment of alternatives
    10600 Develop overall implementation strategy
    10700 Define prototype/pilot activity
    10800 Define phases for implementation
    10900 Review implementation strategy
11000 Define the implementation plan
    11100 Define implementation plan template
    11200 Identify specific implementation issues
    11300 Assess the project management process
    11400 Determine implementation leaders/team composition
    11500 Develop detailed plan and subprojects
    11600 Analyze the completed plan
12000 Implementation
    12100 Hardware setup for E-Business
    12200 Network setup and testing for E-Business
    12300 Firewall/extranet/security
    12400 Development environment setup
    12500 Test environment setup
    12600 Establishment of development standards
    12700 Setup of quality assurance
    12800 Installation of E-Business software packages
    12900 Establishment of external links
    12A00 Testing of E-Business software for production
    12B00 Changes to current application software
    12C00 Interfaces between current and E-Business software
    12D00 Implementation of marketing changes ·
    12E00 Marketing campaigns
    12F00 Setup of web content
    12G00 Software development
    12H00 Integration and testing
    12I00 Quality assurance and integrated testing
    12J00 Procedures and training materials

Figure 16.3 *Continued*

12K00 Operations procedures
12L00 Network procedures
12M00 Changes to current processes and workflow
12N00 Address current customers and suppliers
12O00 Conduct test of workflow and processes
13000 Post implementation assessment
    13100 Gather lessons learned
    13200 Identify unresolved issues
    13300 Conduct usability assessment
    13400 Conduct performance evaluation
    13500 Assess impact on current processes
    13600 Assess customer–supplier relationships
    13700 Perform cost–benefit analysis
    13800 Define recommendations for later work
    13900 Conduct review

Figure 16.3 Template Tasks for E-Business Implementation

Factor	Score	Comments
Alternatives considered for the E-Business strategy		
Alternatives considered for the processes		
Alternatives considered for transactions		
Completeness of transactions from supplier/ employee/customer view		
Alignment of E-Business to the business goals		
How exceptions have been addressed		
Involvement of employees in E-Business planning		
Percentage of employees involved in E-Business activities		
Issues and their severity associated with the current process		
Lessons learned from other organizations in implementing E-Business		
Flexibility in considering changes in policies to eliminate exceptions		

Figure 16.4 E-Business Planning and Organization Score Cards

- Alternatives considered for transactions—here you want to ensure that you have a complete small set of transactions so that E-Business can be initiated in a reasonable time.
- Completeness of transactions from supplier/employee/ customer view—this is the external view of what has been selected;

if there are gaps here, then there will be problems in E-Business operation.

- Alignment of E-Business to the business goals—E-Business must support business goals so that if the business goal is to reduce cost, then E-Business should help in doing this.
- How exceptions have been addressed—if exceptions are included in the E-Business implementation, there will be much greater maintenance and support since exceptions tend to change more and and are unstable when compared to regular work.
- Involvement of employees in E-Business planning—this is similar to the comments and approach in change management earlier.
- Percentage of employees involved in E-Business activities—the higher the percentage, the more there will be an understanding of E-Business; employees will not perceive it as a threat.
- Issues and their severity associated with the current process—managing issues and dealing with the current process need to be addressed; otherwise, they carry over to the E-Business effort.
- Lessons learned from other organizations in implementing E-Business—as with change management, it is important to gather experience and organize it since E-Business is an ongoing program.
- Flexibility in considering changes in policies to eliminate exceptions—as was seen in change management, policy changes can reduce the number and range of exceptions.

The second score card pertains to the implementation of E-Business and the extent to which it was successful. This is shown in Figure 16.5. Comments on the elements are the following:

- Quality and value of Quick Hits surfaced—achieving good value from Quick Hits raises morale and provides momentum to support E-Business implementation.
- Support of Quick Hits for E-Business—Quick Hits have to not only improve the business, but also pave the way for E-Business through simplification.
- Reduction of exceptions due to Quick Hits—since E-Business generally cannot tolerate exceptions, these must begin to be addressed in Quick Hits; you cannot wait until E-Business is implemented.
- Economic value of Quick Hits—the value can pay for the implementation of E-Business and more.
- Schedule performance for Quick Hits.
- Involvement of employees in implementation—this follows from change management.
- Number of surprises in E-Business implementation—surprises can delay the implementation of E-Business.

Factor	Score	Comments
Quality and value of Quick Hits surfaced		
Support of Quick Hits for E-Business		
Reduction of exceptions due to Quick Hits		
Economic value of Quick Hits		
Schedule performance for Quick Hits		
Involvement of employees in implementation		
Number of surprises in E-Business implementation		
Growth of initial E-Business		
Performance in managing issues in E-Business implementation		
Extent and quality of lessons learned gathered during implementation		
Budget versus actual cost performance		

Figure 16.5   E-Business Implementation Score Cards

- Growth of initial E-Business—if you are successful, E-Business will not only work, but will flourish.
- Performance in managing issues in E-Business implementation—this pertains to the mix of open issues that are unresolved as well as to the elapsed time required to deal with issues.
- Extent and quality of lessons learned gathered during implementation— since E-Business is a program, lessons learned and experience are critical for the future.
- Budget versus actual cost performance.

MEASURE E-BUSINESS RESULTS

Of course, you can employ the score cards that have been presented above. Here you should step back and examine E-Business overall. Here are some critical questions to answer.

- Did the implementation of E-Business facilitate change in the regular business in terms of simplification, elimination of exceptions, etc.?

- Were lessons learned in E-Business implementation and operation later applied to change in the regular business?
- Did the Quick Hits help both the implementation of E-Business and the operation of the regular business?
- Is E-Business stable so that there is no deterioration or regression within the regular business?
- Is there is a strong coordination role between E-Business and regular business so that actions in one area are planned in terms of impacts on both?

The danger in E-Business operation is that E-Business takes on its own life and existence and that it starts to deviate in substantial form from the regular business. Then there will be problems in perceptions and market retention with customers. Suppliers may be alienated. Employees may be turned off. Thus, it is imperative that coordination of change and E-Business be linked because after you implement E-Business, it becomes part of the process fabric of the organization.

EXAMPLES

ROCKWOOD COUNTY

Rockwood started into E-Business by establishing standard web sites. These brought little traffic and were often ignored. The breakthrough occurred when intranet applications began to be implemented for employee timekeeping and human resources so that employees could see the benefits. Then, with this experience and lessons learned, better E-Business efforts were made with the public.

LEGEND MANUFACTURING

Legend had established a standard web site for products and ordering. This was used by some large customers. But there was no major impact. The change occurred when management decided to use the web and Internet to attract business from smaller customer firms. Rather than have passive information, the decision was made to provide valued-added services to these small customers in how they could configure, order, install, maintain, and troubleshoot the equipment ordered from Legend. This was the turning point since creating wizards to handle these tasks required large-scale employee involvement. What was even more positive was that the lessons learned to create the wizards was then applied to internal manufacturing and to other processes.

POTENTIAL ISSUES AND RISKS

- One of the biggest problems is that E-Business implementation is often treated as a standard IT project. This is deadly since it does not address change. E-Business should be treated within the context of a change effort.
- The scope and selection of transactions is often performed without sufficient planning and organization. Only in the middle of implementation is it clear that there are missing transactions and work. Then the entire E-Business implementation has to be changed.
- E-Business implementation is often treated as a single project. Then when the initial E-Business implementation is completed, the team is disbanded. The experience is lost. When management then decides to expand E-Business, the entire effort has to be restarted at a high cost in money and time.

LESSONS LEARNED

- As in Chapter 15 with systems and technology, E-Business has to be linked closely to change management to be successful.
- E-Business must not be treated as a large project. Rather it is a program composed of many small projects and efforts involving Quick Hits as well as IT, marketing, sales, and other work.
- The methods of project management defined for change management apply to E-Business. Widespread participation by team members and employees is critical for success. Another critical success factor is to pay attention to issues and to do effective issues management.

SUMMARY

As you have seen, successful E-Business implementation often requires ingredients of change management. As time progresses, change management and innovation will require E-Business to provide for improved process performance with suppliers, customers, and employees. Many failures in E-Business can be traced to the fact that proven principles from change management were not followed. And, after all, E-Business involves substantial change to the organization.

Chapter 17

Common Issues in Change Management

INTRODUCTION

Managing issues and problems related to change is critical if you are going to achieve success in change management. You have to be able to quickly identify and analyze problems and issues. Then you have to work, often in political ways, to get decisions and actions on issues. This chapter contains some of the most common issues that have been encountered in change management. For each, the following are discussed.

- Impact if the issue is not resolved
- Resolution of the problem or issue
- Prevention guidelines

Recall that in each chapter there is a section on potential issues and risk. This section addresses the specific work in the chapter. Here more general issues and problems are covered. These are organized into the following categories for ease of access and use.

- *Personnel issues.* These pertain to the people in departments—both employees and supervisors.
- *Team issues.* These issues relate to the change management leaders and team.
- *Management issues.* These involve upper management and its relation to the change effort.
- *Change effort issues.* These are issues that center on the actual planning and implementation of change.

PERSONNEL ISSUES

EMPLOYEES IN DEPARTMENTS ARE RELUCTANT TO GET INVOLVED IN THE CHANGE EFFORT

The employees may sense that there is risk for them by getting involved. They may feel that they could lose their jobs or that their jobs could dramatically change if they get into the change effort. They may have friendships in the department and fear loss of a friend in the change implementation.

- *Impact.* The impact of reluctance may be resistance to change. They may not volunteer any ideas on either problems or solutions with the work. If this becomes widespread, then the change effort in that department could be slowed or stopped as the change management team hits a stone wall in cooperation.
- *Resolution.* If you sense reluctance, then you should try to find some employees who are willing to participate. In the extreme the person may come from another department. In any case, the person is a peer. The other employees will observe what happens and then when the results are positive, they will be more likely to participate.
- *Prevention.* This issue should be recognized from the start. You might even address and acknowledge it to individual employees. You would indicate that they have nothing to fear. Follow this up with involvement.

A KING OR QUEEN BEE GETS ON A STRIKE FORCE AND ATTEMPTS TO BLOCK NEW CHANGE IDEAS

If you follow many other change management methods, your goal is to get the king and queen bees on the strike force. That is what happens in many cases when there is an Enterprise Resource Planning (ERP) system being installed. Remember that of all of the people in a department these are the ones who have the greatest interest in maintaining status quo for reasons of power, status, and to compensate for what they perceive as lack of recognition by management.

- *Impact.* The king or queen bee will first try to block ideas by raising concerns and issues. It is easy for some people to accept their statements—especially if the people have not been alerted to what is happening. They view their comments as honest concerns instead of what it is—resistance to change. Once the king or queen starts to be heard, the other employees often defer to these people—just as they do in their departments. Now there are few new ideas and a sense of frustration starts to overcome the strike force members.
- *Resolution.* Get these people off the strike force. Make several changes in different strike forces so that it does not appear that you are singling them

out. Go to the manager of their home department and have them request that the person be returned.

- *Prevention*. Do not allow and try to prevent any king or queen bees from being involved in the strike forces. Only use these people for specific rules or instructions. Therefore, it is important to observe the roles and relationships that people have amongst themselves in departments before you identify potential strike force members and solicit involvement.

THE WORK IS BEING PERFORMED IN MULTIPLE, DIFFUSED LOCATIONS

This is a fact of life for many organizations. There can be many branch offices, or the company is a multinational with offices in different countries. The culture in each location is different. Management at each location is different. Hence, there are subtle differences in how the work is performed. This is especially true with manual work, but also true with standardized automated systems in the procedures and policies surrounding the systems.

- *Impact*. You can choose to ignore the differences. Just plunge ahead and force each location to do it the same way. If you do this, you are likely to drive the differences underground. They exist for a reason. Your effort at standardization, if successful, is likely to disrupt the business. Thus, they have to adapt the standardization by creating more informal processes. The results are resentment by the employees, extra work for them, and potentially lost sales and poorer service.
- *Resolution*. If standardization is pushed too far, you can recover. Go to where the change effort is underway and attempt to detect the local nuances and the shadow systems. Then go to the future locations of change and do the same. Begin to identify patterns in how customization is occurring at each location.
- *Prevention*. The best approach is to recognize at the start that there are differences and start to identify these. Acknowledge to the local managers and employees that the standardized approach must be adapted to their culture to be successful. Solicit their input.

THERE IS HIGH TURNOVER AMONG DEPARTMENTAL EMPLOYEES

This can be due to a number of factors. One is that the working conditions are so bad that people leave. Supervisors may have a great deal of power in assigning work and show favoritism, for example. Another reason is that the pay for the work is far below standard. A third reason is that jobs in this department are stepping stones to better jobs so that people clamor to move to better jobs as soon as they arrive.

- *Impact.* High turnover leads to instability. Work may be inconsistent. Productivity may be low. People tend to over-rely on the few employees who remain in the department. These are the de facto queen and king bees.
- *Resolution.* If you become aware of high turnover, you should immediately begin to uncover the reasons for the turnover. Once these are determined, you can decide if you want to address this now and reduce turnover—or wait. If you wait, you can reduce the turnover and improve stability when you implement lasting change. This may be better for the change effort because you are politically taking advantage of the instability.
- *Prevention.* The key idea here is to have turnover as one of the early pieces of information that you collect. Then you can take actions similar to the above.

MUCH OF THE KNOWLEDGE OF BUSINESS RULES AND WORK RESTS IN THE IT GROUP, NOT THE DEPARTMENT

This occurs in departments where there is high turnover. It also occurs where the same system is used over many years. The users accept how the work is done without thinking about the rules. However, the IT group has to be aware of the business rules because they are part of the central core of the programming.

- *Impact.* There can be a disconnect between the user department and the IT group since each perceives the rules differently. It may be more difficult and complex to get at and understand the business rules as a result. Programmers may have to read and understand the old program code that other people wrote and maintained. This exacts a price of time on the change effort.
- *Resolution.* Begin to identify where the business rules come into play in the transactions and work in the business department. Then with this information go directly to IT and start fleshing out the business rules. Move back and forth between IT and the business department to nail down the rules.
- *Prevention.* Early in the change effort, test the business employees' knowledge of the business rules. Then go to the IT group and find out how much input users have to provide IT to get changes made. If there is little input, then there is a problem. Follow the suggestions under resolution.

EMPLOYEES OF DIFFERENT DEPARTMENTS DO NOT GET ALONG

There can be a number of individual or combination of reasons for this. Some people may individually not get along. An example might be two king bees in different departments. Mistrust can be generated by the managers of the departments. A third cause is the nature of the work. For example, there is often a natural tension between sales and accounting.

- *Impact.* On the negative side you would think that the immediate impact is that there would be extensive problems among the strike force team members. This is true but it can be used to your advantage in that you can use the tension to politically leverage for change.
- *Resolution.* If the problems arise in the strike forces and are interfering with work, you might be tempted to try and address the issue. Don't even think about it. You cannot, in a short time, deal with long-seated problems. Instead, keep the strike force focused on details. There are fewer political factors at the detailed level of the work.
- *Prevention.* You cannot really prevent this from happening since it was there before you arrived to do your work. You can prevent it from getting worse by keeping the focus on the detailed steps and transactions.

SOME EMPLOYEES AND SUPERVISORS TRY TO GANG UP TO STAVE OFF CHANGE

As you work with the strike forces and the pace of the work picks up, people will take the change more seriously. There may be individual pockets of resistance as well as organized informal resistance. You should expect some of this as many people feel the greatest comfort in what they do.

- *Impact.* The impact is that the change can be held up. The supervisors can get to managers and raise many issues and questions about the details of the change. Then the managers start to doubt the change effort. They want it throttled back. The impact could be that the change effort is totally halted.
- *Resolution.* If this issue arises, it is best to communicate with management about what is going on. Don't ask management to suppress the supervisors and employees. Instead, hear them out and try to identify specific concerns that can be addressed.
- *Prevention.* You can take the following steps. First, alert management before anything like this happens that it may occur. This prepares them for the event if it occurs. Second, you can indicate to the strike forces and the

change team that this is one of the potential issues that may arise. Indicate that you understand this and have seen it before. A third action is to approach the supervisors and attempt to get them on your side before employees get to the supervisors.

TEAM ISSUES

SOME MEMBERS OF THE STRIKE FORCES DO NOT GET ALONG WITH EACH OTHER

This is similar to one about departments in the previous section. However, here it is typically a more personal problem. For whatever reason there can be personality conflicts in any team.

- *Impact.* A major potential impact is that the strike force work grinds to a halt. Then the problem escalates to the managers of the individuals who do not get along. You then find yourself dealing with these political issues.
- *Resolution.* When this arises, do not pretend that it can be ignored. Meet with each person to understand the characteristics and roots of the problem. Then you can meet with them together. Indicate that you will not tolerate this and that if needed both people will be replaced in the strike force. If they say that they will try to get along, force this by having them perform joint work.
- *Prevention.* Some problems will arise unexpectedly no matter what you do. However, you can meet with supervisors and managers to go over the list of people that you plan on having on the strike forces and see if there are potential conflicts.

YOU FIND THAT YOU ARE HAVING TO OVER-RELY ON SOME CRITICAL EMPLOYEES ON MULTIPLE STRIKE FORCES

Even in large companies this can happen. Why? Because there are critical employees who are pro-change, have a great deal of knowledge or skills, and are not king or queen bees.

- *Impact.* One major risk is that they get burned out from doing their normal work and the strike force work. Someone in this position may also like the de facto power and influence and so may become difficult to deal with. Such a person might dictate opportunities and be resentful when their words are questioned.

- *Resolution.* When you notice this, you should sit down with the individual and try to work out an approach to minimize their time in all but one of the strike forces. Monitor their demeanor in strike force meetings. Try to keep limiting their involvement. Also, remember that you may need them later during implementation.
- *Prevention.* When you identify a critical person in planning the composition of the strike forces, go to the managers and supervisors and see if other people can be employed.

A CRITICAL STRIKE FORCE MEMBER IS REASSIGNED OR IS NO LONGER AVAILABLE TO THE STRIKE FORCE

This will occur if the elapsed time that the strike forces are required is long. However, it can happen early in the effort.

- *Impact.* If the member disappears during the development of the business cases, this is the most critical time. Their knowledge is important to the detail in these cases for change. If the person becomes unavailable at other times outside of implementation, there is a reduced impact. During implementation you will have more people involved so the impact will be reduced.
- *Resolution.* If this problem occurs, you should not try to get them back. Instead, go to the person and solicit some suggested replacements from them. Try to find someone who will add a new perspective to the strike force.
- *Prevention.* Take care to find out what is going on in the department so that if there is major work coming up, you can find out now and can then plan for the person to be away from the strike force. You can make contingency plans with the manager.

A CHANGE LEADER LEAVES THE CHANGE EFFORT. THE EVENT WAS UNANTICIPATED

In any lengthy change effort, this is almost certain to occur. It must be planned.

- *Impact.* If there is only one change leader, the impact can be a disaster. If there are multiple change leaders, the impact is reduced. Moreover, if the departure of a change leader is planned for from the start, the impact can be minimized.
- *Resolution.* When the person announces his or her departure, ensure that there is some overlap with the replacement change leader. Monitor the turnover to see that there is a substantial transfer of knowledge.

- *Prevention.* This cannot be prevented since the overall change effort is a program not a short-term project. Therefore, what you want to do is to periodically assess how the change leaders are doing to see if there is burnout or pressure to return to their home departments.

SOME MEMBERS OF THE STRIKE FORCES CANNOT SPEND TIME AWAY FROM THEIR REGULAR WORK

The manager assigns them to the strike force. They attend some of the initial meetings. Then you find that they are called back to the department. Meetings get cancelled. They are not called back because of their in-depth knowledge, but because their hands and minds are required to deal with volume of work in many cases.

- *Impact.* The immediate impact is to slow down the strike force work. Morale of the remaining strike force members may plummet. They may want to return to their departments as well.
- *Resolution.* When this occurs, go to the department manager to try to get them back as soon as possible. You may also need to identify a replacement.
- *Prevention.* Assume that this will happen. Plan for it. Tell the strike force members that it may occur and have them discuss how best to deal with the situation. Exploit the ties among the strike force members in that one person does not want to let another person down.

A STRIKE FORCE CAN IDENTIFY PROBLEMS IN THE WORK, BUT DO NOT SEEM TO BE ABLE TO COME WITH IDEAS FOR SOLUTION

This is very typical. People who do the work everyday tend to accept their lot in life. We all do this. After some effort the strike force members can often identify problems and issues in the work. But moving from this to coming up with creative solutions is a different matter.

- *Impact.* If something is not done by the change team member(s) assigned to the strike force, the strike force may hit a wall and be unable to go further. Then the schedule for their work slips.
- *Resolution.* When you see this happening, you should step in and make some suggestions for change on your own. Propose some outlandish things to get their reaction. When they react, they will begin to explain why your idea won't work. Then you can work with them to change the idea into

something more workable. They will then begin to take ownership of the idea and develop it. Everyone wins!

- *Prevention*. This is a normal problem. Indicate as such to the strike force. Then you should state that you will help them get started on identifying problems in the work as well as potential change actions. When you later step in and do this, there is no surprise or resentment and work continues.

SOME EMPLOYEES FEEL ALIENATED BECAUSE THEY WERE NOT INCLUDED IN STRIKE FORCES

Change management and the change effort have been given priorities by management. Employees begin to see things happening. They notice that the strike force members will get exposure to management—always useful for career advancement. So it is not surprising that when they are not included, they feel alienated.

- *Impact*. The effect of alienation is not just non-participation, it can also turn into resistance. This is a threat to the change effort since it is these people who will be key allies in turning the king and queen bees around.
- *Resolution*. If you sense that some employees in groups are turning off, you should use the strike force members to reach out to them for ideas and participation. The change management team can facilitate additional sessions and meetings.
- *Prevention*. Prevention begins with discussions with the strike force members. Here you emphasize that some people may feel left out and that this must be addressed. You should also make the effort to involve the employees (perhaps, through focus groups) when the strike force is defining the problems and ideas for change for the work.

MANAGEMENT ISSUES

MANAGEMENT HAS EXCESSIVE EXPECTATIONS FOR THE CHANGE EFFORT

This should surprise no one. In cases where a consulting firm has interested management in change, the managers have typically been hyped up for the change effort. In addition, some managers may have read books or articles that laud the results of change projects.

- *Impact*. There can be many negative impacts. One is that the manager will put unrealistic deadlines on the change leaders and team. This is a setup for failure. A second impact is that the manager will start to really take an interest in the change effort and meddle in the work. As you all know,

when a high level manager is in a meeting, the employees tend to be very
quiet so that nothing really gets done.

- *Resolution.* If you experience the high expectations, bring people down to
  earth by identifying policy and detailed procedure problems in the work or
  business process. This will not be very interesting to the manager who will
  then likely leave the team alone. If the manager sets unrealistic dates and
  schedules, then you have to work to implement the first Quick Hits rapidly
  to buy time for further change. Generally, unless there is a crisis, the dates
  tend to be flexible since there is no compelling business need to meet a
  certain date.
- *Prevention.* Knowing that managers may have high expectations, the best
  approach is to take a realistic tone and downplay immediate results.
  After all, the process and work has been going on for years unchanged.

A TOP MANAGER WHO WAS THE CHAMPION OF CHANGE BAILS OUT

Support from a high level manager is critical for change at several points. One
is when the change effort is launched. Another occurs now and then when political and major business issues must be addressed. It is at these times when you
need upper management support.

- *Impact.* If you lose upper management support for change, then resources
  are likely to be taken away from the change effort. An additional likely
  effect will be that employees will begin to see that management is no
  longer serious about the change effort and so they reduce their efforts and
  move away.
- *Resolution.* If a key manager who supported change leaves and no
  provision has been made, then you have to work through the executive
  change steering committee to begin lining up several additional managers
  to be involved.
- *Prevention.* The best prevention is to expand the support for the change
  effort to several managers. You can approach the champion and explain
  your concern that if he or she leaves, the effort is at risk. The manager
  should then help you to line up other managers.

A MANAGER ATTEMPTS TO MEDDLE IN THE CHANGE EFFORT

This can be related to high expectations. Whatever the cause, the manager has
decided that he can be of value to the change effort and that he or she wants to
demonstrate this through hands-on involvement.

- *Impact*. The effect can be very negative. No one questions the high level manager so that the situation often comes down to one person dictating how change will be carried out. Often, while these are good ideas at a high, general level, they fail at lower levels in implementation. The work slows down and the effort is diverted.
- *Resolution*. When you see a manager meddling in the change effort, you should immediately move to supply them with issues and problems in the business process. This will divert them away from the change effort and may produce some useful results.
- *Prevention*. The two tiered steering committees were designed to handle this issue. In addition, getting lower level employees involved in the change effort will help them become more realistic.

A Top Manager Hears About some New Change Method and Wants to Change the Approach that is Already Ongoing

A top manager may see that the change effort is taking more time than he or she thought. He may then be receptive to new methods or consultants.

- *Impact*. Change is disruptive enough. However, if you replace one change method with another in the middle of the change effort, the results can be chaos. Methods have different perspectives and foci. If you replace a collaborative and open method with a closed one, there will be even more resistance.
- *Resolution*. If a manager indicates interest in some change method, don't turn it aside. Try to turn it into something positive by exploring how parts of the method can be incorporated into the method you are already using. Moreover, there will also be things in common that can be emphasized.
- *Prevention*. In order to prevent this from happening, you can conduct a limited study of various change methods and review this with management. Then when you have started using a change approach, you can point to the key elements that make it useful to your organization. This will help dampen a manager's desire for a new method.

Having Seen some Change Success, Management wants to Immediately Expand the Effort

Like a number of issues this one is natural and should be expected. If you see something working, there is a natural inclination to want to speed things up to accelerate the benefits.

- *Impact.* It is not easy to speed up the change effort once it is underway. The impact of management attempting acceleration will actually slow down the existing change effort. Moreover, a key proven lesson learned from change management is that elapsed time is essential for people to learn from change and to ensure that there is no reversion.
- *Resolution.* If management wants to expand the effort, you can go back to the original opportunities that were developed. Recall that some of these were not pursued because the major attention was directed toward processes that supported the mission, objectives, issues, and other elements. If there are additional resources, some of the better opportunities can be addressed.
- *Prevention.* Communication is the best prevention for this. The more that you channel information and problems in the business processes to management through the change steering committees, the better off you are. You are politically leveraging the committees to head off interference with the change work.

MANAGEMENT DOES NOT FOLLOW THROUGH ON MAKING DECISIONS ABOUT CHANGE-RELATED ISSUES

You approach management with several issues related to the change effort. You immediately sense that they do not want to touch the issues, let alone deal with them. The source of this problem is often that there has been inadequate groundwork laid.

- *Impact.* With management delaying decisions, the change effort can slow down, even come to a stop in extreme situations. Employees in strike forces start to believe that management has lost interest in change.
- *Resolution.* Begin to seek management involvement through the change steering committees. Go to the committees with a range of three types of issues—easy, impossible, and the ones you need resolved. Start with the easy ones to build a successful pattern of behavior in addressing problems. Then move to impossible issues. The managers cannot help you—they feel guilty. Leverage off of the guilt and move to the issues you really need resolved. They will be more willing to help.
- *Prevention.* Once you have established the change steering committees begin to present some issues that are important, but not critical. Get the committees to discuss the issues. Obtain decisions and actions on these issues. You have now established a pattern for management to deal with

issues. Later, when you have other issues, you will find that the work is easier since there is an issues resolution process in place.

MANAGEMENT KICKS OFF THE CHANGE EFFORT AND THEN LOSES INTEREST

The attitude of management depends on the style and culture of the managers and the organization. In some firms the highest executives may have many other pressing issues. Thus, as soon as the change effort begins, they move onto other issues and opportunities.

- *Impact.* Lack of involvement by management should not be interpreted as lack of interest. If management really loses interest, then some of the other issues such as long time lapse to resolve issues will appear.
- *Resolution.* This may not need resolution effort. You do, however, want to test management interest by bringing them information on the change effort and seeing their reactions. You can also surface some issues and see how involved they get and how interested they are.
- *Prevention.* The purpose of the change steering committees is to provide a channel for limited management involvement in change. Also, you are providing a structure for the involvement in the change effort.

CHANGE EFFORT ISSUES

THE CHANGE TEAM AND STRIKE FORCES HAVE DIFFICULTY IN PRIORITIZING THE OPPORTUNITIES FOR CHANGE

There could be many opportunities for change. Moreover, the opportunities may seem to be highly interrelated and interdependent. This gives rise to uncertainty in setting priorities.

- *Impact.* The direct impact is to delay the change effort. More widespread impacts are that the change effort is called into doubt.
- *Resolution.* Get the strike forces to consider the opportunities in groups. Do not set priorities or force the setting of priorities. Start looking at the effects of implementing selected opportunities in Quick Hits so that prioritization begins to emerge naturally.
- *Prevention.* The best prevention is to ensure that the change team is heavily involved in coordination so that the strike force stays focused.

Because of Various Factors, the Change Effort Gets Off to a Slow Start

There is always natural inertia as a new project or effort gets underway. This should not be a cause for alarm. The key is to watch the change effort in terms of the change plan and the issues that arise during the change effort.

- *Impact.* If the pace continues to be slow, then there could be trouble. It may be a sign of early resistance to change.
- *Resolution.* To accelerate the effort get some of the opportunities from the strike forces in front of management early through the two change steering committees.
- *Prevention.* To prevent this, you want to ensure that there are early milestones to show success and results. This will motivate people to speed up the pace.

After Implementing some Changes, the Change Leaders Notice there is Reversion Setting In

This will most often occur with Quick Hits. Why? Because many Quick Hits relate to procedure and work changes as opposed to automation and systems changes that are more difficult to change and revert. Reversion is natural because of habits that employees adopt over many years.

- *Impact.* If reversion is allowed to stand after being detected, then the change team may be diverted to going back and reimplementing the change. The pace and schedule of the change management work is impacted.
- *Resolution.* If there is reversion, you should continue the change effort in other areas. Return to the department where reversion occurred and study it. Why did reversion occur? Gather lessons learned. Then make the decision as to whether you want to address reversion now or wait. Timing is an important factor here.
- *Prevention.* The best prevention to reversion as was stated earlier is to ensure that the lower level employees support the change effort. There must also be sufficient elapsed time after change has been implemented where the work in the process and departments is observed and any lingering side effects or issues are addressed.

PEOPLE BECOME OBSESSED WITH MEASUREMENT OF THE WORK

This is true with some Six Sigma efforts as well as with Total Quality Management (TQM). People get carried away with statistically measuring all aspects of the work and processes.

- *Impact.* Obsession with measurement can lead to a diversion of attention and resources from the change effort itself toward measurement. The impact is that change may be delayed and the entire change effort may be threatened.
- *Resolution.* If you find that there is an emphasis on measurement, you should throttle it back by getting people involved in the implementation of change.
- *Prevention.* Indicate that measurement is only part of the change effort. Measurement contributes to the change effort by generating support for change through negative measurement results of the current work and positive measurements of the impact of Quick Hits. However, you have to make the changes in order to measure the change.

THERE IS TOO MUCH FOCUS ON THE LONG-TERM CHANGE

IT groups and others may see that the real change will only occur when there has been completion of major change work. They may feel that the Quick Hits are not that important and that they divert attention from long-term change.

- *Impact.* If more resources are put into the long-term effort and less goes into Quick Hits, then there will be less visibility of the change effort. There will be fewer short-term benefits. This could put the credibility of the change effort in question. Moreover, people will start going back to their regular work. Momentum is lost. The key lesson learned is that there must be a balance between short- and long-term change.
- *Resolution.* If you sense pressure for the long-term effort, point out that the change approach is one of sequential, substantial change. Also, emphasize that the Quick Hits lead and lay the groundwork for acceptance of long-term change.
- *Prevention.* Always relate long-term change to Quick Hits. Show how they are interrelated.

Emphasis is Placed on Quick Hits

Many people like fast results—like fast food. So it is not surprising that when the first wave of Quick Hits is successful, there is a push to get more Quick Hits. Attention toward long-term process change is diminished.

- *Impact.* If you divert resources from the long-term change into Quick Hits, you will likely begin implementing Quick Hits that are inconsistent with the long-term change. This makes the long-term change more difficult to implement.
- *Resolution.* Whenever you sense a lot of enthusiasm for Quick Hits, you should always indicate how these Quick Hits relate to long-term change.
- *Prevention.* Keep the long-term change as the known and obvious goal. Indicate that the Quick Hits while giving benefits may not be lasting. Lasting, persistent change often only comes through the long-term change that typically will involve systems and technology.

Issues are Taking too Long to Resolve, Affecting the Work of the Change Effort

Even in the best of cases, it will take time for issues to work through the change team and the change steering committees. To employees and managers outside of this it may appear that nothing is going on with respect to the issues.

- *Impact.* If employees and supervisors sense that it is taking too long to resolve issues, they may feel that management has lost interest in the change effort. They may feel that their future efforts are tied to the resolution of the issues. Work slows down.
- *Resolution.* Keep employees and supervisors informed about issues. Try to decouple their immediate tasks and work related to change from the issues. Most of the time there is plenty of work to be done before you really need the issues resolved.
- *Prevention.* Inform the strike forces about the process for resolving issues. Indicate to the steering committees the political damage that will occur if issues linger too long unresolved.

Appendix 1

The Magic Cross Reference

Area	Topic	Pages
Benefits of change	Specific factors	6–7
Change implementation strategy	Development	144–145
Change implementation strategy	Selection	154–155
Change management	Elements	9, 10
Change Success	Factors for change	29–31
Data collection on processes	Analysis	115–116
Data collection on processes	Initial data collection	112–114
Dimensions of change	Specific dimensions	6
Failure of change	Myths	26
Failure of change	Reasons	27
Implementation of opportunities	Grouping, analysis	128–129
Interfaces among processes	Types, nature, importance	21ff
IT and processes	How IT changes work	20
Long term change implementation	Deciding on direction	198–204
Long term change implementation	Implementation	205–210
Management of change effort	Issues and lessons learned	75–80
Measurement	Change score card	43
Measurement	Processes	226–227
Opportunities for change	Definition and evaluation	95–102
Opportunities for change	Selection	102–104
Organization of change effort	Method of change management	72
Organization of change effort	Steering committees, strike forces	68–70
Organization of change effort	Team formation	83
Planning	Analysis tables	53–55
Planning	Business planning elements	49–50
Planning	Change objectives	59–61
Planning	Change strategies	62–64
Planning	Goals of change management	58
Planning	Relationship of planning and change	23
Quick Hit implementation	First round	180–183
Quick Hit implementation	Successive rounds	190–191
Resistance to change	Factors behind resistance	37–38
Resistance to change	How to overcome	40–41

Appendix 2

Further Reading

Anderson, D. and L. A. Anderson, *Beyond Change Management*, Jossey-Boss, 2001.
Beer, Michael, *Breaking the Code of Change*, Harvard Business School, 2000.
Conner, D. *et al.*, *Project Change Management*, McGraw-Hill, 1999.
Fullen, Michael, *Leading in a Culture of Change*, Jossey-Boss, 2001.
Holman, P. and T. Devane (eds), *The Change Handbook*, Barrett Koehler, 1999.
Olsen, E. E. *et al.*, *Facilitating Organization Change*, J. Wiley & Sons, 2001.
Senge, P. M. *et al.*, *The Dance of Change*, Doubleday, 1999.

About the Authors

Bennet Lientz is Professor in the Anderson Graduate School of Management, University of California, Los Angeles (UCLA) where he teaches courses in process improvement, change management, and information technology. He has consulted with over 110 firms in change management in over 35 countries over the past 20 years. He is the author or coauthor of over 45 books and over 50 articles. He has managed over nine IT and business groups.

Kathryn Rea is President of The Consulting Edge, Inc., a leading consulting firm in the area of change management and process improvement. The methods in this book have been applied to over 120 clients in over 40 countries. She is also the author or coauthor of over 20 professional books in management.

Index

Other Titles Available from
Bennet P. Lientz and Kathryn P. Rea

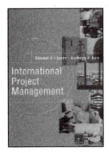

International Project Management

-Presents over 150 specific lessons learned and guidelines for managing international projects
-Explains how businesses can effectively address cross-cultural, social and political issues
-Shows how a business can select the right vendors and outsourcing across national boundaries

ISBN 0124499856 ♦ 2002 ♦ 277 pp ♦ $44.95

Achieve Lasting Process Improvement:
Reach Six Sigma Goals without the Pain

This book enables you to:
-Establish sustained and lasting process improvement
-Achieve the results of Six Sigma without the pain and expense
-Implement process improvement without risking business

ISBN 0124499848 ♦ 2002 ♦ 281 pp ♦ $59.95 ♦ Hardcover

Project Management for the 21st Century, 3rd Edition

-Each chapter contains guidelines and next steps
-Common project examples are included across chapters
-Modern and historical examples are provided

ISBN 012449983x ♦ 2001 ♦ 395 pp ♦ $44.95

For convenient ordering go to http://books.elsevier.com

ELSEVIER
BUTTERWORTH
HEINEMANN